AMAZON EXTREME

Colin Angus &
Ian Mulgrew **AMAZON**

THREE ORDINARY GUYS,
ONE RUBBER RAFT, AND
THE MOST DANGEROUS
RIVER ON EARTH

EXTREME

BROADWAY BOOKS

NEW YORK

BROADWAY

A hardcover edition of this book was originally published in 2001 by Stoddart Publishing Co. Limited. It is here reprinted by arrangement with Stoddart Publishing Co. Limited.

Broadway Books titles may be purchased for business or promotional use or for special sales. For information, please write to: Special Markets Department, Random House, Inc., 1540 Broadway, New York, NY 10036.

BROADWAY BOOKS and its logo, a letter B bisected on the diagonal, are trademarks of Broadway Books, a division of Random House, Inc.

Visit our website at www.broadwaybooks.com

FIRST BROADWAY BOOKS EDITION PUBLISHED 2002

PRINTED IN THE UNITED STATES OF AMERICA

Book design by Pei Loi Koay
Maps: Crowle Art Group
Photographs: Courtesy of Colin Angus

Library of Congress Cataloging-in-Publication Data
Angus, Colin.
Amazon extreme: three ordinary guys, one rubber raft, and the most dangerous river on earth / [Colin Angus, Ian Mulgrew]
—1st Broadway Books ed.
p. cm.
Originally published: Toronto, Ont.: Stoddart Pub. Co., 2001.
Includes bibliographical references.
1. Amazon River Region—Description and travel. 2. Rafting (Sports)—Amazon River. 3. Angus, Colin—Journeys—Amazon River Region. I. Mulgrew, Ian, 1957– II. Title.
F2546 .A584 2002
918.1'10464—dc21
2001043024

ISBN 0-7679-1050-8

10 9 8 7 6 5 4 3 2 1

To Ben Kozel and Scott Borthwick.

We all need friends to

accompany us on our journeys.

CONTENTS

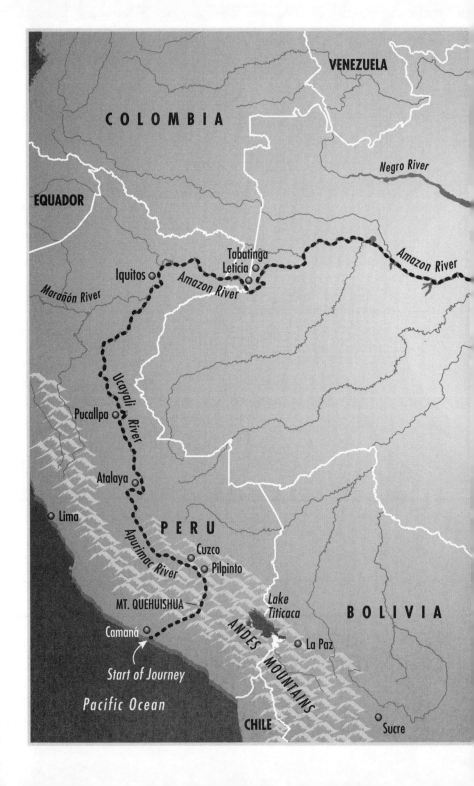

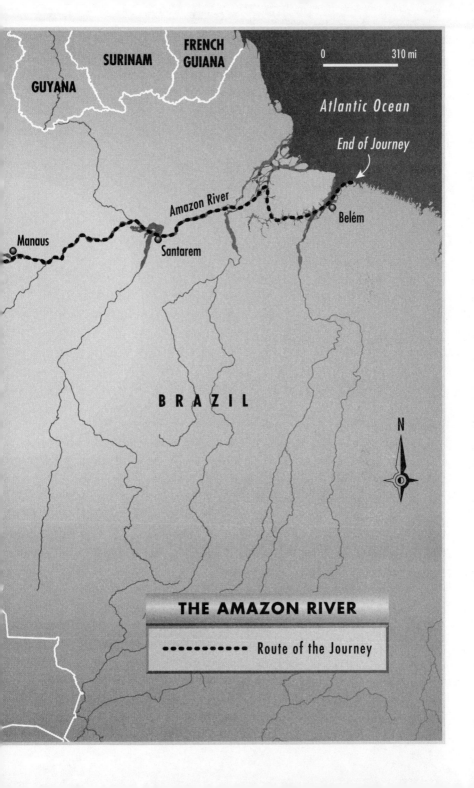

AMAZON EXTREME

PROLOGUE

Day 9: September 21, 1999

I didn't expect to die of thirst—certainly not at twenty-seven. I knew it was a possibility, an inherent risk in any adventure, but I thought we had minimized our risk through careful planning, training, and a set of modest goals. Today, I was not so sure.

If you looked around, you saw packed dirt, sand, and rock everywhere. It was lunar and we might as well have been on the dark side of the moon. We had no way to summon help. No one knew precisely where we were in Peru, and no one would report us missing for weeks—if then. Our journey across South America was supposed to take six months, and no one expected us to check in. It was difficult to believe that, within two weeks, we found ourselves in such a predicament.

We began our trek from a soiled Pacific Ocean beach, hiking up the lush Río Camaná and Río Majes river valleys as far as we could. Leaving that narrow strip of water and life behind, we hiked across a slightly tilted tabletop plateau on the western shoulder of the Andes. At first, the topography of the upper-highland desert was a vast plain strewn with boulders. Thousands of large, sienna-colored rocks littered the landscape. Gradually they became less numerous, until now they could be seen peeking out from the folds of the land or balancing on the larger ledges. It was as though someone had spilled a bag of marbles up ahead and most of the alleys had rolled down the incline, except those that hit a fissure, an outcropping, or a ledge.

The landscape was a spectrum of sandy tones and hues, with the horizon a gauzy pale blue above the jagged line of the hilltops. By 1 o'clock the sun was white hot. We were walking across an open-air oven—a constant dry heat accompanied by an incessant wind that scoured the land. There was no life but the occasional cactus. We were three gringos in a foreign desert, slowly dying. The sand would preserve us perfectly if we collapsed—just like the many centuries-old mummies found here.

I decided to abandon my pack because it was too much to carry as I got weaker. Scott and Ben dumped theirs, too. Appearances be damned, we were in serious trouble. We probably would not survive the two-and-a-half-day trek back to the Majes Valley without water. Our only chance was to push on and trust the dated maps.

We rested, briefly. I sat, my muscles throbbing with pain, yearning for a drink. We didn't talk because it took too much effort. Besides, our tongues were swollen by dehydration. I thought about our prospects and how ill-prepared we seemed to be. It was almost comical: Don Quixote saw reality more clearly. I would have laughed, but I was afraid I would crack my lips. I decided to save the mirth for later.

For more than a year I had thought about crossing South America from one coast to the other, mostly by running the Amazon in a whitewater raft. I was living in southwestern Alberta, at the foot of the Rocky Mountains, chopping wood in a forest of burned pine to pay the rent. Snow swirled around my feet when it hit me: Explore the Amazon! Go explore the Amazon. Yeah, that's the ticket. In the middle of a North American winter, thoughts of a hot, steamy jungle warmed my soul, and the prospects of riding rapids from the Andes to the Atlantic fired my imagination. Yippee-kiyay, cowboy!

The more I thought about it, the more alluring an Amazon adventure became. Almost no one had gone down the entire river and no one had rafted it from start to finish. I wanted to be the first.

This was the initial leg of the trip, a relatively short hike from the Pacific Ocean into the mountains. We wanted to reach the continental divide and the source of the Amazon River, the planet's most mystical waterway. We planned to extreme raft the Amazon, from the headwaters to the mouth on the Atlantic Ocean.

Oh, how the road to hell is paved with good intentions! Here we were in the high desert, the prospect of even seeing the source of the Amazon seemingly more remote than when I was in Canada. Scott, Ben, and I were parched, likely lost, and beginning to understand from the soles of our burning feet to the tops of our scorched heads that we had been very foolish. I looked around. An inexorable sun singed our retinas as it crossed the barren landscape like a blowtorch caramelizing sugar. We were in imminent danger of becoming condor chow.

Western Peru is a narrow, desolate, coastal desert lying at the base of the Andes—among the planet's tallest mountains. We knew that—it's in all the books. The southern hemispheric weather patterns are the reverse of North America's, so the rains fall on the eastern side of the mountains, not the Pacific side. Western Peru is in a rain shadow, parched and nearly lifeless. We knew that too. Yet here we were dying of heat prostration.

I envisioned the worst:

CUZCO, PERU (AP) — The bodies of Scott Colin Angus, 27, of Canmore, Alta., Ben Kozel, 26, of Australia, and Scott Borthwick, 23, of South Africa, were recovered yesterday from a barren, isolated area about 200 miles southwest of this fabled Inca city. Ironically, they died of thirst on their way to raft the world's second-longest fresh-water river from its source to its mouth.

This part of the trip was supposed to be a cakewalk. The Amazon almost bisects the continent. It starts only about 100 miles from the west coast and there is some evidence in pre-history that it might have emptied into the Pacific Ocean. As the two tectonic plates under the continent collided, they caused enough geological dislocation to reverse the drainage pattern. Our plan was to start at the coastal town of Camaná, hike to the continental divide, and ride the Apurimac and the Amazon to the Atlantic Ocean. Our focus had been entirely on the river: it was extreme whitewater for much of the journey, a courage-testing descent from 17,000 feet in the Andes to the 5000-foot level of the Upper Amazon basin. We had not put much thought into this hiking segment of the journey.

We arrived in Peru two weeks ago, flying first to the old Inca capital, Cuzco, where we deposited our river gear with the South American Explorers' Club. The equipment consisted primarily of our 13-foot self-bailing raft, five paddles, tent, back-up butane stove, throw-bags, four 115-quart dry-bags, smaller personal dry-bags, water filter, climbing gear, ropes, repair kit, cam straps, two pumps, water containers, cooking utensils, video tapes, and fishing gear. With the gear in storage, we headed back to the coast by bus to make the climb into the Andes on foot.

We started full of assurance. I had already taken off alone on a tiny sailboat to challenge the mighty Pacific. It wasn't an ego trip, and on my return I hadn't gone around bragging about my feats of derring-do. Yet, though I didn't consider the things I had done particularly special, I knew I was different from most people. I found opportunities where others saw obstacles. Daydreaming is my favourite activity. I regularly get lost in reverie—fantastic scenarios unfolding in my mind with such clarity that they rival reality. These dreams have led me to travel.

The Amazon evoked such strong feelings for me that I thought it was calling me. This was an adventure I felt compeled to undertake. I'm a doer, not a couch potato or an Internet geek. I decided to go down the Amazon not because the journey would be cited in some book of records, and certainly not to make people respect me or look up to me. I decided to extreme raft the Amazon because I wanted to—desperately. Heck, I wanted to have some fun, and everything I read told me this would be the adventure of a lifetime. Besides, what better way is there to learn about the world, yourself, your friends, and your character?

From the moment the first Europeans encountered the Amazon, supernatural stories have been attached to it. The earliest reports were filled with fantastic visions of female warrior tribes and Cities of Gold, the legendary El Dorado. Conquistador and pirate alike portrayed the sprawling Emerald Forest as an Eden and a Green Hell.

The Amazon teems with spiders, vipers, crocodiles, ants, jaguars, anacondas, parrots, parakeets, scorpions, sloths, monkeys, boas, toucans, fish, and insects of all kinds; it shelters varieties of poisonous flora and fauna alongside species that may provide the cure to the most debilitating diseases. Just listing the plant life would require a book. Some 18,000 plant species can be found in the Amazon, with classification pending on many more. A tropical-tree entomologist found 1,500 beetle species, 163 of which specialized on a single leguminous tree. The verdant carpet of Amazonia's vegetation—one of the few places where the term "biomass" seems particularly appropriate—is said to be responsible for replenishing half the world's oxygen. The Amazon is unique: a rain forest so dense and impenetrable that it cloaks and nurtures people still clinging to a neolithic lifestyle.

The Amazon drainage basin, with its attendant tributaries, occupies half of South America and represents one-fifth of all the fresh water on the planet. That's the thing about the Amazon—its staggering size. It is a continent unto itself: the drainage area is almost as big as Australia. Ocean liners and riverboat steamers ply the river offering popular cruises from Belém, Brazil, on the Atlantic coast, to Iquitos, Peru, in the heart of South America—the equivalent of taking a cruise ship from New York to Denver. In learning about the Amazon, I also recognized that people everywhere remain fascinated by it: environmentalists want to save it, politicians want to develop it, and scientists want to study it. There are news stories, magazine articles, web sites, television programs, hundreds of books at Amazon.com, and even an Imax film.

Surprisingly, only a handful of people have ever made the entire journey from the source of the Amazon to the massive mouth and mazelike delta. That's partly because, up until the second half of the twentieth century, no one was certain where the source actually was. Before aerial mapping in the 1950s, the Marañón River system in northern Peru was considered the source of the Amazon. Recent topographical maps created by Peru's Instituto Geográfico Militar, however, show that the Apurimac River system is the longest Amazon tributary.

Apu Rimac was the Lord Oracle or Great Speaker of Peruvian mythology who predicted the coming of the Spaniards and the end of the fabled Inca Empire. The roar of the river's monster rapids and savage cataracts, according to the locals, is the thunder of his voice. You can still hear that voice today, and only the foolish are deaf to its warning. Kayaker J. Calvin Giddings, who led a group down some of the gut-crunching, sphincter-tightening sections, was overwhelmed by its savage intensity. He entitled his book on the experience *Demon River Apurimac*—and said that description was an understatement.

There is still debate about which of the springs feeding the Apurimac represents the true source of the Amazon, but much of the conflict centers on semantics. What is the "true" source of a river anyway? Is it where the bulk of its water comes from, or is it the spring of the feeder stream farthest from the mouth?

In 1906 the English adventurer Major J. Orton Kerbey explored the Urubamba and followed the Inca trail from Lake Titicaca toward Cuzco. He considered that a pond in the mountains near the continental divide was the source of the Vilcanota, Urubamba, Ucayali, and Amazon rivers. He was the first to go down the river. But he lost his canoe in the Pongo de Manique, the vertical-walled canyon of the lower Urubamba, and was forced to hike out. In 1953 the Frenchman Michel Perrin journeyed to Lake Vilafro and proclaimed it the ultimate source of the Amazon. But his attempt to journey down the river ended in tragedy when his partner, Teresa Gutierrez, died in the rapids below the confluence of the Apurimac and the Río Pampas. That was the history of the river. People set out to conquer it and died, or were forced to abandon their attempts because of catastrophe.

A *National Geographic* team went looking for the source, vainly, in 1969, and U.S. adventurer John Ridgeway tried to find it in 1970. He was stricken with crippling *soroche*, the dreaded bends-like altitude sickness. It wasn't until 1971 that the American Loren McIntyre led the supposedly definitive *National Geographic* expedition. McIntyre traced three headwater streams to the continental divide and reported:

> On October 15, 1971, we reached an ice-edged river above Carhuasanta, longest of the five headwater brooks. The Indians call that 18,200-foot summit Choquecorao . . . Here at 17,220 feet is the farthest source of the Amazon—more a pond than a lake, just a hundred feet across. My partners named the lake after me, more or less in fun, knowing it may not always be the most distant water of the River Sea. It could disappear in a single sea-

son. The Andes are new mountains; they still buckle and break.

The expedition followed the river as best it could—sometimes by jeep, sometimes by air, and sometimes by boat, but McIntyre did not attempt to run the Apurimac or the lower tributaries of the Amazon. An American-financed group claimed to be the first to do that in 1985. It was their description of that first successful descent of the river from source to sea that hooked me. If anything stoked my enthusiasm for my trip it was reading *Running the Amazon* by Joe Kane, a spine-jarring, mind-blowing adventure story.

Kane went along to document the journey of an international expedition that intended to travel the Amazon from source to sea. His book evokes the acrid smells of jungle towns and creates such a sense of mood that I was spellbound—especially when he wrote that he thought McIntyre was wrong about the headwater streams and speculated that an ice-wall on Mount Minaspata was the true source of the Amazon. Kane based his belief on the opinion of Nicholas Asheshov, a British journalist who made the Peruvian Amazon his beat. Asheshov considers McIntyre's pond little more than "a marshy lake where everybody goes and has a pee."

In 1996 an international team of scientists led by the Pole Jacek Palkiewicz claimed that the source was an underground glacier near Arequipa, an icy creek known as Apacheta Crevice at the 16,961-foot level on Volcán Chachani. And the *Encyclopaedia Britannica* continues to list Lake Lauricocha as the source because it contributes the most water to the main river.

I liked the idea that the true source of the Amazon was an open question and that the map was not fully filled in. I relished the thought of venturing into a dark place to illuminate it. I was intrigued and excited by the prospect of following in Kane's footsteps. I wanted to see things for myself. And I was determined to run the wild and woolly Apurimac in a white-water raft, coursing our way the entire length of the serpentine river system that was the Amazon.

I knew I'd need partners who were motivated, fit, affable, and willing to pay their share of the costs. Only two friends qualified: Scott Borthwick of South Africa and Ben Kozel of Australia. I had met them both in London, England, but they had not met each other.

Scott had been born in Pretoria, South Africa, but he had called London his home since 1997. His family was originally from Newcastle, but had emigrated to South Africa, where his father owned a bakery. Scott worked in the Purchasing Department of the Imperial College of Science and Technology and had grown up a boy's boy. He could be recognized from the thighs down by his tattered shoes, grazed knees, and plum-colored shins. If he wasn't visible, you could guarantee he was somewhere using a magnifying glass to spark a blaze or dissecting a frog. He saw himself as Tarzan, and he'd never completely abandoned that idea of himself or his love of a dare.

Scott's parents split when he was a teenager and his mother moved back to Britain, leaving Scott and his older brother with his father. Living in South Africa was problematic for Scott as he grew older. He loved and hated that country. The political instability and economic uncertainty finally forced him to follow his mother back to the United Kingdom.

I knew Scott as a generous stand-up guy with a sense of humour and a zest for life. He liked photography, flying kites, music, reading, sports, and considered himself scientific and practical. His philosophy, like mine, was simple and direct: "There must be only a single goal in life, and you must want nothing and believe nothing to arrive there."

Scott also had experience in the wilderness. In June 1997 he hiked by himself from Reykjavik, in southern Iceland, to Isafjorour, a small fishing town above the Arctic Circle and one of the most northern points on the island. With a three-season tent and sleeping bag slung over his shoulder, the trek took him two weeks—and the experience marked him. He was a newly minted adventurer and, since he had traveled all over Africa, Europe, and the Americas, he'd be a great addition to a small team. So would Ben.

Born in Adelaide, South Australia, Ben stood a strapping 6 foot 6. He was in Europe on an extended working holiday when I met him. His mother was English and his father Czech, and they had met as fellow immigrants down under. Times were hard with the communists, and his father, who worked as a border guard, arrived in Australia after using his connections to escape from the Eastern Bloc. He was housed in a government-subsidized hostel for immigrants, and there he met his wife. Ben's father became a foreman in an aluminum frame plant and his mother worked in the Adelaide Public Library. To this day they remain happily married.

Ben grew up in the working-class suburb of Holden Hill. Like every other athletic young boy, he played Aussie-rules football, soccer, or cricket when he wasn't daydreaming about visiting exotic places. He told me he had considered joining the navy, so strong was his wanderlust. "That or a national park ranger, working somewhere in lonely outback Australia," he added.

But Ben's father frowned on travel. The only good life, he said, was a big home, a good job, a family, and the respect of your neighbors. His son had the potential to be a doctor, and that was what he dearly wanted. At the University of Adelaide, Ben studied zoology, botany, and ecology, but he became passionate about conservation. At twenty he joined the Australian Trust for Conservation Volunteers and soon found himself working as a team leader supervising international volunteers on environmental projects—orchestrating reforestation, weed-control measures, and trail construction across Queensland.

Inspired by the stories the volunteers told of their home-lands, Ben went backpacking around Europe for a year in the Pyrenees Mountains, Scotland, Norway, and Turkey. We met while he was in London for several months. Afterward, he returned via Southeast Asia to Australia in early 1998 and went back to work in Queensland.

I knew Ben as an intellectual with a cynical wit. He also had a keen mind for geography. As a child he spent hours poring over atlases and maps. He loved tales of great explorers such as Sir Francis Drake, who went around the world in the *Golden Hind*, Sir Charles Darwin, who explored the Galapagos in the *Beagle*, and Sir John Franklin, who searched for the North West Passage, only to die when his ships, the *Erebus* and the *Terror*, became entombed in the ice. I still haven't met anyone else with such knowledge of the physical world. He could not only rattle off countries and capitals but also discourse on mountain ranges, plateaus, rivers, and natural or man-made features—he was a geographical savant. I tried hard to stump him, but he was always right. At the same time, Ben was passionate about protecting the environment.

Ben and Scott would be fabulous crewmates. I sent letters to each of them, proposing that we mount an expedition to cross the continent of South America under our own power. We would hike from the Pacific Ocean to the source of the Amazon, and raft downriver to the delta. If successful, we would be the first to extreme raft the Amazon. In addition, Ben would be the first Australian and I would be the first Canadian to travel the length of the river. Scott would be following in the paddle-strokes of fellow South African François Odendaal, a legendary adventurer who had been the instigator of Kane's expedition, but who quit in the face of escalating personality clashes. I waited with fingers crossed for their replies.

Both wrote back and said they were interested: we should begin preparing immediately. I was ecstatic. Ben told me he was supervising local trainees as part of a long-term federal government program. The work was intense and stressful, but not as fulfilling as his earlier job, so he was keen to go. Scott, too, thought an extended break was just what he needed.

We decided to follow the same route as Kane, but nothing

else about our journey would be similar. I could only hope we'd see none of the knock-'em-down, drag-'em-out fights that had broken out on Kane's trip. Their big-budget safari had degenerated into a mire of personal recrimination and animosity. Of the nine men and one woman who began that well-equipped descent, only two of the original party completed the journey. Relations deteriorated and became so acrimonious that Odendaal later published his own account, in many ways contradicting Kane's. He describes a soap-opera of caustic disagreements between Kane and Piotr Chmielinski, a Polish mechanical engineer who had made the first recorded descent of the Colca Canyon in 1981. Odendaal says the group came close to fistfights, and he maintains that Kane exaggerated his adventures. So does the expedition's main sponsor, Jack Jourgensen, a fifty-one-year-old Wyoming millionaire who got rich selling the U.S. government yellow paint for highway lines.

Who knows? It's a good read and I learned a lot from it. But, for me, the story of their expedition was not really about descending the Amazon; it was about the need for a chaperone on a school trip. We three, in contrast, were acquaintances heading out on an extreme vacation without hang-ups about making history or ambitions to become the world's biggest adventure boors. No one would mistake any of us for Sir Richard Burton. More likely the Three Stooges or Bart Simpson!

This trip wasn't going to cost us much. We planned on taking the kind of gear you can get at the local outdoors store and we wanted to traverse the continent entirely by foot and whitewater raft. We intended to descend the Amazon's 4,007 miles from the moment the snowmelt and runoff swelled its longest tributary, the Apurimac, large enough to carry us. Call it the world's longest, most interesting roller-coaster—and we wanted to ride it.

PART 1 THE DESERT

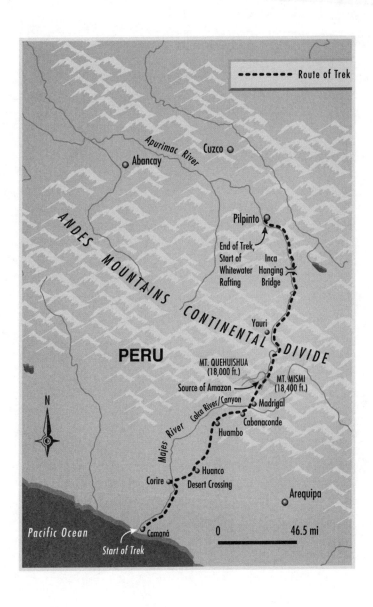

September 11, 1999

We arrived by bus late in the day at Camaná, a tiny town north of the Chilean border. The famed Nazca Lines, those massive and inscrutable geometric patterns carved by some ancient civilization, are a few hundred miles to the north. I was looking forward to seeing the area's famous beaches.

Camaná is set back from the water about 3 miles, so visiting the sea immediately after our ride was not possible. Instead, we booked into a cheap hotel and went exploring.

Western tourists and even Peruvians are said to flock to this town during the searing summer heat, but they were nowhere to be seen. We were the only gringos in town, and there didn't appear to be many native Peruvians holidaying there. Market stalls lined many of the streets as vendors hawked everything: balls of twine, avocados, bananas, oranges, slabs of beef, planks of ribs, chicken feet, pineapples, fish, gewgaws, and spices. Fowl, pigs, and donkeys rooted everywhere and were as numerous as people. To our eyes, imported merchandise was fairly expensive; local products cheap.

We had to carry enough food for about a week. After that, we figured we would reach Corire, a town where we could re-supply. We stocked up on rice, dried beans, lentils, oatmeal, salt, flour, a kilo of rank-smelling cheese, some equally redo-lent salted meat, onions, potatoes, garlic, peppers, powdered milk, sugar, spices, and some Nescafé coffee.

Across from our hotel a young boy sat beside a blanket dis-playing multicolored combs. I watched him for a long time. No one gave him a glance. In the evening I bought a bright-orange comb. The boy grabbed the money wordlessly with a dirty, scabby hand—the blank expression on his face did not change even though I gave him five times the price and de-clined change. His cold indifference saddened me. Later, I gave the comb to a crazy old woman with thick, matted hair who was delighted with it and smiled with tea-colored teeth. Welcome to Peru—a country so grindingly poor that teachers officially earn about US$2 a day.

Peru is the third-largest country in South America. Lima is as sophisticated and spectacular as any European capital, yet the country has been an economic and social mess for more than a century. Two guerrilla groups intent on revolution re-fuse to die. Millions live in abject poverty, and the entire insti-tutional infrastructure is decrepit. The senior political and intellectual elite is corrupt or complicit. To me, it is unfath-omable how a nation can survive like this. But government never was my strong suit.

Day 1: September 13, 1999

Outside the *hostal* a beat-up 1970s Toyota Corona presented it-self in a cloud of dust, just after sunrise. We loaded our packs in the lidless trunk, and the decrepit automobile lurched to life. The driver did everything at top speed, and we arrived at our destination within minutes.

My visions of a Hawaiian-style beach were shattered by the

long stretch of dirty, foul-smelling sand that greeted us. The driver grinned, exposing a row of yellow, rotting teeth as we unloaded our gear.

"*¡La Punta Bonita!*" he gestured at the sand, cackling at the incredulity pasted on our faces.

Garbage spilled across the sand like dirty socks strewn about a dormitory. The air was clammy under a canopy of high haze, a reminder of the foggy weather that guidebooks warned us plagued the area. Numerous buildings lined the beach, but they were not the holiday homes I had envisioned. Some were roofless, and the walls of others were crumbling.

At first it seemed as though we were on the edge of a ghost town. But soon I noticed an urchin slipping among the apparent ruins and, far in the distance, two men dragging a gnarled dead tree. It was as if we'd walked into a set for Beckett's *Waiting for Godot*.

"I guess we won't be having that beer in a seaside bar to celebrate our departure," Scott said.

"What on earth brings the tourists here in high season?" I asked.

"Let's test the stove and get on the road," Ben retorted.

We had not been able to find naphtha the day before, so we bought gasoline as a substitute, hoping it might work. We didn't want to test it in the hotel room in case it erupted in a fireball. I turned so Ben could get the small Coleman from my pack.

He pulled out the stove, gingerly filled it with the fuel, and tightened the cap. Scott anxiously primed the pump with a few quick motions, opened the jet, sparked the lighter, and jumped back, anticipating an explosion.

He chuckled—"See, nothing to it"—as small bright-blue flames flickered and the stove hissed contentedly.

We high-fived each other, shut it down, and repacked it. We were off. Suddenly, a little girl appeared.

"What are you guys doing?" she asked in Spanish.

"We are going to cross South America," I replied.

She stared at me for a while.

"My daddy sells cigarettes."

"Ciao," we nodded.

We left her standing there and went to dip our boots in the Pacific Ocean, a ritual to mark our departure.

There were enormous breakers. Trying to get the timing right, we ran after the receding water like three loaded camels, splashed momentarily in the water, and retreated. Scott was too slow and the wave caught him. He laughed, but that was before he knew of the blisters the wet leather would gnaw into his feet by lunchtime.

With that inelegant two-step, we strode down a misty dirt road, our journey begun. We were free. We were self-contained. We had only to follow the path far enough and we would cross a continent.

We had plotted our route using a series of topographical maps purchased in Lima, the colonial Spanish capital of the country. We spent hours poring over the detailed charts, trying to determine the most direct route to the continental divide from the coast. It was impossible to follow a straight path.

The topography of southwestern Peru is a washboard of mountain ranges. The landscape consists of hellishly deep canyons separated by mountain badlands and endless stretches of *puna*, the savage alpine desert. The mountain ranges are arrayed in a series of cordillera, or spines, running parallel to the coast from north to south. Each successive picket of peaks is higher than the last, until they crest and plunge into the Amazon jungle. We would ascend and cross every range until we reached the almost 18,000 mile divide.

The roar of the ocean faded as we walked into the Río Camaná Valley. The birdsong and insect drone provided a soft fluctuating hum of white noise. Occasionally the bark of an underfed, abused dog pierced the air. Viewed from above, the river valley was a green ribbon of irrigated farmland running across a strip of desert scrubland that extended up and down the coast. Virtually no rain falls here, and the water brought down from the mountains by the Majes River originates far away. Laborers paused from working the fields and watched us stroll past. They didn't often see three gringos with enormous bags on their backs.

My mind wandered as my legs settled into the routine. Everything seemed slightly unreal. I had dreamt about this day for so long that it was difficult to believe it was actually here. Every minute brought us closer to the Atlantic Ocean. I tried to imagine what obstacles we'd encounter, what kind of people we'd meet, what hardships we would endure. Would any of us bail? Ben's voice interrupted the thought.

"There's a picture opportunity that could speak a few thousand words," he said, pointing at a billboard for VISA that loomed over a wrinkled old man in tattered clothes hoeing corn with a bent stick. As we walked by, the *campesino*'s eyes did not rise from the soil.

After a few miles, the 70-pound weight of my pack made my shoulders ache. I reassured myself that my muscles and joints would gradually adapt. The morning fog burned off, but a thick haze obscured the sun. Our conversation quickly became sporadic, each of us lost in his own thoughts as we passed rich fields of corn, melons, tomatoes, and onions. Occasionally, we saw lush jade-colored levees choked with rice.

As we got farther away from Camaná, the small, self-contained farms gave way to sprawling ranches. We could see the makeshift bamboo-and-mud hovels of local farm workers clinging to the valley's encroaching gravel walls. The dirt road gradually became a rutted lane, skirting the edge of the fields, winding toward the head of the valley. The rich loamy earth smelled good, and clouds of gnats rode the breeze.

Periodically the lane stumbled upon a cluster of adobe-and-thatch shacks. Children paused, mouths agape, when they caught sight of us. Sometimes nervous mothers snatched the children up and ran inside. We could feel their eyes watch us as we passed. The men we encountered were inquisitive and less afraid. "Where do you come from? Where are you going? Why don't you go by bus?" We struggled to understand and answer in broken Spanish.

Toward mid-afternoon we met two women sifting corn in front of a home that squatted beside the lane. They warily watched us approach, but held their ground. They were native Peruvians wearing black bowler hats and sweaters of vivid blue and pink. I found it impossible to tell their age within a generation: one was older, and the other could have been her daughter.

"Hola," I said, smiling.

The twentysomething broke into a broad smile, but her elder companion maintained a businesslike tone: *"Buenas tardes."*

You could feel the tension. The two women spoke quickly to each other, the younger one apparently more inclined to be hospitable. After a moment she turned and asked us to excuse her friend. She explained that she was more familiar with gringos.

They wanted to know what brought us so far from the main highway and where were we going? We explained as best we could, but it was clear the older woman wanted nothing to do with us. "I'm surprised you are here," she said ominously. "No fear bandits?" Her rough, callused hands continued to sift the corn. "Many bandits up ahead," she said, "a-a-e-e . . ." She wailed and shook her head at the thought of some tragedy. She spoke rapidly to the younger woman.

"She's right—they did terrible things," the younger woman said. "You must be careful."

"Gracias."

I looked at Ben and Scott. "Let's move," came the clear message from their eyes.

"Muchas gracias," I repeated.

We walked debating among ourselves how much credence to put in the woman's warning. We presumed she was exaggerating.

Soon we were on the lookout for a good spot to camp on our first night. We found a perfect place overlooking the river. Scrubby brush grew among the pebbles and sand. It was inconspicuous and invisible from the road. Although no one would acknowledge it, the old woman's cry still echoed in our minds.

I made a dinner of rice, veggies, and dried beef while Ben pitched the tent. Scott went to the riverside to pump water through our filter into empty plastic Coke bottles. We were true neophytes, fumbling and hesitant with the new equipment.

Soon after it got dark, we turned off our lights so we were invisible to anyone coming along the lane. We sat under a starless sky, the firmament obscured by the high haze, talking softly. The gnats, which had devoured us throughout the day, vanished with the setting sun. We sat peacefully for an hour. Then, while I was brushing my teeth, I spotted the flickering light of two lanterns drawing near. I held my breath nervously, as they grew larger, passed by, and finally winked out.

Day 2: September 14, 1999

The morning was gray, thick with haze. Shortly after leaving camp we passed through a small village—if that's what you call a scrum of shacks in a dust bowl. The villagers stared warily when we appeared, and kept their distance as we walked past.

About five minutes after passing the settlement, Scott noticed a large bone sticking out of the sand. We looked closer. There were clumps of mealy white flesh clinging to the jawbone. I nudged at the sand with my foot, scraping to expose more of the clearly human remains. Scott coughed uneasily. "Take a look back," he said in a whisper.

About twenty men clutching hoes and scythes had followed us along the trail and were watching us intently. It was a Hitchcock moment—the gloomy light, the remains, and the silent, stone-faced sentinels.

"Maybe we should get a move on," I said.

"Yeah," Ben and Scott muttered in tandem, and we began to stroll away.

It was difficult not to bolt, but we maintained our usual pace. I glanced back a few times, nervous that the villagers might be following us like demented Children of the Corn. They weren't.

"Where did that old lady say the banditos were?" Scott asked.

"I'm not sure," Ben replied. "Somewhere up the valley."

"How far up?"

"I don't know."

"Maybe here."

We fell into silence. We were only about 18 miles from Camaná, the closest police office.

"I say we forget about it," I ventured after a while. "None of our business."

We walked in silence. I felt nauseated. I didn't want to think about what had happened back there. It wasn't pretty, it sure wasn't lawful, and we didn't want any part of it.

The haze created a greenhouse effect, turning the valley into a sweaty sauna. The gnats swarmed and feasted on any bit of exposed skin. The bug repellant worked for only a few minutes before it was washed away by the waves of sweat that rolled off us.

In the early afternoon we came upon another village at the end of the lane. Only a footpath continued beyond. We met up with a few people around the huts and they treated us in a friendlier manner. They smiled when we approached and were gracious when we asked directions in our limited Spanish.

It was late in the day when we encountered steep cliffs that cut across the trail in the narrowing valley. The only way to continue was to ford the river and walk along the other bank. But the river was 100 yards wide, the current swift, and, as far as we could tell, the water at least waist deep. There was no way we could carry our packs across.

Leaving Ben and Scott with the gear, I scrambled up the cliff to see if there was any way to continue on the same side of the river. The angled granite rose into a vertical wall. With our gear, we could never hope to scale it.

I returned to find Ben and Scott with two teenaged boys. I understood only bits and pieces of what they were saying. Scott said they were offering to get us across the river. We nodded dumbly and the boys disappeared.

We were about to give up and make camp for the evening when the adolescents returned with a large inner tube, probably from a tractor tire. They placed it on the water and, using lengths of cane, created a small raft. Grinning from ear to ear, the taller of the two boys picked up my bag and placed it on the makeshift platform. He picked up the other bags and stacked them in a pyramid. The inner tube supported the weight easily.

Pushing their floating cargo, the boys nimbly picked their way across the shallowest spots in the river and directed the inner tube toward the other side. Our gear safely reached the far shore. The boys waved goodbye, jumped on the tube, and, laughing and hollering, disappeared downriver riding the current.

We pitched camp, thinking we were alone on the riverbank. Ben was cooking rice, beans, and corned beef when a boy of about eight emerged from what looked like a pile of driftwood and came over to us. He carried a cracked, faded-yellow bucket. Inside, I saw a mess of squirming pink crayfish.

"You want buy?" the boy asked.

"How much?"

"Thirty centavos."

About a dime. I pulled the coins from my pocket. In a moment our dinner went from being staggeringly boring to gourmet. The boy declined a dinner invitation and ambled back to his dwelling.

We ate like kings and, after dinner, lounged around reflecting on the day. Ben decided the stove was acting up and took it apart, while I studied the maps.

"We've gone 12.5 miles so far," I said cheerfully. "We're averaging just over 12 miles a day—right on schedule."

Ben looked up. "This stove is fucked," he said. He pulled out his multi-tool and started dismantling the Coleman. "I think the gasoline is blocking up the lines. There's no gas coming out the jets." He pulled off the brass tube leading from the tank to the burner. The little jet appeared to be blocked. He withdrew a long slender wire and began fiddling with it. After a moment or two he stopped and put the stove back together. It worked, but the flame was weak.

"I dunno," he mumbled.

"I'm calling it a night," I said.

Day 3: September 15, 1999

The wind shrieked good morning, scouring everything in its path with sand stripped from the surrounding hills. We built a windbreak with a few logs and rocks, but the ailing stove continually blew out as it struggled valiantly but unsuccessfully to heat the porridge.

After finishing our tepid gruel, we continued up the valley under a sky hazy and dark with airborne sand. A few hours further on we met a sullen man maneuvering his bicycle through the rocks.

"Hola," he said, exposing a mouth of black and gold stumps.

"Hola," Ben replied.

The man stared at us. After an uneasy minute of awkward silence, he told us he had never seen a gringo in the highlands before. "Would you like to buy some cocaine?" he asked, as he pointed to a burlap sack about the size of a loaf of bread in his bicycle basket. "Primero. Primero. Primero. It will get top dollar."

"No, no," we declined.

He shrugged.

"Goodbye," we said.

We wondered whether the man was having us on. Who knows? We continued hiking up the valley, the wind buffeting us throughout the day.

The stove wouldn't work when we stopped for supper, and no amount of tinkering would revive it. We sat in the tent to escape the relentless sand. The wind clawed at the fabric and, at times, a gust would flatten the dome completely, but always it sprang back. We passed the stove around, each taking a futile turn trying to fix it. The air stank of gasoline.

Ben and I gave up and opted for a cold meal of dried pork and mushy tomatoes. Scott was beginning to feel sick and couldn't face food. He spent most of the night vomiting at regular intervals. I know; I was awake much of the night, too, feeling equally queasy. By 3 A.M. I was racing Scott for the exit, praying I'd make it before my insides exploded out of both ends of my body. This is why they call it the Inca Quickstep. It was a ritual scurry every twenty minutes as I shuddered and shivered through the night.

Day 4: September 16, 1999

Scott felt better in the morning. I lay in my sleeping bag hoping my burning belly would settle down. Ben cooked porridge over an open fire. I watched with glazed eyes as Scott dug a hole and buried the Coleman stove. From now on, we would depend solely on campfires.

I felt drained in every sense. Keeping up with Scott and Ben was excruciating. By noon I could eat only crackers and cheese, and the diarrhea was constant. Shortly after lunch, Ben started to succumb as well, and the three of us stumbled on down the track.

We arrived in Corire shortly after dusk. The town sat on the edge of an arid highland desert that rose into the cordillera. The dividing line between the irrigated fields and the surrounding wasteland was drawn as if with a razor. Away from the river's groundwater and life-giving irrigation, the unforgiving land was bone dry, a dead hardscrabble wilderness of cacti and reptile.

I was feverish and had developed a cough. Ben and Scott were similarly strapped. Lacking the energy to explore, we booked into the first *hostal* we found and retired to the dingy room. In spite of the flaking lime paint, bare light bulb, and unyielding beds, it was a welcome sanctuary. We could rest, lick our wounds, and feel sorry for ourselves.

Day 5: September 17, 1999

Corire was a veil of sickness: diarrhea, vomiting, and hacking coughs. The small communal bathroom down the hall was soon decorated with a fine spray of feces. Twice a day the *hostal* owner cleaned the toilet and, within minutes, the bathroom would be a stinking mess again. I'm sure he hated us.

We occasionally ventured from the *hostal* to buy food or water, not trusting anything out of the taps even after passing it through our water filter. We believed local water to be the cause of all illness.

By our standards, Corire was the Third World. Water flowed out of the taps, electricity was available for part of the day, and there were even late-model automobiles. But modernity was a veneer. Scratch ever so slightly and the underlying rot and decay were visible. It was a decrepit town.

Day 6: September 18, 1999

We all felt bad, but we decided to go to see the ancient hiero-glyphs that the locals boasted were nearby. Ben dragged him-self out of bed for the trip even though his face was pale, his eyes puffy, and he walked like a stiff-legged zombie.

The Toro Muerto Petroglyphs, as they are known, were less than 2 miles into the desert. They are believed to be the most visible 1,200-year-old remains of the Wari, a people who in-habited this part of South America before the Incas.

The etchings are abstract figures—stylized lizards, deer-like creatures, and people carved into hundreds of VW-sized boul-ders that litter an otherwise open sandy plain. At the side of the largest, which created an excellent windbreak and shelter from the incessant westerly, I dug into the sand with my hands. About a foot down, I exposed the charcoal remains of a fire. Further excavation revealed some dried beans, bone frag-ments, and crayfish claws. Although it was impossible to de-termine the age of this little midden, I imagined it had been left by the Wari Indians.

We spent an hour looking at the weird and wonderful im-ages before deciding we had better get supplies for the next part of the journey. Buying water and other provisions con-sumed the rest of the day. We bought eighteen full bottles of water, three of them carbonated because that was all that there was in town. If we didn't like soda, there was always Inca Cola.

As we lay in the room at the end of the day I was still plagued with a terrible cough. All of us were feeling the stress brought about by days of sickness.

"Mate," Ben said to me sharply, "would you mind putting your hand over your mouth at night when you cough? I don't want to catch whatever godforsaken lung disease you've picked up!"

Snippily, I ignored him.

"Asshole!" he insisted. "Cover your mouth."

"You're right," I submitted. "I'm sorry."

Scott remained silent. It was the first spat of the trip.

It was juvenile and we knew we couldn't afford to lose any more time, especially over sulky bickering. We had spent only four full days on the trail, but it seemed like an eternity—an eternity regularly punctuated by liquid bowel movements.

We couldn't delay because of the approaching rainy season. If we started rafting the Apurimac too late, the engorged river could prove too much. It is a death trap at the best of times and an impossibility at high water.

I was also worried about our budget. The heat and diarrhea meant we were consuming large amounts of water. Since we drank only bottled water in the hopes of keeping illness at bay, our contingency fund was literally draining away. Potable water is expensive.

We had intended to stay in Corire for just one day, but already we had spent three nights there. Unfortunately, it took more time to heal than we had anticipated. Ben still felt extremely weak, but we acknowledged the pressing need to move on. On the fourth morning, Ben, looking better than he had the previous day, went downstairs to drop off the key. He returned chuckling, an ear-to-ear grin pasted to his face.

Roberto, the owner of the *hostal*, had quizzed him on how gringos have sex. Roberto's girlfriend was bored, he said, and he was curious to learn some new stuff.

"Mano-a-mano, how you gringos go to it?" he asked.

Ben gave a shrug, lifted an eyebrow, and said, "Ah, you know, the same as you."

"No, you tell me your tricks, your special twists."

"I can't give you the finer points in my pidgin Spanish," Ben tried to convey.

But Roberto became increasingly impatient. "Never mind, never mind," he said, his arms waving. "Here, you show me, you show me."

He tugged Ben by the arm as he gesticulated to the next

room. As he pulled away, Ben said, he saw an obese woman sitting in an armchair.

"No, no, no," Ben stammered. "Must go . . . we are headed out now, early, must go. Thanks."

We were still laughing as we headed down the street toward the far side of the valley. The orange glow of the desert in the distance was a stark contrast to the verdant Majes.

We carried a minimum of equipment: one tent, three sleeping bags, one pot, cups, plates, and pocketknives. For clothing, I had a pair of long pants, one pair of shorts, a T-shirt, a couple of long-sleevers and sweaters to ward off the mountain cold, and completely unnecessary rain gear. As we traveled inland, the valley narrowed and rose ahead of us toward dusty foothills, the precursors of a distant wall of mountains, the cordillera that run from Colombia to Drake Passage.

At the edge of town, before heading out into the desert, we showed a few of the local men our map. One, his face a mask of nearly black leather, looked at it blankly.

"¿Habla inglés?" Ben tried.

"¿Dónde está pueblo?" I asked.

There was not a flicker of recognition.

"¿Cómo se dice . . . oasis? ¿Aquí?"

He could have been deaf and dumb. No matter how insistently we pointed to the patch of green the map identified as an oasis—"¿Agua?"—there was not a glimmer in his flat anthracite eyes. Finally, he shook his head.

"No entiendo," he shrugged.

We held out the map, pointing like apes, but the others too shook their heads. Our handbook Spanish was useless.

"¿Dónde está agua potable?"

"¿Está lejos?"

They clearly didn't get it.

We kept saying to each other, there it is on the map—it must be there. The men watched us discuss it, but offered no guidance. They didn't even seem amused at our confusion.

The seven maps covered the landscape from the coast to the continental divide. They were very large scale. Each half-inch represented about three-quarters of a mile. But they were old and we weren't sure how accurate. We figured the tiny green patch, together with the five black circles that, we presumed, represented dwellings, was apparently 35 miles from town. A day's hike, maybe two at most.

Twenty minutes after leaving the town we were alone in a dry, dusty world of rock, sweat, and pain. The occasional tiny cactus blended into the rockscape and, every so often, we spotted a stand of spiny plants, some 6 to 9 feet high. No other vegetation was visible, and there was no indication of humanity. I walked behind Scott and Ben as we hiked through the flat expanse of boulders. The gray-brown rocks ranged between five inches in diameter to about a yard. The ground was strewn with them as far as you could see across the plain, stretching to an undulating line of pale-orange hills.

From a distance the hills reminded me of a rumpled sheet draped over a piece of furniture. I noticed a few lighter smudges, sandstone cliffs that looked like fading scar tissue. Beyond the foothills, much higher mountains rose gray and forbidding. At first we followed an ancient riverbed across the desert. The ground was covered with dun-colored rocks and boulders, some turning to powdery sand and scree that blew away in the incessant wind. Late in the afternoon the distant hills slowly transformed themselves into a painted landscape, radiating red and violet, scarlet and blue. I'd seen a similar iridescent effect at Australia's Ayers Rock and on coral beaches of the south Pacific as they reflected the magic-hour's rainbow-hued light.

I bedded down thinking that the landscape was really beautiful—minimalist as opposed to barren and empty. It was the first time I'd been in a true desert and I was smitten by it. I was also optimistic that, in a few days, we would be at the source of the Amazon. I foresaw a melting snowfield at 17,700 feet, one shoulder of the mountain draining toward the Pacific, the other spilling northeasterly, the ground water gathering to form the Apurimac, the Ucayali, and ultimately the Amazon.

I slept fitfully. I kept waking desperately thirsty, but I held back. We had left Corire with 6 quarts of water each, and already we had consumed about 2.5 quarts of our personal supply without thinking much about it. We had begun to cut back today and I wanted to save a bit as an emergency reserve, in case our calculations were wrong. Something in the back of my mind nagged about rationing. I didn't realize how wrong we had been.

Day 7: September 19, 1999

We rose at dawn, hoping to beat the heat with an early start, and left camp at 6:30 while it was still dusky. By 7 the sun had crested the hills and the valley was again an incinerator.

We knew when we stopped for lunch that the map was off or that we were seriously misinterpreting it. We would not reach the oasis as expected. The grade was increasing as the desert rose into the mountains, and our pace was slackening. We camped for the night at the head of an *arroyo*. High cliffs rose up on both sides and the canyon floor was rock and sand. Morale was low as we sat and stared at our remaining dregs of water.

I had about a pint left and my thirst was excruciating. We guessed that we had about 9 to 12 miles to go and faced the toughest climb yet. As we sat there with cracked lips and parched mouths, the precariousness of the situation hit us. If the map was wrong or our navigation off, we were going to die. Perhaps we had taken the wrong valley.

I slept badly, dreaming of sparkling pools with big fences around them.

Six quarts is ample, but not a lot of water for two days in a desert with a climate like the inside of a clothes dryer. I say that in hindsight. None of us had any desert experience and we weren't really aware how much water our bodies would consume carrying 70.5-pound packs. As we followed the river valleys from the sea, we had not bothered to monitor our water consumption: we simply stopped and refilled our bottles whenever they got low. Our naïveté was proving painful.

We were now in our third day and we did not have a drop of water left. We ate the last of the bread and strawberry jam we had bought in Corire for breakfast. Again, this morning, we started out early, hoping to avoid the worst of the blazing heat. It was scant relief.

The Zen-like beauty of the desert went by unnoticed and conversation was completely absent. By 11 we were worn out and fried. Our faith in the map was shaken, to say the least. We didn't think we should still be walking by this point. Yet, looking at the distinguishing features on the map, we guessed we still might be only halfway there. We were not sure how far off we might be.

"What if the oasis no longer exists?" Ben asked.

Scott and I didn't have an answer.

The map indicated that a road and villages should be within sight. We hadn't seen sign of man, machine, or beast since we left the last farm, back at Corire. There were other little inconsistencies between what the map indicated and the terrain we were crossing. Plus, we all expected we'd be there by now.

We kept going nevertheless, climbing the ever steeper slope.

I was in a pair of long pants and a long-sleeved shirt, hoping to save myself from sunburn. I also sported a fashionable, broad-brimmed dark-green hat I'd bought in Canada. Ben and Scott wore baseball caps, dirty shorts, and T-shirts, the same Day-Glo outfits they had been wearing when we set out.

About 1 P.M. I broke the silence. "I'm dropping my bag," I said.

Ben and Scott stopped and turned to look at me. They nodded and their packs slid to the ground. We sat on the ground. Scott opened a can of tuna and we passed it around, sipping the water in which it was packed. Nectar.

"When we get to the next village I'll buy you a Coke," Scott joked.

Ben looked as though he had a witty reply, but gave up because it wasn't worth the effort. He went back to rummaging in his pack.

We stored our empty water bottles into small day-packs and continued up the interminable rocky incline. We left behind the sleeping bags, some dregs of food, our tube of maps (except the one covering our current location), a tent, compass, pocketknives, *The Lonely Planet Peru*, three cameras, a video camera, spare batteries, video cassettes, a dry-bag for the camera, and an extensive first-aid kit.

Without the pack, it was a bit easier to continue, but each step still required extreme concentration and willpower. One foot after another. The desert stretched ahead, steeply rising to a ridge beyond which we believed lay a valley in which we would find an oasis. My tongue was swelling and speech was impossible. We walked, lost in our thoughts.

Lifting each leg over and over and over again up the slope was agony. The muscles did not want to respond. Taking a break did not help, either. Unlike a pause when you're tired, the rest didn't bring relief or ease the inflamed muscles; rather, it accentuated the precariousness of our situation. I didn't want to go on, but neither did I want to stop. That meant inevitable and painful death.

It took what seemed like forever, but we finally reached the summit. The view inspired disappointment and fear. I could not believe my eyes. Our maps indicated an oasis on the other side of a ridge. We had climbed all day toward this ridge. All day. And now we were there. Surely we were there?

No. We weren't at the top. We hadn't crested a ridge. We'd mounted a rise, a veritable speed bump on the way to the far-off summit of the main slope. All day, as we hiked up the hill, beyond our line of sight, the land continued to rise. Another long, steep, desolate slope lay before us, rising higher still.

I would have cried if my body had allowed such a frugal waste of liquid. I figured this is where the guy on the *Lonely Planet* television show sits down and dials 9-1-1 on the satellite phone. Our budget precluded such amenities. Ouch! My right leg began to shake uncontrollably, like a pneumatic drill, the overtaxed muscles cramping and seizing. The tiny pile of equipment we had abandoned was lost behind us in the heat haze. Nowhere on the 360-degree horizon could I see a stick to indicate water. We were on one of the most arid and isolated plains on the globe, and damned if I knew what we were going to do.

We were out of water, slowly broiling to death under a pitiless sun that was staring down unblinkingly from an aquamarine sky. With more money, we wouldn't have been in this condition. We could have called for help. With better planning, we wouldn't have been in this predicament. We would have brought more water.

"I think the map's off," Ben said.

Scott and I smiled. "No kidding," I replied.

"It is," he insisted.

There was nothing else to say. We kept going toward the next rise. But we were moving at a snail's pace, and the ridge just didn't seem to get any closer. I began thinking irrational, strange thoughts completely unrelated to the situation.

"The map's off," Ben repeated.

"Yes," I replied, "we know that."

"No, we should be going more easterly," he said.

Scott and I looked at each other. "Let's have another look."

The map came out and we stared at it in puzzlement. I was so addled from the lack of water that I couldn't make head or tail of it. Neither could Scott nor Ben. It was difficult to focus or to think clearly. After a moment or two, I didn't even want to look at it, as the symbols swam in front of my eyes. Trusting my previous judgment, I insisted we continue in the same direction.

"No," Ben said, "we should be further east. If we keep going this way, we'll miss the oasis."

"I don't think so," I said.

I was too tired to argue, and my mind refused to reason. Scott stood gape-mouthed. I insisted we keep going in the same direction. And I said that, over and over. Scott didn't have much of an opinion, but he opted to follow me. Not wanting to go off alone, Ben dejectedly continued along with us. He wasn't happy.

"The map's off," he continued to mutter.

"No kidding!" I said.

"How old were they?" he wanted to know.

"The maps?"

"What do you think?"

"The old guy said they were from fifty-year-old aerial photographs. It says on the corner, 'Updated 1951.'"

"They were based on aerial surveys that are fifty years old!" Ben shouted. "We should have spent more money on maps. But no-o-o-o."

He was working himself into a lather.

"There have been a lot of inconsistencies," he added. "What if the oasis isn't even there?"

"Don't think like that."

It was difficult not to. My mind recalled scenes from bad films of parched men staggering and crawling across sandy expanses, dying of thirst. It hadn't crossed my mind before we embarked that we wouldn't even see the source of the Amazon or that we'd die of thirst.

Gazing across the rocky expanse, I thought, What a mess! My lips were beginning to bleed. I couldn't even get up the energy to whine. The acetylene sun blazed down and the grueling routine continued—left leg forward, right leg forward, left leg forward . . .

Two weeks before I had been with my mother and sisters in Canmore, Alberta, almost atop North America's Great Divide. Clint Eastwood filmed *The Unforgiven* in the Rocky Mountain foothills near there. All we had talked about was how great a trip this would be, the knowledge I'd glean, the fun we'd have. Now I was praying that somewhere over the ridge we'd find an oasis—or I was dead.

I stopped and pulled out an empty bottle. I had heard stories about drinking your own urine in times of desperation. I was going to give it a try. My bladder felt empty and I had to push before any urine came forth.

The pint bottle filled up about a quarter full with a chocolate liquid. My piss had become so concentrated it was the color of Guinness. I put the bottle to my lips, but the ammonia smell made me gag. I couldn't drink it. I returned the bottle to my pack—maybe later.

We reached the top of the second ridge—and again were greeted by a slight dip and a continuation of the upward slope. We were beyond despair. We could see yet another ridge ahead. But how were we to know if that was really the summit, beyond which lay the oasis? Maybe the dry barren slopes just didn't end. Maybe they kept going and going.

We sat despondently for perhaps twenty minutes. I wasn't really thinking at all. My mind spun and I was aware of only one thing: my thirst. A cactus was growing nearby—a big juicy cactus. I stumbled toward it and slashed it with my knife.

"Don't do that," Ben warned.

I ignored him. A pale-green translucent fluid ran from the wound and I licked it up. A few seconds passed before a burning sensation filled my mouth and throat.

"A-a-i-i-i-e-e-e!"

I stepped back, spitting what I could out of my mouth.

"I don't think it's poisonous," Ben said.

"Let's just keep walking," Scott added.

We staggered onward and upward toward the next ridge. Ben continued to mumble about how we were going the wrong way. I turned toward another large cactus and said, "Ben, we're not going that way. Be quiet and keep walking."

It took a moment for me to realize I wasn't speaking to Ben. He and Scott laughed. My mind was fucked. Concentrate, I told myself. Left foot, right foot, left foot. My legs were slow to move and I was beginning to hallucinate.

"Stay focused," Ben said. "The oasis can't be much farther. Stay focused."

Without Ben or Scott to keep me motivated, I would have sat down and given up. More than anything else in the world, I wanted just to collapse.

It gets very difficult to walk when you become dehydrated and your joints begin to swell, but we managed to keep going. Time slipped by and we slowly gained altitude. Still, the closer we got to the next ridge, the more reluctant we were to let ourselves believe it was the summit. For the final 15 yards or so, I kept my eyes low for fear of seeing another ridge rising up.

None did. The land fell away into a valley. I crested the ridge, looked at the far horizon, and saw a violet wall of mountains with the peaks shrouded in clouds. I let my eyes fall down the faraway mountainsides into the valley. The rippled landscape turned brown, copper, bronze, burnt sienna—dry, dry, dry.

My heart stopped beating as I lowered my line of sight still further. I scanned the valley in a panic before spotting the splash of green. There it was! A picture-perfect oasis in the middle of the high desert. A thin dirt road snaked up from the southwest, turning sharply at the oasis toward the mountains—just as the map indicated. It wasn't a mirage. I knew it wasn't.

We grinned at each other, our lips cracking.

We quickened our pace, stumbling, tumbling down the

gentle slope toward the oasis. You cannot believe how good an algae-filled pond crawling with mosquito larvae can look. We fell into it, whooping with delight.

To be alive! Yes! This was why we came. To revel in the moment, completely outside ourselves in the ecstasy of being alive. We had made it. Lying in the tepid pond, I could think of nothing more satisfying. Well, a few things, but nothing at that moment would compare.

Water had never tasted as fine as that lumpy green liquid I scooped up and slurped down. Disease, forget it! For the next few hours I slowly rehydrated, lying in the shade of a eucalyptus tree, happy in quiet contemplation. That's what it's all about—to be here and now, completely in the present and aware of every molecule in your body. Yeah!

It was still mid-afternoon and, when we felt we had recovered enough, we decided to retrieve our bags. It's surprising how quickly we were able to bound down the incline, get the bags, and return happily along the route that had been agonizingly difficult only a few hours before.

Back at the oasis, we discovered a handful of ramshackle dwellings inhabited by suspicious people who refused to sell us supplies. Huanco, as the oasis was officially known, offered us only water. But we were in no danger of starving. We had some rice and soup left, and the locals said another larger village lay only 3 miles down the road.

I sat that night incredibly satisfied. I looked at the Southern Cross hanging in a sky bejewelled with constellations New York and Europe will never see. They are the same stars that the Portuguese, Spanish, and English explorers followed to their destinies. I knew they were also pointing me to mine.

We had nearly died that day. I hated to admit it, but that was why we had come—to ride that adrenaline rush as much as to ride the river. Before we had finished, we would roll the dice again, again and again. It was going to be a rollicking whale of a ride. With too much traffic on the roads for a good game of ball hockey today, young people must look elsewhere for thrills. Right?

Tomorrow, I thought, we will get up and continue our journey to Mount Quehuishua, Mount Mismi, and the sacred birthplace of the Amazon. At this point, I couldn't wait to get into the river. I was looking forward to the six weeks it would take us to run 560 miles of the most dangerous whitewater in the world. For no matter what happened—we might be bucked into roiling maelstroms, tossed by tumultuous turbulence and currents—no matter how we were manhandled by the river or the terrain, we wouldn't die thirsty.

Day 10: September 22, 1999

We rose early and headed down the winding dirt road that led away from the oasis, up into the Andes, and on to Arequipa. It didn't take long for the road to contort itself into an intestine of switchbacks as it climbed the grade. Sometimes we scrambled up the steepening slopes to avoid the arduous back-and-forth route of the backcountry highway. It was a tough, relentless climb. We moved like crabs.

My mind wandered as I walked. Conversation among the three of us seemed superfluous. We had spent so much time together that it felt as though we knew each other's thoughts. Of course, it wasn't true. We were different—just like everybody else.

I spent a lot of time thinking about the Spanish conquistadors, the first Europeans to cross South America. Their direct descendants could be traced to families that were still in positions of power throughout the continent. How tough and ruthless they must have been—no maps, no inkling of what lay ahead. But they had superior technology to the local inhabitants—horses, wheels, metal armour, and, of course, gunpowder.

Francisco Pizarro was the first to arrive in Peru, according to the record books. He is to South America what Christopher Columbus is to North America. Every kid in the country can tell you what he did—and the continent has never been the same since. He is held in mixed regard, as the herald of Western civilization and as the barbarian who sacked and destroyed one of the most advanced and sophisticated indigenous empires the New World had produced.

All the guidebooks and encyclopedias reiterate the salient events in his life. Pizarro left Spain for the West Indies two years before Henry VIII was crowned king of England. He lived for about a decade in Hispaniola, the main Spanish base in the New World. In 1513 he served as Vasco Núñez de Balboa's chief lieutenant for the famed march by the Spanish military explorers across the Isthmus of Panama to the Pacific Ocean. They founded Panama City, and Pizarro became one of its the most powerful and wealthy elite.

In Panama Pizarro continued to push down the northwestern coast of South America, chasing rumours of an Indian Empire of gold. Fierce native resistance hampered him from finding the fabled Inca for years. But, as only the greedy and gold-fevered can, Pizarro persevered and succeeded in late 1527 or early 1528. You can imagine his awe as he looked at the jig-saw architecture of Inca cities. Without mortar, they designed multi-story stone buildings that withstood the earthquakes in this geologically young area. I had an idea of what these cities might have been like from the ruins I'd seen so far on the trip, and the ubiquitous pictures of Machu Picchu I'd seen over the years.

Walking along a road that was probably in use back then, a landscape steeped in such rich history, I couldn't help thinking: This is where some Monty Python character pops up and says, "Cor, it's history come to life, isn't it?"

Although the Inca never invented writing, they were a sophisticated people with a highly stratified society, advanced communal services, and an efficient state government ruled from the capital, Cuzco—reputed to be the oldest city in the Americas. It was a large and rich sovereignty extending more than 2,400 miles along the western coast, including parts of present-day Colombia, Ecuador, Bolivia, Chile, and Argentina. Like the Romans, the Inca understood that an empire required infrastructure. They constructed a public road and trail system and maintained an elaborate civil service that communicated via *quipu*—pieces of macramé that conveyed information through a complex code of knots and colored threads.

Pizarro knew immediately that such organized political structure meant wealth. He returned to Spain and persuaded King Charles I to name him governor of Peru, raised a lot of money, and headed back to milk his new possession. In 1531 Pizarro sailed from Panama City with about 180 men and, when they landed in what is now Ecuador, they started a war. The Spaniards fought south, following the Inca trail system back toward the heart of the empire. With swords, horses, and a smattering of muskets, they slaughtered the Inca.

By the end of 1533 Pizarro and his army controlled the empire, including Cuzco. Two years later Pizarro founded Lima, which became the center of the government in South America as the Spanish forces looted native treasuries and appropriated gold and silver mines. When the conquistadors arrived, there were about 6 million Inca; within the first fifty years of conquest, the population declined to fewer than 2 million.

From Peru, Spanish settlers infiltrated south and east. It was during these years that they made the first attempts to cross the continent by land in search of an easier route back to Europe. Those efforts were the historic roots for our journey. We were following in the footsteps of Francisco de Orellana, the first Spaniard to cross the continent, though we were using a more southerly route. When he descended the Napo River in 1542, he was the first European to run the Amazon system. It was, in fact, one of the people who accompanied him, Friar Gaspar de Carajal, who named the river with his fanciful account of women warriors. He said the women were "very white and tall, and have hair very long and braided and wound about the head, and they are very robust and go about naked, but with their privy parts covered, with their bows and arrows in their hands, doing as much fighting as 10 Indian men."

I could understand why such visions would occur to the good friar. As I trekked up the side of the Andes, my shoulders aching, my pack stuffed with modern marvels, I considered the conquistadors and their contemporaries as true heroes—men physically and mentally capable of enduring hardships that no modern individual could handle.

We humped our way through the dun-colored, treeless world, as if we were on a treadmill. Upward, upward, upward sloped the plain, seemingly stretching to infinity. Hours would pass, and we still seemed to be in the same spot. At least, the backdrop didn't seem to move or change. Perhaps it was the lack of contrast. The landscape was a sepia-colored print—a brown-hued, textured rock garden. There were cacti, but they added to the dreamlike, Daliesque quality of the geography. Or perhaps it was my desire to get to the river. We, unlike the conquistadors, had a destination. We were at about 8,600 feet and still breathing fairly easily. The summit of the first line of mountains, which we hoped to cross the next day, was about 13,800 feet. That would be the first real test on our bodies: how they responded to the thin air and the lack of oxygen at high altitude. We knew we were taking a risk by climbing to the divide without taking the time to allow our bodies to acclimatize.

As we climbed higher, small alpine flowers began to appear, then larger blooms. There were plants with bright yellow petals like nasturtiums, and others with smaller, more delicate pink, purple, or blushing blossoms. The splashes of color were incongruous in the monochromatic desert high country.

Nine hours after leaving Huanco, we reached the crest of the next major ridge and stood facing a plateau. The village, we had been told, was about 3 miles away. We strained our eyes scanning the horizon. Scott spotted some irregular man-made-looking objects and we took them to be our destination. As we got closer, I could distinguish six circular buildings, but there was no sign of life—no people, no dogs barking, nothing. Instead of lush fields, the land was as dry and hardscrabble as the slope we had just ascended.

It was clear the town had been abandoned. I groaned, slumped my shoulders, and let my bag slip to the ground. The buildings, each about 10 feet in diameter, were decrepit and rotting. Cracks and holes pierced the loose-fitting rocks that formed the walls. Each was roofed with a dilapidated frame of dried cactus that had once supported thatch.

I went from once hut to the next, hoping to find a stash of food—a can of beans, anything. But each interior was the same: dark, dirty, and empty.

Scott and Ben set up camp while I searched for water. I found a dried-out stream just below the village. I assumed the area had been abandoned when the water dried up. Then, again, maybe nomadic herdsmen used the site when water was more abundant. I retraced the course of the former creek to a fissure in the face of a nearby cliff. A canyon, carved over centuries by the water, led back into the cliff-face. Maybe there was water up there.

I stepped into the mouth of the *arroyo*, its sides so high that no sunlight reached its floor. It was almost dark, and the air was distinctly cooler. I felt as though I were in a cave, so close were the sides of the walls and so high the upper lips of the cliff. The walls rose up on both sides about 2 yards apart. The gray canyon floor was polished smooth by water. I pressed deeper, enjoying the break from the searing heat. Yet if there was water, surely people lived here? After all, every inch of arable land was exploited in Peru. Llama herders lived at more than 14,000 feet, farmers grew corn in desert conditions beside minuscule springs.

The canyon twisted and turned as it cut back into the hillside. I looked up at the ragged slice of azure. Suddenly hun-

dreds, perhaps thousands, of startled birds swarmed past me—
Andean geese, cormorants, terns, coots, and other species,
squeaking and squawking. They seemed to be everywhere in
their confusion to escape. Wow! Talk about Hitchcock's *The
Birds!*

I walked deeper into the canyon. It was a natural garden. A
range of plants thrived on the damp cool air and abundant fer-
tilizer. Verdant Spanish moss hung from some ledges. Guano,
the build-up of years, covered any other visible rock face and
dripped from the canyon lip like so much gray icing. Flowers
blossomed in every hue. Vines crept over the rocks, and there
were even small bushes. Ahead, I could see a pool of stagnant
water. It stood in a deep bowl carved in the canyon floor by a
waterfall long silent. The water was lime green with algae and
smelled of decay. It could be the remains of a stream run dry
years past or rain from a month before.

I returned to camp to tell Ben and Scott.

We discussed the situation over rice and soup for dinner.
We had a quart of water left and it was 25 miles to Huambo,
the next town on the map. There wasn't even a farm until
then. We didn't want to repeat the near-death experience of
the desert. We decided to subsist the following day on rice
alone, cooking a big batch at breakfast and eating it cold for
lunch and dinner. Ben and I would return to the canyon to assess the water.

Ben's jaw dropped as we left the desert and entered the cool,
colorful canyon. The birds again startled us as they fled. The
stagnant pool glistened, a jade gem in the dusky light. We decided to strain the water through a shirt, filter it with our water
purifier, and boil it. Ben's biggest concern was toxins that
wouldn't be affected by the heat.

The first stage worked fairly well. The T-shirt removed a lot
of slime, but the water still looked like murky olive oil. Our water filter choked on the muck and plugged up after only two
squirts. In spite of a vigorous scrubbing, it was useless. So, boiling it was. We set the pot of water over the fire and, after twenty

minutes at a brisk roll, we removed it from the flame and let it cool. The process turned the water a chestnut color. It looked vile.

Scott took the first sip, swishing it around in his mouth before swallowing. "Tastes like shit, mates," he said jovially. "The question is, Will it kill me?"

Ben and I shrugged. The pot was passed around, and we each had a swallow. It didn't taste too bad—a slightly fishy flavor, but not overpowering, not as strong as Asian fish sauce.

"This is pretty good considering there is practically more bird shit in it than water," Ben said, water dribbling from his chin. "Maybe there are some nutritional benefits to all that algae."

We repeated the process, filled our water bottles, and cooked the rice and soup using the same water. The next day would be a long one, and I wasn't really looking forward to it.

Day 11: September 23, 1999

I woke at 5 and lit the fire Scott had built the night before. The air was freezing and I practically climbed into the boiling rice to keep warm. Ben and Scott got up when the rice was ready and we ate big steaming bowls when it was cooked. We stored what was left, still in the pot, in Ben's pack.

Just the faintest glimmer of pearl-colored light could be seen on the horizon. Dawn was not far off.

We reached the summit at about 11 A.M. To celebrate, Scott pulled out the rice and we wolfed down the tasteless carbohydrate. I was gasping for breath. We would descend slightly into the famed Cañón del Colca for the next part of the trek, and I couldn't wait to get a good breath.

On the other side of the ridge there was more life. Occasionally we spotted wildlife—a fox trotting along the fringe of the chaparral, a couple of *vizcacha* (indigenous chinchilla-like rodents) sunbathing on a rock, a vicuña grazing, or a lizard enjoying the day. By late afternoon my stomach was constantly rumbling. It wanted more than rice. Oooh, what I would have given for a good Thai restaurant! I even began wondering how *vizcacha* would taste slowly roasted on a spit, crisp and evenly cooked all over. Probably like rabbit. Or maybe more like rat.

It had been six days since we had left Corire. We had planned to resupply after only two or three days. That miscalculation meant our food was stretched to the limit. The prospect of buying a chocolate bar or a Coke made me drool.

When we arrived in Huambo, the sun was setting. Children ran along beside us chattering in Spanish, eagerly directing us hither and yon or cursing us silly. Who knew? They took us down cobbled streets past sizable adobe houses. An old man with a donkey joined our procession as it spilled noisily into the town's central square. An impressive stone church dominated the scene and there were two café shops. We entered the nearer one and slid into the three chairs that surrounded a single wooden table.

An elderly native woman greeted us with a kind smile.

"Hola."

We ordered the menu of the day and she brought us each a big bowl of soup, a plate of rice covered with a chicken and corn stew, hard-boiled eggs, and a glass of orange juice. Dessert was a Sublime, a small square of chocolate and peanuts produced by Nestlé in Peru. After days of eating practically nothing but rice, they were heavenly.

Sitting on those wooden chairs, the mud walls decorated by a few racks of Indian corn and dried gourds, we calculated how far we had come. The old lady looked at the map spread across the table and giggled when she recognized the name of her town. From Camaná to Huambo was almost 124 miles. We were doing well. Huambo is one of a series of villages along the lip of the Colca Canyon.

Before saying goodnight, we bought supplies from the shopkeeper and splurged on Sublimes for the road. We set up camp just outside the village.

Day 12: September 24, 1999

I awoke and stepped outside the tent at about 8 A.M. The view stunned me. Until recently the Colca was regarded as the deepest canyon in the world—its bottom at one point 11,000 feet below the upper reaches. But recent opinion has it that the nearby Cañón del Cotahuasi is deeper.

Whether the Colca is the deepest or second-deepest canyon, it is spectacular. We hadn't seen it when we arrived because it was dark. In daylight, it yawned back at me—a giant chasm that could swallow the Grand Canyon. I felt as though I were looking into the bowels of the earth. Steep, folded, cinnamon-colored cliffs tumbled to the darkness below. The Colca River, presumably flowing at the bottom, was invisible. Sunlight lanced into the canyon, only to die in the murky sea of shadows below. The walls climbed above me, rising perpendicular before making the subtle transition to steep mountain slopes. These slopes rose much higher to become snowcapped peaks. I didn't know what was more impressive— the jagged mountains towering over my head or the great emptiness below.

After the Spanish had subjugated the Inca Empire, Pizarro's brother ended up with control of the Colca Valley. He pillaged and stripped the land and resources until they were exhausted.

For the next few days we would follow the canyon until we reached the base of Mount Mismi. I was looking forward to this stretch: it would be relatively easy because a road followed the canyon's rim, and the scenery was breathtaking. We struck camp in record time—less than twenty minutes. Dismantling the tent and stowing the gear were now mechanical routines. We were seasoned travelers.

Our goal for the day was a town called Cabanaconde, about 11 miles away, a fairly relaxing stroll and just what we needed after the previous day's trek. People frequently passed us on the well-groomed gravel road. The women wore heavily embroidered jackets, black dresses, and distinctive white-felt bowler hats often adorned with lace, sequins, or badges. The vivid dyes in their clothes, particularly the pinks and blues, fairly burned with intensity. An old farmer coaxing his donkeys along touched his hat as we passed. Some giggling young girls walking with books under their arms greeted us. Most of the young people we saw dressed in Western-style clothing, though many of the older ones wore garments of hand-woven cloth. Both men and women walked with their shoulders back and their heads high. The land was no longer empty and barren.

Amazingly, although the terrain was anything but flat, there were farms everywhere. The lush hillsides were terraced like natural amphitheatres. We could see men and women working the fields. Occasionally we saw a man plowing with a bull or a team of oxen that dragged an elaborately carved wooden plowshare. Tools and crops were carried in and out of the fields by patient donkeys.

Most of the inhabitants of the Colca Valley are Indians. More Indians apparently live in Peru than in any other country in South America and make up nearly half the country's population of 26 million. The rest are primarily *mestizos*, people of mixed Indian and European (mainly Spanish) ancestry. Roughly half of Peru's population lives along the coast, and almost all the other inhabitants, including most of the country's Indians, eke out a living as subsistence farmers in the highlands. The Himalayas is the only other place in the world where people live at such high altitudes.

The road clung to the canyon rim, and I was glad I was on foot. Passing vehicles came within a few feet of the precipitous edge and the deadly drop. Every so often a car hurtled past, its occupants seemingly oblivious to the danger and the driver merrily tooting his horn as he fishtailed around the next corner. Four out of every five vehicles was a mini-bus, usually a Toyota Hiace stuffed with brown laughing faces.

Cabanaconde was nearly identical to Huambo. A beautiful

whitewashed church sat in the middle of the town, with a manicured square in front. The canyon here was even more impressive—3,900 feet deep. Mount Mismi stood magnificently on the other side, its snow-dusted summit 10,500 feet above the canyon. But what really caught my attention were the gringos. It had been a fortnight since we last saw a tourist. Here, at least half a dozen milled around the square. *The Lonely Planet* listed this town as a must-see spot, and they had come. There was a local lookout called Cruz del Cóndor, and rumour had it that, occasionally, there were Andean condors in the area. We didn't see any.

Tourism brings more facilities and higher prices. Our hostel cost three times what we paid elsewhere, though, for $3.30, we were living in style. Our beds had soft pillows, the food in the dining room was borderline gourmet, and the *agua caliente* truly was hot, not tepid or just plain cold. Tourism had also transformed the locals. They looked at us not with genuine interest, but with a greedier look in their eyes. We were the same as an ATM machine and they were concerned only with our wallets.

It was good, however, to talk to other people again in English. Ben, Scott, and I were traveling like a troupe of mutes. Because of our broken Spanish, we had barely interacted with the local people, repeating the same phrases over and over again.

"Mount Mismi."

"Camaná."

"Canada, Australia, y Inglaterra."

"Sí, a pie." ("Yes, by foot.")

We spent most of the evening chatting up two American girls, Sarah and Sarah from Portland, Oregon. They were doing volunteer healthcare work in Peru, had a few weeks off, and were spending it backpacking throughout the mountains. We were smitten.

Day 13: September 25, 1999

We were slightly disoriented as we left the hostel, in part because it was situated on a small side street. I asked a young man wearing a baseball cap which way to Maca, our destination.

He gestured with a nod toward a trail at the end of the street. We walked to the head of the path and unrolled the map. It indicated that a road led to Maca, not a footpath.

"Maybe the trail was created after the map was surveyed," Scott suggested.

"Maybe it's a shortcut," I said.

"The road is filled with switchbacks and this is more direct, maybe," Ben volunteered.

I spotted a woman hanging her laundry.

"Señora, Señora," I called, gesticulating to get her attention.

She looked over. I pointed down the trail in pantomime: "Maca? Maca?"

"Sí," she nodded and went back to her chore.

"I guess this is it, boys," I said.

At first the trail skirted mounds of fetid garbage at the edge of the village and picked its way across the terraces. We hadn't gone very far when a woman who looked to be in her nineties and what seemed a slightly built teenaged boy began to overtake us with two donkeys.

"Hola," I said. "Is this the trail to Maca?"

"Sí," the woman replied.

I waved gracias and we continued to walk. The old crone turned to us: "Would you like to use our donkeys?"

"How much?"

"Five soles."

Scott, Ben, and I looked at each other and eagerly pulled off our packs. Walking easily, we soaked in the scenery. I couldn't help thinking about my family and how my mother would have gasped at these vistas.

My dad, Colin Angus Sr., is dead now and I really didn't know him well when I was growing up. My mother, Valerie Spentzos, an extraordinary woman whose courage is probably the source of my own chutzpah, reared me. She loves learning and, even at the age of sixty-nine, is making plans to go back to school. I think I got my drive and insatiable curiosity from her.

My mother was born Valerie Bremner in Edinburgh in 1932. When the war broke out, her family moved to the Isle of Coll to escape German bombers. Later, she went to university in Glasgow to study literature and languages, met my father there, and briefly dated. But he joined the merchant navy and became a sea captain; she immigrated to Canada and became a high school teacher, their love unconsummated.

In Thunder Bay, Ontario, my mother married a Greek colleague, George. They had three children while they were both teaching there. After six years of marriage, however, they split up. My mother took my three siblings and moved to British Columbia.

My half brother, George, is the eldest—seven years older than I—followed by Jane and Patty. They all look alike, with strong Greek features. My mother found a job in Golden teaching junior high, but she hated it and moved on as soon as she could to the coast, in Port Alberni. It was there, in that working-class pulp-mill town and deep-sea port, that she met my father again.

They had corresponded with each other over the years and he was working for the Canadian federal government as skipper of the hydrographic vessel *Parazoa*. His first marriage, too, had just broken up. I learned later that his ex-wife lived in Victoria and they had a baby daughter, but his relatives adopted the little girl after their divorce.

By the end of my mother's year-long fling with my father, their infatuation had cooled but she was pregnant. I was born in Victoria a few months after my father had sailed away, leaving my mother. With four hungry mouths to feed, she tried to trace him. She wrote to his relatives in Scotland, but no reply or child support ever came her way.

Worse, the school board was unwilling to hold her job for the two-month maternity leave while she bore me and she was forced to find another. She was given a teaching position in Hope, but it took two years before an opening allowed us to move back to Alberni.

When I was about to begin first grade, my mother took an unpaid year's leave of absence, borrowed a lot of money, moved to Victoria, and got her Master's degree. Then, at the age of fifty-six, when I was still a teen but all the other children had left home, she sold her house in Alberni and moved to Comox, on the eastern coast of Vancouver Island. Although not a bustling city, it was a step up from decaying Port Alberni. I came to realize that there is more to the world than work and houses. My mother still jogs six miles every other day and takes accordion lessons. She passed her zest for life on to me. It was that nomadic life as a kid that gave travel its allure and led directly to my being on an Inca trail headed for the source of the Amazon.

As we descended into the Colca Canyon, the terraces disappeared and the slopes became more steep. The trail made a dizzying descent, with hundreds of steep switchbacks disappearing down into the darkness. It required focus to stay on the path and maintain balance.

I thought it odd that the trail went all the way to the canyon floor. Wasn't Maca on the upper lip?

"Are you sure this is the way to Maca?" I asked the old woman.

"Sí," she said.

Her companion nodded his head. Even under close scrutiny it was difficult to tell his age. He could have been a very small man. Perhaps he was a dwarf. This was clearly David Lynch country. Down. Down. Down. For two hours we descended that steep, toenail-crushing trail carved into the cliff. A sheer drop on one side, a vertical wall on the other. The direct rays from the sun disappeared below us. Down we went until, eventually, the Colca River came into view, a few huts clinging to its side.

I could see that the trail did not continue on this side of the river. It was impossible, as the canyon walls were too precipitous, slicing perpendicular into the Colca. The river sluiced through this part of the canyon with the force of a fire hose. I realized we had been duped.

"Stop!" I shouted. "This trail doesn't lead to Maca."

The woman turned and held me with her eyes.

"No," she said matter of factly, as if everyone knew that.

"We want to go to Maca," I insisted.

"Well, this isn't the way," she shrugged. Turning away from me, she tapped the donkeys and started to walk again.

"Stop, stop, stop," I stammered. "We don't want to go down any further."

Grudgingly she stopped. She and mini-man watched as we unloaded our packs. As we were about to leave, the man-boy stuck out his hand. "Money."

"We didn't want to go this way," said Ben. "Why should we pay you any money?"

"You used our donkeys," replied mini-man.

"That's because you lied to us and said this trail leads to Maca."

Ben started back up the trail. The midget, for he stood no taller than 4 feet, sprinted in front of Ben and blocked his path. He was fearless of Ben's imposing 6-foot-6 frame, which towered menacingly over him.

"Money!" mini-man demanded, his obsidian eyes blazing with a diamond's cold intensity. No matter what his age, the midget had left childhood long behind.

The old woman stood silently with the donkeys, her eyes burning with anger.

"Tell you what," said Ben, "take our gear back up this goddamned cliff and I'll pay you the money."

"NO!" mini-man yelled. "We're not going that way."

Frustrated, Ben threw up his hands in defeat. He pulled from his pocket a handful of crumpled soles and thrust half the agreed-upon price toward the midget. Three soles. "That's all you're getting."

Mini-man snatched the grimy notes and shoved them in his pocket. He walked back to the old woman muttering curses. We ignored him, but his guttural shouts followed us up the canyon, echoing off its walls and pricking our ears until we had out-distanced the reverberations.

Ten sweaty hours later, we arrived at the town of Maca. Once again, it was after dark. We found our way to the central square and saw the bell tower of the church collapsed in the heap of rubble. A middle-aged *mestizo* selling alpaca sweaters lingered.

"What happened to the tower?" I asked.

"Earthquake. Many dead—more than a thousand. A big catastrophe."

We nodded empathetically. "Café?"

He pointed across the square.

We entered the dimly lit adobe building and found a dozen men around a long wooden table watching a small black-and-white TV. A second wooden table sat empty. The men looked up for a moment, then turned back to their Arequipeñas—the local beer. A teenager eyed us as he pulled on a bottle of pisco, Peru's answer to Tequila. A matronly woman appeared bearing plates of food on each arm—like a tree laden with steaming fruit. She put one before each of us—corn gruel on rice with a pair of chicken feet. It wasn't much, it wasn't fancy, but it hit the spot.

After we had finished, the men asked if we would buy them

a round. They were used to tourists with bottomless pockets. We explained that our budget didn't allow it and said good-night, heading into the night to pitch camp on the outskirts of town.

Day 14: September 26, 1999

We rose early, before dawn. We wanted to cross the canyon and reach the village of Madrigal. From there we would make our climb to the source of the Amazon. The canyon here is not nearly as deep or as steep, and we made our way to the bottom without difficulty.

We arrived at the Colca's edge late in the morning. It was the tail end of the dry season, so the river was at its lowest ebb. We couldn't agree where to ford it, so each of us chose his own path. I found an area where, although the current was swift, there were numerous boulders breaking the flow that could be used as stepping stones.

I divided my gear into two loads so I wouldn't be overburdened and picked my way across, getting only my shorts wet. Ben made it across successfully, too, and together we headed downstream. The two of us had fallen back into the close friendship we had enjoyed when we first met in England. We found Scott cursing and soaked. He spread the contents of his day-pack out on a rock to dry it in the sun. "God-damn slippery rocks," he growled.

Soon we were on our way again, this time climbing out of the canyon. As we hiked up the steep slope, we came on a series of hot springs. A handful of young girls splashed in the water, making a game out of the laundry they were cleaning. When we neared the rim of the canyon, we found ourselves back in a cultivated landscape. The trail to Madrigal ran parallel to a small channel used to irrigate the fields. I marveled at the simplicity and efficiency of the tiny aqueduct. It branched into hundreds of smaller channels, capillaries to nourish the terraces. Miniature mud dams held the flow back when necessary. If water was needed, these dams could be broken with the kick of a foot, and the water would bubble through the furrows into the terraced fields. Gravity, combined with the natural incline, pulled the rivulets down one terrace after the other. When sufficient water had been released, the dam could be rebuilt with a bit of mud and a few rocks. It was a system devised by the Incas, who used several methods to make their farms more productive, even though historians say they did not have wheels or plows pulled by animals. Here, they cut terraces into the hillsides to reduce erosion and make irrigation easier. The main Inca crops were corn, cotton, potatoes, an edible root called *oca*, and a grain known as *quinoa*. They are still being cultivated.

Entering Madrigal, we were immediately greeted by the local police officer. He was a friendly fellow. He noted our personal details in his report book and allowed us to leave our gear in the office while we looked for a scout and for donkeys for hire.

Madrigal sits at an altitude of almost 10,000 feet. The divide is only a short distance away, at 15,700 feet. The climb would be much easier if we had donkeys to carry our gear. It's tough to carry a 66-pound pack up a 45-degree incline at such an altitude. We couldn't find anyone willing to accompany us up the mountain. Most men we asked declined, saying they had crops to tend—obviously, they didn't need the money. We went back to the police officer and asked him for help.

He led us a few blocks and knocked on a door. We were ushered inside a smoky, airless room where eight or nine men with the demeanor of casting-call thugs sat in heated debate. They wore felt hats pulled low over their eyes and immediately fell silent on our arrival. All eyes turned toward us.

In the corner, a man at a desk went back to a pile of papers. The policeman addressed a stocky middle-aged man in a black cloak. They spoke in rapid-fire Spanish, or perhaps it was a blend of Spanish and Quechua, the preferred Indian language of the highlands. Occasionally, one of the others interjected excitedly.

The swarthy man turned, talking so softly you had to lean forward to hear what he said. Everyone listened. In painfully slow, concise Spanish, he said with great seriousness: "So, you want to get to the top of the mountain?"

We nodded. I wasn't sure whether we had stumbled upon the local Mafia or a regional acting troupe. The man in the cloak continued with the *gravitas* of a stand-up comedian.

"You want donkeys?" he said conspiratorially.

We nodded again. The other men in the room leaned forward, watching us intently. The man in the cape stared at us.

"I have donkeys"—he looked around for effect—"many donkeys," he nodded.

From the sober looks, I was sure they were pulling our legs. "Can we rent a couple?" I asked.

"Perhaps," the man said, and fell into silence.

Heads around the room nodded. I waited. One beat, two beat, three beats. No one said anything.

"We really need to know," I continued. "We'd like to leave tomorrow."

"I will have to think about it," the man replied, as if I had asked to marry his daughter.

"How much will it cost us?" Ben interjected.

"We can discuss that when the job is finished," the man said gravely.

"We'd really like to know before we go," I told him.

He nodded his head. "Mmmm."

"How much?" I pressed.

"Hmmm," he said, continuing to nod.

The conversation was clearly over. We turned for the door.

"Goodbye then," I ventured.

The man waved dismissively: "I'll see you tomorrow morning in the square."

It wasn't a question. We weren't expected to answer. We closed the door behind us.

"That was weird," I said.

"I don't like it," Ben replied. "I don't like going without knowing the cost."

We were all unsettled by the encounter. As we walked toward the edge of town, looking for a place to spend the night, we met a youngish man headed home with his donkeys.

"Hola," Scott called.

"Buenas tardes," the thin man said.

We asked if he would like to accompany us up the mountain with his donkeys.

"It is Sunday tomorrow and I must go to church. Why do you want to climb the mountain?"

Once we explained our quest, he offered to accompany us with two donkeys for $25 a day. It was expensive, but we agreed.

"My name is Willie," he said.

We shook hands.

"If you like, you can sleep behind my place."

Day 15: September 27, 1999

We were rousted out of bed about 5 A.M. by the sound of hectoring Spanish blasting from loudspeakers in the church. After a half-hour of denunciation so distorted it was impossible to understand, tinny marching music was provided as a reveille.

"Every morning we have this," Willie told us as we packed. "It is beautiful, isn't it?"

Willie's wife stood at the doorway holding their baby, swaying to the sound of drums and trumpets.

"What happens to the people who want to sleep in?" Scott asked.

"Nobody sleeps in. How could you when there are fields to tend?"

Willie secured our bags to the donkeys with several ropes of braided leather. The larger beast carried Scott's pack and mine. The other bore Ben's bag and some separately packed provisions. We carried our own day-bags with water, lunch, and sunblock. Willie, who was barefoot, also carried a bag, made from a colorful woven blanket folded to make a comfortable carrying sack. It contained several pots of corn gruel—the local staple.

A vast network of trails, most dating back to the Inca Empire and before, still link every inch of Peru. The automobile of the people remains the donkey—the perfect means for navigating the rough, steep paths. We were headed for a col, a low saddle on the divide, with an elevation of 15,700 feet.

The initial stages of the trail were lush. We passed plots of corn, onions, potatoes, zucchinis, and other vegetables. Although we were at tropical latitudes, the altitude created a temperate climate. Soon we were climbing steep switchbacks. Although donkeys can ascend much steeper slopes than a car, there is a limit to what they can safely descend.

At 11,800 feet the landscape was barren and brown. There was no irrigation here and the primary vegetation was a straw-like grass called *ichu*. There were dwarf trees called *quinua* in Spanish, and shrubs genetically evolved to survive in a landscape of cloudless days, extreme solar radiation, wind, and cold. This high country is called the *puna*—a barren alpine region that makes up much of Peru. It is an environment stalked by the most fearsome of the supernatural Inca demons, equivalent to the Land of Cain. Only the hardiest of plants live at these altitudes, and the hardiest of people.

The men we met now were alpaca herders. These indigenous animals, similar to llamas, are genetically designed to withstand the rigours of their alpine home. They graze on the golden *ichu* or any other vegetation they find. The herders trade meat, leather, and wool for fruit and vegetables produced below.

At 13,800 feet I was gasping for air. I looked thankfully at the donkeys that trundled along without complaint. Willie followed behind them, occasionally tapping their rumps with a piece of rubber fashioned from a car tire. When he wanted them to pick up the pace, he muttered, "Burro vas burro." Like the donkeys, Willie was accustomed to the altitude. He had lived his life above 9,000 feet.

The precarious trail skirted the top of several cliffs. Sometimes it was washed out, leaving only a slope of loose gravel and scree tilted toward a precipitous drop. I crossed such strips with speed, hoping my momentum would carry me to the other side before I lost my footing and plummeted off the cliff. Willie told us that the previous week an alpaca herder coming down to the village had slipped in this very area. He and his donkey had fallen to their deaths.

At 2 o'clock we were at roughly 14,000 feet and frequently stopping to catch our breath. It seemed we were continually gasping. Even during our breaks I felt out of breath. On one of the many stops I took out the Sublimes. I asked Willie if he wanted one, but he declined. He said he had never tasted chocolate—"too big a luxury." Instead, he slurped back his corn gruel while the donkeys grazed on the brown grass.

"You sure, Willie?" I pressed. "These are damn fine chocolate bars."

I held one out and he relented. He took a bite, hesitant at first, grinned, and wolfed down the square.

We still had 1,500 feet to gain in altitude. The distance was only about 3,000 feet, but with the elevation so steep, we covered it slowly. Every half-hour we stopped. Willie offered us some of his coca.

We chewed on the leaf with a sliver of *llipta*, a chalky mixture of mineral lime and ash that acted as a catalyst, causing the saliva-moistened leaves to release the drug. Coca is supposed to give a slight buzz and relieve hunger and fatigue. The locals insist it's a cure-all. The bolus numbed my mouth and throat. If I persisted on chewing the leaves for a long time, my mouth started to burn, as though I had eaten too many sour candies.

We reached the divide at 4 o'clock. In the crux of the pass sat a large cairn topped with a cross. We were 15,700 feet above sea level and there was no plant life, only sharp-edged rock.

There was no snow on the trail itself, although it ran beside a great white glacier and a field of snow and ice. We had been looking at the Colca Canyon all day. Now a vast expanse stretched before us, sloping imperceptibly toward the Amazon Basin. If we looked north and south, our view was limited by very close, towering mountains.

Scott stepped behind the cairn to urinate.

"Careful, mate," Ben said with a wry smile, "you're polluting the Amazon."

Willie was transfixed. He had not been up here before. He had never considered the idea of a continental divide, but he seemed to understand the concept. The donkeys couldn't have cared less. They looked miserable, braced against the icy wind that howled through the pass like a banshee.

Dark clouds were rolling in from the east, and we decided to move on. We wanted to descend at least 980 feet before setting up base camp. Not only was the col extremely exposed but the altitude was too high for our bodies. Ascending from 9,800 feet to 15,700 feet in one day is pushing the envelope of acceptability. The rule of thumb is that, above 11,800 feet, it takes a day to acclimatize for every 980 feet in altitude.

Scott and I were already suffering from *soroche*, the dreaded altitude sickness that felled Ridgeway and Odendaal during their trips to the source. If we remained at this height overnight, we could end up really sick or even permanently maimed. Above 14,700 feet you risk pulmonary and cerebral edema.

We didn't have the time, though, to wait until we were acclimatized. We were already running behind schedule and feeling pressed. We had to get our raft in the river. The rainy season was approaching and it would be suicidal to run the Apurimac when it was swollen. Navigating the rapids at high water was out of the question. We must ascend Mount Mismi and Mount Quehuishua as quickly as possible.

The two mountains that represented the controversial source of the Amazon reached skyward to the south of us. The volcanic cone of Quehuishua was directly above us. Beyond was Mount Mismi. Snow began to fall as we made our way down the eastern side of the divide. Willie, in bare feet, stumbled but didn't complain. During a break, Scott pulled from his sack a spare pair of running shoes. He handed them to a grateful Willie.

About five feet of snow had fallen and the wind shrieked. Willie maintained there was a hut in the area where we could shelter, but it was 6:30 and the light had almost gone. It was impossible to see in the gray-whiteness of the squall. We heard the barking first. A large black-and-white dog bounded into view. We looked to follow its tracks—surely its home was nearby. But the wind had erased the dog's trail.

"Go home," Scott said, but the dog wagged its tail.

"Let's camp here," I said. "We're never going to find the hut. We can squeeze four people into our tent."

Willie, who had no tent or bedding, shook his head.

"Willie can wear all our clothes—that should keep him warm," I ventured.

He was already shivering, and I could see he had no faith that our tent would shelter us from the storm. "OK," I relented. "Let's go for another twenty minutes."

I felt sick. My body wanted thick, rich air. My head was pounding from the lack of oxygen, and melting snow dripped down my neck. The wind howled.

"¡La casa!" Willie cried.

A dark object loomed ahead—perhaps a boulder. Staggering closer, I saw it actually was a hut—a sturdy-looking, windowless stone structure. The gaps between the rocks were chinked with mud and the roof was thick thatch. We found the low wooden door. Like Goldilocks, we walked in.

Ben pulled out his headlamp flashlight and shone it around the small room. Just to be out of the squall was welcome. It had a packed dirt floor and a chimneyless fireplace. A pile of llama skins lay in a corner. Beside the fireplace was a bundle of dried twigs, which must have been carried up from the valley. There was no wood at this height. The ceiling and walls were black with soot.

Willie lit a fire and, seconds later, I was outside in the snow, tears streaming from my eyes. I was overcome with a coughing fit. Weakened by the pounding headache and nausea brought on by the *soroche*, I gulped fresh air. Moments later, Ben and Scott were smoked out, too.

We pitched our $99 Coleman tent in the lee of the hut while Willie happily cooked dinner inside over the fire. Eventually, the cold drove us back into the smokehouse. I buried my head in my jacket, but it was still asphyxiating and I was nauseated. Willie, looking as healthy as ever, announced that dinner was ready—a plate of rice drenched with tuna swimming in a tomato sauce. I managed to swallow a few spoonfuls before calling it quits and heading to bed. I was going down for the count.

Day 16: September 28, 1999

I awoke with a great wet weight on me. The tent had collapsed under the newly fallen snow and my $34 Sears sleeping bag was soaked. Shivering, I struggled from the soggy cocoon, but as soon as I was upright my head was pummelled by some fiend with a mallet inside my skull and my stomach somersaulted. I staggered into the snow, vomiting, clutching my forehead. It was excruciating. Where were the miracle analgesics when you needed them? The extra-strength Tylenol was useless.

Scott, looking no better, wriggled out of the collapsed tent and grimaced. Even the donkeys, tethered 10 yards away, appeared unhappy. Several inches of snow lay on their backs, and they hadn't eaten since the previous afternoon. Scott shook the snow off the tent and the walls sprang back to life.

I stumbled into the hut to find Willie cooking another batch of rice and tuna sauce for breakfast. Only Willie and Ben had been able to keep last night's version down. I tried a few mouthfuls of leftovers, but they came right back up.

After breakfast, Ben spread out the map. We were camped at the bottom of a V created by two valleys running away from the continental divide. Each of the valleys contained a feeder stream. But which was longer? The longer was the true source of the Amazon. The streams drained two mountains—Mismi and Quehuishua. We planned to climb to the summit of each so we could honestly claim to have reached the Amazon's most distant headwaters. Today Mismi; tomorrow Quehuishua. Willie would remain in camp while we made the ten-hour ascent of Mismi, which at that moment we couldn't see for snow.

My head was still taking a beating as we started up the valley. I stopped to vomit, but brought up only bile. Scott colored the snow with his own liquid laughter. Ben remained unaffected. He was gasping for air, but healthy.

At about 15,700 feet Scott vomited again. "I can't go on," he said, wiping his mouth. His face was gray. "You guys keep going, I'll wait at the hut." He turned and staggered back down.

I continued, but it was impossible to maintain pace with Ben. Every twenty or thirty steps I stopped and dry-heaved, my body racked with convulsions. Lights flashed in front of my eyes. My head was splitting. What was the name of those Inca gods who were said to inhabit these dead zones? The *apus* and *wamanis*? Powerful Andes deities, described as bearded white men, who live inside mountains and must be placated. It felt as though they were cleaving my skull for trespassing. My lungs were on fire. I could go no farther.

"I can't go on," I shouted at the disappearing shadow of Ben, his tall shade leaning into the screeching wind and snow. He didn't seem to hear me.

"I'm going back!" I screamed again. "I'm going back!"

The shadow halted, turned, and gave me a wave before it disappeared into the maw of snow.

Back at the camp, Scott and I spent most of the day lying in our sleeping bags, slipping fitfully in and out of consciousness. My head hurt so much it was impossible even to write in my journal or read. I thought of the danger we were in if the sickness got worse. I tried to suppress the welling paranoia.

At one point I got up and found Willie inside the hut chatting to the owner, a shepherd who turned up to find us there. I wanted to join them, ask about life in the mountains, listen to his experiences, but I was too ill. A few minutes upright was all I could manage.

About mid-day the snow stopped and the sky cleared. Scott and I both wondered how Ben was doing. He needed this break in the weather if he hoped to reach the summit. I ate nothing all day and, at five, I forced down some of the pasta Willie had prepared. It wasn't pleasant, but I was able to hold it down.

By six it was getting dark and I shuddered with the first wave of anxiety about Ben. It was impossible for us to search for him if he didn't make it back. Scott and I were too sick. Willie was physically capable of a search and rescue mission, but he had made it clear he was reluctant to venture any farther up the mountain. What should we do?

The snow started again and we waited. We huddled in silence, shivering in the tent. I began to wonder what I would say to his mother if Ben didn't return. It was a dangerous mountain, 18,500 feet high. With bad weather, like any mountain, Mismi was a death trap. I thought of the other Amazon expeditions that had lost members.

Eight o'clock came and went, with the snow forming drifts

and the wind caterwauling relentlessly, like a fingernail raking a chalkboard. We had to do something. Armed with flashlights, Scott and I headed into the wicked night. Willie refused to budge: foolhardy rescues weren't covered for $25 a day.

It was a nightmare. Pitch black, snowy, windy, without a star or a moon—scarier than hell. Take a wrong turn and you could fall into a crevice, plummet off a cliff.

"Be-e-e-e-e-e-e-e-en!" I yelled.

Not a sound but the wind.

"Be-e-e-e-en!" Scott yelled.

Nothing.

We flashed our lights on and off, pointing them in one direction, then another. Nothing. It was like looking for extra-terrestrial life. Scott and I soon realized that Ben would not find the camp in this lumpy darkness. The hut was all but invisible. I decided to head farther up the valley, hoping to stumble into Ben. Scott stayed near the hut to direct us back with his flashlight.

The physical effort brought back my nausea. Bass drums pounded in my head. I leaned into the wind and snow. I was sure Ben was gone.

"Be-e-e-e-e-e-e-en!" I hollered. "Can you hear me, you fucker!"

I flashed my light on and off, on and off, as I staggered up what I thought was the trail. I shouted as I stumbled.

"Be-e-e-e-en!"

I was losing faith and worrying about the flashlight batteries giving out when I saw it. Yes. There it was. The flicker of a light. Faint, but undeniable.

I started toward the blinking star. Half an hour later I met a cold, tired, hungry, but triumphant Ben. He had made the summit and was jubilant. The bad weather rolled in after he got to the top, he explained breathlessly.

"It was way worse than this," Ben bragged, gleefully, in the teeth of the wind. "I couldn't see a foot in front of me. I was blind, stumbling through waist-deep snow. Every so often I'd nearly step into space. Cliffs everywhere. I must have staggered around up there for hours, looking for a way down. Like a blind man I was."

He was oblivious to the danger now. The adrenaline had given him a natural high. The fear that had gripped him evaporated with the first embrace of safety. He was coasting on the body's own equivalent of heroin. Fuck the storm!

I grinned with him. Why not! This was our first accomplishment as a team.

"It was wild," he said.

Ben described climbing down a number of small cliffs, only to come across an especially daunting precipice. It was twilight. "I knew if I climbed back up, I would never get off the mountain," he said. "Once dark, there wasn't a hope in hell of getting down. So I started down this god-awful cliff," he continued excitedly. "I got about halfway down and ran out of holds. With the wind clawing at me I hung on the rock wall for four or five minutes, trying to decide what to do."

He paused for his breath.

"That's when I slipped," he said. "Thought I was a fucking goner. Sliding, grabbing at anything I could, arms flailing. It would have been a sight. Well, as you can see, I managed to grab an outcropping before I had slipped more than about three yards. Jesus, I was lucky!"

He was able to make it to the bottom unscathed.

"At the base of the cliff the terrain leveled out and I just started making my way down the hill. I figured I'd eventually hit the camp."

Three hours later he spotted my light.

Back in the hut, as he gobbled pasta and tuna, Ben said he would pass on tomorrow's ascent of Mount Quehuishua. "Your turn for glory, boys," he grinned. "I've done my bit."

Hearing of his harrowing journey, my body aching from the continuing affects of *soroche*, I wasn't enthusiastic.

We really needed more days to acclimatize, but we had neither the time nor the supplies. One can of sardines and some rice were all that was left. We asked the owner of the hut if he had any spare food to sell. He hadn't.

It would take us another week to go down into the valley to purchase provisions and return acclimatized. We couldn't afford a week. We had to climb Quehuishua the following day.

Day 17: September 29, 1999

I awoke feeling a little better. I managed to down half a bowl of Willie's rice and tuna. In the last thirty-six hours I had eaten a single bowl of food.

"Ben, would you mind getting our Sublimes out of your day-pack?" I asked. The chocolate squares were to be our lunch.

He rummaged in his pack for a moment and looked confused.

"We packed them in there yesterday for the trip up Mismi," I said. "Remember. We didn't eat them because we turned back."

Ben looked at me blankly and went back to searching his pack, seemingly flummoxed. "I can't find them," he said, stone-faced.

"What do you mean you can't find them!" I said. "Your pack is tiny and there's hardly anything in it."

"Actually, mate," he said sheepishly, "I ate them."

My mouth fell open.

"When I was coming down the mountain last night . . . I was hungry . . . I thought maybe I'd die." He turned away.

"Those were going to be our lunch," I whined.

Scott pulled some hard lemon candies out of his backpack. They would now be our lunch. There would be nothing tonight.

I was pissed, but what could I say? If I had been up on the

mountain yesterday I'd have eaten them too, especially if I thought they might be my last meal.

Willie, Ben, Scott, and I left camp together, heading toward the ridge. The first part of Willie's journey home lay toward Mount Quehuishua. Ben decided to accompany us on the initial stages as we followed the small feeder stream that was the humble beginning of the Amazon. It was about a yard wide, murmuring as it meandered through the snow. Wreaths of mist rose from the water and dissipated in the breeze. We would trace it to where the first drops began their 4,300-mile journey.

The incline for the first 3 miles was not steep and we made good progress. The snow melted rapidly under the bright sunshine. Our insouciant little stream bubbled and gurgled merrily as it swelled with the snowmelt. It formed miniature oxbow loops, and higher up we could see it cascade down the mountain's flank. A nearby glacier glimmered Prussian blue and gold in the morning sun.

My stomach churned and the jackhammer continued to pound at my skull. I took some extra-strength Tylenol pills and they seemed to help—a hell of a lot better than the coca leaves. I wasn't vomiting—and that was a good sign.

At the pass, Scott and I prepared to veer to the left to ascend the flank of Quehuishua. Willie and the donkeys were going back over the pass and down into the Colca Valley. Ben would return to wait in camp.

The stream had about the same force and volume as a fire hydrant. Farther up we could see it, reduced to a trickle, disappearing altogether underneath the loose sharp shale. I drank some of the icy cold water. It tasted beautiful, exciting. The water I was drinking was a beginning, the birth of the world's mightiest river. The complexities of the ecosystem that began here were staggering to comprehend. The cool water slid down my throat.

"Goodbye, amigos," Willie said, shaking our hands.

"Good luck, guys," Ben added—and he was gone, too.

Scott's health was about the same as mine—not very good. Ahead of us stretched a steep slope and a series of slate-gray cliffs. About half the route was covered in snow and the rest was a bed of loose, jagged boulders. The wind had stopped and we could hear the water gurgling as it seeped through the rocks.

At sea level I could have bounded up this slope. At 16,400 feet, without proper acclimatization, I could barely stand. The lights continued to shimmer and flash in front of my eyes. Frequently, loose boulders gave way and I slid backward. We slogged on, scaling a series of small cliffs until we stood on the mountain's shoulder. We could see the summit plainly, perhaps a mile or more from where we stood.

Scott pulled out a couple of candies. I sucked on mine, careful not to inhale it as I wheezed and gasped. The view was incredible—a panorama of jagged, snowcapped peaks surrounded us. In the valleys below, you could never see the mountains in this way. Those in the foreground always eclipsed the peaks beyond, producing a limited vista. Here the view was unimpeded and incredible.

We followed the trickle of water, now hardly more than a wet stain seeping over the bedrock. Where the surface rocks were loose, it disappeared altogether. Near the summit, we came to the last spot where it could be seen flowing. The small glacier sat just above the trickle, weeping in the midday sun.

Scott proclaimed solemnly, "Every river starts as a single drop."

I placed my hand under the icy tears and filled my palm. I drank the melt-water down. "Cheers! Here's to finding the beginning of the mightiest river on this planet."

I looked around. The towering spire of Mount Quehuishua, majestic and proud, provided a silent benediction. "Wow," I gasped. "It's more beautiful here than I could have possibly imagined. Everybody in the world has heard of the Amazon River. Yet no one knows this place exists. This is the birthplace of the Amazon."

We were at just under 17,725 feet. I threw up.

Fortunately, it didn't take much longer and we stood triumphantly on the summit. Panting, I admired the 360-degree panorama. To the west was the Pacific drainage basin, to the east the Atlantic. Far below, out of view behind the mountain's shoulder, Ben was lying in the tent reading a book: *Immortality*.

That was it. I felt immortal now—that was the feeling. I felt in touch with the Inca and all those who had come before and looked out over these peaks, spires, and turrets. I felt connected to the Spaniards, who must have gazed with equal awe at the continent before them. It was a transcendent kind of feeling, but I couldn't indulge it.

It was already 3 o'clock and we had to hurry to get off the treacherous mountain by nightfall. We threw caution to the wind, clambering down over loose boulders and slippery scree as fast as we could go. It felt as though I was breathing into a plastic bag. I frantically inhaled and exhaled, to no avail.

For the next few hours we went full out, until a sharp pain pierced Scott's chest. We stopped and rested. When the pain subsided, we continued down. My face was roasted. In spite of my hat and sunblock, the sun reflecting off the snow and the ultra-violet radiation had blistered the skin. Scott's face, too, was a mess of blisters.

About 6 o'clock the sun slipped behind the peaks. At first it was almost a relief not having its fire scorching our faces. But the twilight faded quickly to black, leaving us blind and terrified.

We were off the upper shoulder of the mountain and, if we maintained the right direction, we faced no more cliffs—or so we told each other. I could hear Scott's stomach growling ferociously. But we had no food and none awaiting us in camp—just damp sleeping bags.

Our flashlights illuminated a pencil-thin slice of inky blackness, but only a few yards in any direction. We had no idea of what lay beyond the 3-yard beam. As a result, we stumbled down two dead-end canyons and nearly walked off one of those cliffs that didn't exist.

Terrain that seemed flat and featureless in daylight was unfathomable in darkness. At one point I stumbled and, as I fell on my face, launched my flashlight into the night. It hit a rock and blinked out. We searched, but it was gone. What was more frustrating was that the spare batteries I carried were incompatible with Scott's flashlight, and his light was growing dim. With only one light, I repeatedly stumbled over the rocks littering our way. When Scott's light winked out, too, we inched along like blind men.

We were beginning to think of curling up until daylight when I saw a flash in the distance. It must be Ben. We couldn't signal back. Keep flashing, I begged. But he stopped.

Once the light disappeared, we quickly became disoriented. Without reference points, we were lost in a midnight sea. For the next hour or so, we stumbled in what we thought was the direction of the light.

It flickered again—this time much closer and almost parallel to us.

"Be-e-e-e-en!" I yelled.

He heard me. "Over here!" he replied.

We were overcome with relief. "Keep flashing the light!" I shouted. "We have no flashlight." We stumbled toward his flashing light.

"You guys look like shit," Ben said. "Did you make it?"

"We sure did," Scott replied.

The three of us were back at the hut by about 10 o'clock. We collapsed onto the llama skins.

"So, any luck finding those Sublimes?" I asked dreamily. My *soroche* wasn't nearly so bad now and I was starving.

"Sorry, mate."

We were bone-weary, hungry, but aglow with self-satisfaction. Our descent of the Amazon River had begun and I could not wait to get on the water. Fully clothed, I climbed into my saturated sleeping bag. In a few minutes, I was fast asleep.

Day 18: September 30, 1999

We were up early, driven out of bed by starvation and the elation that comes from knowing it's all downhill from here on. My body felt as if a bus had hit it and my face was burned. Camp was quickly struck and we began following the stream that meandered peacefully near the camp. About 1,000 feet down it joined with another brook, descending from the slopes of Mount Mismi. Ben smiled as we passed "his" stream.

"The true source of the Amazon," Ben said, nodding toward Mount Mismi, now hidden behind a rise.

"Well, we've stuck to our time schedule," Scott said, limping along.

"But only by beating the shit out of our bodies," Ben added. "Next time we climb a mountain over 14,500 feet, we spend ten times as much money on gear, bring more food, and spend time acclimatizing."

He looked back at the mountains and at the brook beside him. We were finally descending the Amazon. "Oh, fuck it!" he said. "We'll just do it with whatever we've got."

As we descended, vegetation remained scarce. A large broad valley, sloping gently eastward, fell before us. Brown grass alternated with rocky slopes. At one point the stream we were following disappeared into acres of bog covered by a spongy, sphagnum moss. We walked around the perimeter of this marsh, as skirting it was certainly easier than crossing it. In the distance we saw alpacas grazing.

By noon we expected to see the collection of huts that Willie had told us about. And we did. Outside a huddle of four huts a group of men skinned a freshly killed alpaca. They saw us coming and we could see them calling inside the hut. A few more men appeared.

"Hola."

"Hola," one of the men replied. They looked nervous, but not aggressive.

"Could we buy some food?"

They said they didn't have anything to sell, but would be happy to share with us. One man, wearing a grimy llama-skin jacket and a pair of old black, pleated pants, asked if we would like to join him and his family for dinner. I could have kissed him.

We followed him into the nearest hut, almost identical in design to the one where we had spent the last few days. Three children sat on the floor on llama skins; a woman hovered near the mud fireplace, which belched smoke into the already thick air. I coughed as Ben asked the man why they didn't use chimneys.

"Wood is scarce," he said. "A chimney lets out all the heat. When the wood has to be carried up on the back of a donkey, a chimney is too much of a waste. Besides," our host said with a wave, "the smell of the smoke is pleasant."

With streaming eyes, Ben coughed his agreement.

Our first solid meal in a long, long time was boiled potatoes adorned with hefty chunks of llama meat. I bolted the stringy protein down, forgetting about the smoke. I licked the tin plate, sure that our hosts wouldn't disapprove. The wife smiled and dumped more hearty food into my plate. I was in heaven. My nausea was gone and my stomach was full.

Later, the children watched in awe as we set up our dome tent. They had never seen such strange materials. Their world was made up of whatever the harsh land provided. Our world looked complex and difficult by comparison. They didn't like it.

We had dropped about 9,800 feet from our base camp, but the air felt much thicker. Or maybe it was just my body slowly acclimatizing.

Day 19: October 1, 1999

I awoke at 5:30 to the sound of llamas nibbling on the tent's fly. The woolly, skittish animals bolted as soon as I emerged. The sky was milky white, the same color as the llamas scampering far up the hillside.

Fernando, one of the children, came and invited us to have breakfast with the family.

After another meal of llama and potatoes, I gave our hosts a T-shirt. It was a rather meager present and perhaps a cliché, but it was all I could spare from my limited gear. They seemed delighted, anyway, and the father took off his llama jacket so he could sport his new shirt.

We left after pleasantries, aiming to reach Yauri, a village about 25 miles away, where we were assured we could get dried alpaca meat and rice.

Wet flakes of snow began falling, later turning to rain as the temperature warmed in mid-morning. Our altitude was still 12,800 feet, but my body felt recovered from the *soroche*. I was weak and tired, though. After many days of pushing myself to the limit with minimal nourishment, I was bone-weary with fatigue. I relished the thought of climbing into a big soft bed and sleeping for a few days.

The Río Hornillos, as this tributary of the Amazon was called, ran along our right side, the water muddy and tumescent from the downpour. This was the first rain we had seen. We were now on the "wet" side of the Andes, and the rainy season was approaching. I was thankful I had continued to haul the rain gear for these last two weeks.

The rain bucketed down into the valley as we trudged along, the trail never straying far from the stream's edge. We passed a number of stone huts, each with an interchangeable collection of reticent children, ill-tempered alpacas, barking dogs, and curious adults.

We reached Yauri well after dark. The rain, which abated briefly in mid-afternoon, continued to fall in torrents. We pitched our tent beside a roofless, abandoned stone hut on the outskirts of the community. Our efforts to start a fire were fruitless. Everything was too wet. We ate salty, dried alpaca, chewing the pemmican in a tent that stank of mouldy sleeping bags. We hadn't had a chance to dry them out for days. We were a sorry lot.

Day 20: October 2, 1999

Shivering and hungry, we awoke to find a crowd of wide-eyed locals surrounding the tent. They had been waiting to see what would emerge, and they seemed genuinely disappointed at us. I don't know what they expected, but our disheveled, smelly, bearded bodies and blood-shot eyes clearly appalled.

"Hola," I said through chattering teeth.

Some of the adults smiled. The children looked scared.

"Is there a store here?"

A man stepped forward. "I am a shopkeeper. Follow me."

We were led past rows of mud buildings to a small, tidy house, slightly larger than the others. A Coca Cola sign was peeling from the outer wall. Only the image of the distinctive Coke bottle endured to identify the poster.

Inside, a wrinkled woman sat on the floor, mumbling. A small dog gnawed playfully at her toes. She seemed unaware of the puppy or of us. Across from the woman were three shelves, two empty. The other sagged with two bags of rice, two bags of pasta, a withered onion, five cans of tuna, two cans of sardines, a large vat of beans, and a small jar of bubble gum.

All we left behind was the bubble gum and a cup or two of beans. The woman continued mumbling, the dog nibbled on her feet, and the proprietor smiled broadly.

Plunked down in the middle of an isolated moonscape, Yauri was a fairly large settlement—about 700 people—a real village compared with the tiny outposts we had encountered. It also had an impressive church. It was anything but friendly.

We ate at the local *casa comida*—the corner of someone's house where dinner was offered for about 80 cents. The meal was soup, potato with some sort of meaty gruel on it, and a glass of cordial juice.

At the junction of the Hornillos and the Apurimac, the river was deep enough to support kayaks. We were following the Apurimac proper now as it flowed across a broad alluvial plain flanked by menacing volcanic peaks. Most of the houses and small villages were set back from its banks because of fluctuating water levels and steep, inhospitable terrain. Our trail kept to the top of the cliffs bordering the river. Sometimes we would lose sight of the water altogether; other times we would see it below, thrashing along at the bottom of a 380-foot cliff.

Walking became a grueling endurance test. We averaged thirteen hours a day on the trail and we were obsessed with covering ground. The harder I pushed myself, the more I disliked it and the harder I tried to get it over with. I didn't like the blisters, I hated the aches and pains, and I despised our bland diet of rice, beans, and tuna. I loathed how skinny I was getting. I was tired of the monotonous routine.

Nearing mid-day, we came on a man and his two sons building a mud hut beside two others each the size of a small shed. As we passed, they made gestures of swigging a liquid, asking us if we would like to join them for a glass of *chicha*, the homemade brew. We accepted the offer.

The father, Martilo, explained that they were building a home for his eldest son, who had just recently married a girl from Yauri. It would take about three days to build the structure. The bricks were made from a mixture of straw, manure, dirt, and water. A donkey stomped the pile, his hooves pounding it to the right consistency. The resulting mud was poured into rectangular cubes and placed in the sun to dry.

We sat on the hardened mud bricks and, as the man spoke, a plastic bottle of *chicha* was passed around. Then we cooked our pasta.

"My son José is the best fisherman around here," Martilo said proudly.

José wiped his mouth on his sleeve and said: "There are not

as many fish in the river anymore. I will have to start farming llamas to feed my wife and children." He talked of llama farming disdainfully, as though it was much more honorable to earn a living from the river. It was dangerous: to reap riches from the Apurimac was the test of a true man.

As we headed back down the trail, José called out to us. He was going to name his first son after us—"Gringo."

Poor kid.

It wasn't long before the trail we were following stopped abruptly, as the river cut to the canyon wall. We would have to ford it and continue on the other side, where the terrain was less taxing. Scott made it to the far shore first, jumping across on the slippery rocks. I followed, slipping once, but regaining my balance before reaching the other side.

Ben wasn't so lucky. He slipped. Surprisingly, no bones were broken and his pack remained dry. He walked with a painful limp, however.

At 8 o'clock that evening we reached the Inca Hanging Bridge—a landmark suspension structure that was maintained by the locals as a ceremonial centerpiece. In the dim light we couldn't really see it. We could see the nearby village, Hurinchiri, and the nearby modern bridge, but we were too exhausted to visit.

As I lay in the tent I pinched the skin on my back and my stomach. There was no fat whatsoever. My body felt weak and emaciated. I could see the drawn look in Scott's and Ben's faces and I knew my face must be a mirror. The whitewater promised an end to this purgatory. Every day would be exciting, and the rapids would provide a constant adrenaline rush. It would be paradise.

It had been a long time since I had even had a Sublime— too long . . .

Day 21: October 3, 1999

I awoke hungry, the burning emptiness of my belly pushing me from what little warmth my sleeping bag offered. All night I had dreamed about food, about Cuzco and the range of restaurants it offered—Chinese, Italian, Hare Krishna, pizza. I was starving to death, I was sure of it.

I got out of the tent and was immediately astounded by my first sight of the Inca Hanging Bridge. Its wood-and-vine structure—with grass cables as thick as tree trunks—was anchored by stone abutments originally put in place by the Incas. It was said whole armies could cross.

The Inca burned such bridges as they retreated before the Spaniards, hoping the Apurimac gorge would prevent invasion and protect them. This hurdle only delayed the inevitable.

We skipped breakfast in an effort to get to Pilpinto, the end of our trek.

Above the hanging bridge the land had been good for little more than herding llamas or alpacas. Below, there was more topsoil, and the runoff from the many tributaries of the Apurimac, and the river itself, provided enough water to support numerous farms. The river almost had enough volume for us to start rafting. Unfortunately, many parts were still clogged with huge boulders that made it unnavigable.

We turned a corner of the trail and were confronted by a chilling and grim apparition. An Indian man stood hammering a shrieking donkey over the head with a shovel. It took me a moment to realize it had fallen from the cliff above, slipping on the steep switchback. Both forelegs were broken. The hurt, terrified animal, its nostrils flaring, was propelling itself about on its chest with its hind legs, desperately trying to escape the shovel-wielding assassin.

The man slammed the spade down again and again, pounding on the donkey's head. He wanted to kill it to end its suffering. But the donkey brayed more frantically with each bash. Its

guttural anguish swallowed the noise of the river and everything else in the world. It was a fearful, hellish scene.

Ben picked up a huge rock and lifted it high over his head.
He stepped forward quickly and hurled it down on the donkey's skull with an almighty whack! The animal's glossy black
eyes, wide as saucers, went flat and rolled back into its head. It
was dead.

There wasn't a sound. I slowly became aware of the river
and the donkey's last breath, a low whistle like a boiling kettle
being removed from the stove. A chill wind gusted, ruffling the
animal's dull gray fur.

The man looked at us, his face a mask of indifference. He
said nothing, but waved and walked off.

Scott eyed the carcass: "Well, drop the dead donkey. Any-
body fancy some big fat steaks tonight?"

"I'll pass," I said.

We continued walking for another two hours, pitching
camp just before the village of Surimana. I felt cheerful. After
studying the maps, we decided to push through to Pilpinto the
next day.

Day 22: October 4, 1999

Pilpinto is one of the few villages actually on the Apurimac
River. The Apurimac gorge widens here, so at the base of the
steep walls there is some land that grows a few crops. There are
no terraces, as the canyon walls are too steep. On the south
side of the valley we could see a jagged, zigzag scar—the road
descending the cliff in a series of thirty or so switchbacks.

The buildings of Pilpinto were mud, some with tin roofs
and others thatched. The only one of significance was the
stone church. All the streets were dirt. Most of the inhabitants
seemed to have nothing to do but watch us, the circus of the
moment, and we gathered spectators by the minute.

With a population of about four hundred people, the village doesn't see many tourists. Only recently has vehicle access arrived in the form of a long, treacherous dirt road. So, people stared—and they weren't very friendly.

I refused to let the stone-faced residents depress me. Our progress down this side of the mountains had been astounding, and I knew we would sleep that night in Cuzco, the fabled capital of the Inca.

We hobbled toward a beat-up Toyota Hiace van that served as a local bus. There was just one departure a day for Cuzco— at 8 P.M.—so we were just in time. I relished the thought of a day in the big city, a good restaurant feed, and the rest of the journey in a boat. I lay back on my seat and fell asleep.

THE DESERT

PART 2 THE WILD APURIMAC

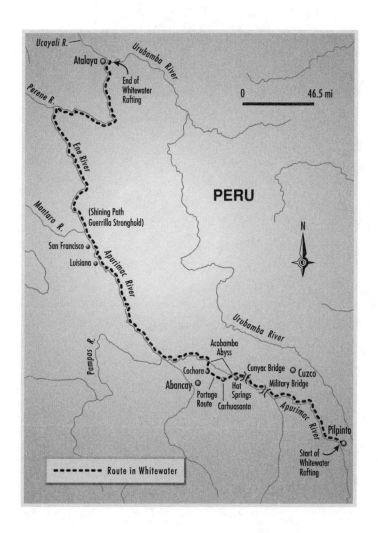

Day 23: October 5, 1999

Riverrunroundedenroundroundgurglegurlgegurgle. Ever listen
to a river? I think they all have distinctive voices and personal-
ities, just as writers or people do. They're all different characters. The Thames, the Hudson, the Ganges, the Nile, the
Irrawaddy, the Yangtze—each one has spawned a civilization,
and each evokes a different ethos. Rivers play a central role in
our culture today, as they did in the past.

Images and pictographs of rafts adorn the tombs of ancient
Egyptians. From Nepal to Venice, the ferryman is a universal
figure. Charon wears many guises. There is a curious warning
recorded in the book of *The Teachings of Amenemope*: "Never
leave behind a man in the passage of a river when you have
space on the ferry boat. Do not build a boat and try to get the
toll: Ask for the toll from those that have it and refuse it from
those that cannot afford it." There are the river of life and the
river of death, the river of knowledge, and the river of forget-
fulness. Alexander the Great crossed rapids using inflatable

boats made from cow and horse hides sewn together and waterproofed with animal fat. The coracles used by Irish monks were just variations on a theme. You'll find exactly the same kinds of craft in use today around the globe—for exactly the same reasons.

Rivers are important communication, trade, and political routes. People invaded along them, dispatched emissaries of good will, and sent their goods to market. As we hiked over the mountains, I anticipated getting to know the Apurimac River well. We would start at its tail and slide all the way to its mouth.

Lying in bed, well rested and well fed, I thought about the trip and what lay ahead. There is something about the water and the mystical attachment it evokes for me. From my earliest memories, water hasn't been just another element: it's my element. I'm not sure why. Rivers and the sea fascinate me. Maybe it's something in all of us. In any case, that was why I was on this trip.

Like other boys, I loved pirate stories and *Treasure Island*. Although it's corny, I really enjoyed Farley Mowat's *The Boat Who Wouldn't Float*. Like two stubborn lovers, the protagonist and the boat are constantly butting heads. *Paddle to the Amazon* by Don Starkell is one of the most original adventure stories I ever read. It's the tale of a father and son who paddled a canoe for two years from Winnipeg to Belém, Brazil. What they shared and went through together! I thought of my own dad, a sea captain, and what it could have been like for us to have shared a trip. But it was not to be.

Although I bore his name, my father was a mystery figure to me. My mother referred to him as "Uncle Colin." I wasn't really aware of his absence growing up because I'd never known his presence. I didn't know anything different; to me, that was just the way things were.

My mother sent my brother off to St. Michael's boarding school in Victoria when he was fourteen and I was seven. After that, it was just Mum, my half-sisters Jane and Patty, and me. So, for most of my life, I was brought up in an all-female household. I never learned how an engine worked or how to fix a bike. The only tool in the house was a chipped, slotted screwdriver. I also had no interest in any team sports. Aside from that, I was a fairly normal little boy. I was fascinated by airplanes and spent hours making the tissue-covered, balsa-framed planes powered by rubber bands. I loved gliders, water missiles, kites—pretty much anything that went aloft. The ultimate would have been a gas-powered radio-controlled plane, but there was not enough money for that.

I never hung around with large groups, but always had one or two really good friends I could relate to. When I was twelve I read *Dove* by Robin Lee Graham, and more than anything else it got me off the couch. It is the five-year saga of a sixteen-year-old American who circumnavigated the globe. It made me realize that the world wasn't all picket fences and station wagons. I immediately planned my first adventure—a solo crossing of the open Pacific Ocean.

God, what a trip! I have so many memories, and it led directly to this moment, here in Cuzco, high in the Andes. The world unfolds in mysterious ways.

I decided while I was in high school that I wanted to get a sailboat and explore the world. Flying was too boring, too easy. The thought of sailing in my own boat appealed strongly to my sense of adventure. I imagined myself poring over charts of little-known areas, crashing through horrendous storms, or relaxing under palm trees with beautiful Polynesian women as my boat floated out in the bay.

I didn't tell many people this plan. The few I told would look at me and smile. It was too far-fetched for them even to waste their breath on. But, to me, I couldn't see anything that would stop my dream. Hard work would bring the boat, hours of studying would bring the knowledge, and the only other thing that was needed was a brisk wind. It was all so simple.

I had a good friend, Dan Audet, who had just moved west from Quebec. He was the only person with whom I discussed my plan in detail and the only one who believed it possible. Soon after entering eleventh grade, I bought a 13-foot Enterprise sailing dinghy with money I had saved from my paper route and a dishwasher job. I learned the physics of sailing on this boat, and it was an environment very conducive to daydreaming. Dan and I would pack camping gear in the boat and spend weekends sailing among the islands of the Georgia Strait.

My plan originally was to go to university, get a degree of some sort, and go sailing. While in my first year at the University of British Columbia, studying science, I began to question the logic of my choice. I was enrolled only because society, my mother, and my peers expected this of me. But I wasn't happy being cooped up in boring classes. I didn't enjoy what I was learning. I remember sitting in English class (my only classroom with windows) looking out at the bay while the professor's voice droned on monotonously. Fishing boats, proud though weather-beaten, churned past, and sailboats scudded across the harbor. They represented the way I wanted to explore and learn. From that day on I devoted my efforts to sailing books and making plans.

I dropped out of college at the end of my first year and left some months later in my sailboat across the Pacific. People thought I was giving up a lot, but I felt I was giving up nothing. If I never got rich, I didn't care. If I never owned a home, I didn't care. I had to forget what society dictated and do whatever it was that made me happy. Sailing off in a sailboat made me happier than anything else in the world. Not everyone agreed, of course. People told Dan and me that we were simply too young to put to sea in our own boat. "Cruising isn't a sport for kids. You need twenty years' experience under your belt and $200,000 in your bank account to keep things rolling." No wonder people stay at home and ashore!

At the yacht club a nautical man of indeterminate age in-quired, "You guys planning on sailing around the world?" I nodded, knowing what would come next.

"I don't mean to put a damper on your trip," he said, the capillaries across his cheeks and nose flushed with Scotch, "but you'll never make it. You have neither the experience nor the finances to pull off such a long journey."

"I'll put it out of my head immediately," I said. Why argue with the already committed?

The fact is that a number of people in their late teens and early twenties are exploring the globe because they enjoy the luxury of few responsibilities and good health. Aside from the independently wealthy and the aging baby boomers, we are a generation with time on our hands, disposable income, and, Bart Simpson be damned, wanderlust. I wouldn't erase a mo-ment of our trip, and it proved to me that the naysayers were often wrong. Navigation turned out to require a lot less alchemy and pixie dust than I'd been led to believe.

Dan and I financed the trip on a limited budget. It was my first experience mounting any kind of expedition, and the les-sons I learned were a blueprint for planning this trip down the Amazon. First, we took a few sailing lessons. Next, for $15,000, we bought a 26-foot full-keeled sloop. Sure, it was a handy-man's special, but it was sound and the diesel engine was in good shape. Three months of hard work and a few more thou-sand dollars had our *Ondine* looking like new and equipped for offshore cruising.

We set sail on July 1, 1992, a dismal and chilly day. Among the small knot of well-wishers was the mother of another friend who brought dire warnings of horrible death in the open ocean. It was a bit like Cyrus the Sea Serpent when the old man stands on the dock and warns, "You'll never make it, you'll never make it. If the doldrums don't get you, the storms will. If the storms don't get you, the pirates will. You'll never make it."

We got off to a harrowing start. We weathered a major storm off the coast of Oregon, ran out of funds, and had to survive in Alameda. I remember the fear as we drifted without power in the shipping lane, rising dramatically and falling into the deep troughs of the big swells under the Golden Gate Bridge. No engine, no wind, no radar. Freighter traffic plowed past so close that their horns seemed to come from directly overhead and I swore I could reach out and touch their hulls in the pea-soup fog. We survived. But days later off the coast we were buffeted by 50-knot head winds and taken on a wild ride. My mother was so worried watching the damage reports on TV that she tried frantically to reach me.

I'll never forget the feast we had at the Isla de San Francisco near La Paz. We had spent four days on the island hiking, swimming, fishing, and exploring. We had a tremendous celebration the night we left. Boats from around the nearby islands joined in, along with Mexican fishermen who provided fresh tacos. The feast around the bonfire lasted well into the night as we exchanged stories and downed glasses of punch. I looked across at the broad range of faces encircling the flickering flames. There were old faces and young, from many different parts of the world. We would go our separate ways, many never to see each other again, but for one instant we were united. These are the moments when the true magic of traveling is revealed.

After a thirty-two-day passage from Mexico to the Marquesas, we moved the boat west from Tahiti to New Caledonia. We spent the next seven months traveling through Papua New Guinea, Palau, China, and Hong Kong. Along the way, Dan decided to stay in the South Seas, working on a cruise ship. In late February 1994 I sailed the *Ondine* solo to Brisbane, Australia. It was on my way back to Canada via London, a year later, that I met Scott and Ben.

We ventured out into Cuzco refreshed. The city featured splendid broad avenues at its finest and warren-like slums at its worst. The ancient Inca capital was full of beggars. It boasted of being the oldest inhabited city in the New World, laid out originally in the shape of a jaguar, a revered Inca deity. In a fertile valley surrounded by splendid mountains, its cobbled streets must once have sparkled with sunshine and dazzled visitors. But that was a long time ago.

Gonzo writer Hunter S. Thompson was here in the early 1960s and talked of the Inca peering into the tourist-filled restaurants. Tumis and other archetypal indigenous images grinned from placemats and door knockers even then. Nothing has changed. The disparity between rich and poor remains abysmal. The ruins and the guano-splattered statues memorialized glories long past, for the present is a scandal. A drab, sprawling Andean metropolis, Cuzco has lost even the charm that usually accompanies antiquity.

We went to the South American Explorers' Club and retrieved our equipment. I was impatient to get on the water, and couldn't believe how excited I was to get going. To be on the water after all that hiking—that's more my style.

Day 24: October 6, 1999

We rumbled out of Cuzco at 5 A.M. in the dark. By 11 we were back in Pilpinto, pulling our gear off the roof rack of the small bus.

The weather was hot and dry. A crowd gathered in the square as the bus driver wrestled with the raft, paddles, pumps, dry-bags, wetsuits, and other containers stuffed with equipment and food. The mounds of high-tech gear fascinated them. I felt a twinge of conscience pulling the children off our bags. In their culture, everything seemed to be shared. But we needed it all.

Ben, Scott, and I set up a chain to relay the gear down to the river's edge. I don't want to suggest Peruvians are any less honest than other people, but why tempt fate? We were ready to disembark about 2:30. The fire-engine-red raft was inflated and our gear was carefully stowed into the 115-quart dry-bags, our large durable sacks that were made of the same rubberized material as the raft.

The raft represented the latest technology. It had six independent inflatable chambers constructed of two layers, like a bicycle tire and inner tube. The outer layer, or sheathing, was made of a hypalon-coated fabric. It was extremely tough and durable. Heavy-duty zippers provided access to the inner-air bladders of rubbery plastic. If one of these chambers was damaged, the others would keep the raft afloat—as the designers of the *Titanic* had also planned. It was a self-bailing boat, which meant that, if it filled with water, the fluid would drain in less than four seconds. The floor was an independent unit inflated like an air mattress and secured, via a cord that ran through grommets around its edge, to the porous webbing that made up the bottom of the raft. When the boat filled, the inflated floor rose and the water drained underneath through the webbing. The cam straps attaching the gear to the boat ran through the lacing in the floor and over the bags.

The boat was wide enough to lay two dry-bags lengthwise, side by side on the floor. Two more were stacked on top. Two spare paddles, a pump, an aluminum stretcher (used for carrying the deflated boat), and sleeping foamies were arranged around the bags and cinched as tight as possible with long cam straps. The precious video camera and tapes were packed into double dry-bags—just in case. The boat could rock, buck, even flip, and the gear would not escape or get wet. Or so we hoped.

Our paddles were made of a combination of plastic and aluminum. They were durable and inexpensive, and were used by commercial rafting companies. The "guide paddle," used to steer the boat from the stern, was slightly longer than the others.

Each of us was in the basic "uniform": a helmet, lifejacket, neoprene booties, and something to ward off the chill from the water. I wore a splash jacket and pants made from water-proof nylon with neoprene seals at the wrists, neck, waist, and ankles. I was a walking sauna. Ben and Scott wore wetsuits, which were equally sweaty.

Before we pushed off, Ben got into conversation with an elderly well-dressed man in the assembled crowd who appeared to be a village elder. "What is the river like downstream?" he asked.

"*Este río aquí es tranquilo,*" the man began, "but farther downstream it is not the same. It is violent, full of waterfalls and cataracts. No boat can make it through."

Ben patted the side of the raft: "This boat is designed for exactly that kind of water. We will make it."

The man shook his head and turned away. Gringos! The people behind him shook their heads, too, and laughed nervously. How could we know what lay downstream?

Extreme rafting is a relatively new sport. The Georgie White Company organized a run down the Colorado in 1951, and for years only wealthy thrill-seekers pursued it. Like downhill skiing, which was once the domain of the most adventuresome bushwhackers, extreme rafting has attracted more and more people.

In 1972, for instance, so many people were rafting on the Colorado River that the U.S. National Park Service had to cap the number at 17,000 a year to limit the environmental damage. The sport has taken off—in 1985 there were 400,000 registered rafters and 150 outfitters in North America. Today it's impossible to quantify how many more there are. Even President Bill Clinton, daughter Chelsea, and the secret service ran rapids in an inflatable. A recent U.S. national survey suggests that 15.2 million people now go rafting. There is a seven-year waiting list to go down the Colorado River in Grand Canyon National Park. The sport is similarly popular in Europe, with

French and Italian outfitters offering trips downriver in the Alps and the Massif Central.

I spent one season as a commercial rafting guide, so I had some experience on the water. Ben came to Canada about two months before our departure to prepare and plan the trip. Scott was supposed to come, too, but he went on safari in South Africa first. His late arrival meant that Ben and I did all the prep work and purchased all the supplies. Ben and I also spent time practising on the rivers of the Canadian Rockies—the Kicking Horse, the upper Bow River, the Red Deer, the Kananaskis—learning how to maneuver and gaining an understanding of river hydraulics. We also began our education in reading a river. It is an almost impossible skill for novices to master, one that builds with confidence and practice. When the adrenaline is pumping and there is whitewater chaos all around, it is important to make cool, firm decisions. You must calculate the speed of the current, your own speed, and the angle required to reach a destination.

When scouting the river, it is essential to establish the flow, the state and gradient of the riverbed, and the presence of obstacles. Flow corresponds to the quantity of water that goes through each section of the river. Together with the gradient change and the conformation of the bed, the flow determines the speed of the river. The average speed of the river increases with the gradient and decreases with the roughness of the riverbed. An increase in speed and ruggedness can make the flow very turbulent.

Fast and turbulent rivers are able to cut deep valleys, creating impressive natural arches and cavities in the rock. They create their own landscapes over lifetimes measured in millions of years. Waterfalls result from collapses in the riverbed. As water flows over and around large obstacles, it causes vortexes and whirlpools.

Every river is a universe unto itself, unique with its own quirks, eccentricities, and pace. Look closely and listen. For an exciting extreme-rafting run, the minimum is an average drop of between 10 and 33 feet per mile, with a minimum flow of 53.5 to 70 cubic feet. A river rarely flows faster than about 6 miles per hour. A slow river is below .8 feet per second, and a fast river is 1.6 feet per second. A fast river in the mountains can flow as much as 10 to 13 feet per second in big water.

Making an assessment of the river also depends on the color of the water. When it's clear, or relatively free of silt, the rapids themselves, with the attendant spray, waves, and foaming mist, are difficult enough to parse. When the water turns the color of coffee from highland runoff, it is impossible to distinguish salient features, hazards, and traps.

Extreme rafting is a sport where experience and judgment are paramount, given the difficulties in discerning what lies in wait from shore or, in a worst-case scenario, as you're barreling down a set of rapids. A kayak is sprightly and maneuverable in rapids, while an inflatable is slower, more cumbersome, and less acrobatic.

Whitewater comes in all sizes, shapes, colors, and ferocity. Some rapids pose no danger; others become raging nightmares of chutes, waterfalls, killer holes, boulder sieves, and hydraulic traps and pitfalls. The chance of dying is high if you don't know what you are doing. In Europe a scale helps rafters to evaluate a river and its current:

Class I: Easy. Open spaces, run is regular, obstacles are obvious and easily missed and any waves or breakers are limited.

Class II: Not Very Difficult. The river is relatively free of rocks and most obstacles but is fast moving, creating small waves and simple breakers. Some maneuvering might be necessary but since the rocks are visible and the gradient is not excessive, it's not tough. Risk to swimmers is small.

Class III: Average Difficulty. The river may have bends obscuring views of the rapids; it could have a fairly steep gradient, with rocks in the current and small drops. Tight bends and strainers may be present. There are breakers and high, irregular waves.

Class IV: Difficult. The route is hard to see, there are big, continuous waves with strong rollers, there are rocks in the main current with drops, and holes with a backwash, together with restricted and obligatory passages. It is necessary to have a thorough knowledge of rescue techniques because some rollers can capsize an inflatable and rocks could cause a wrap.

Class V: Very Difficult. It is a run for expert paddlers who must scout the route before descending. The rapids are violent and may contain large, unavoidable waves. There are keeper holes and the chutes and waterfalls have difficult entries and exits. It is preferable to descend only if precautions have been taken for eventual rescue.

Class VI: Extreme. There are a succession of jumps with keeper holes, siphons, possible wraps and violent backwashes. The mass and speed of the water make controlling the raft difficult. Detailed scouting is necessary and the dangers must be weighed carefully. Because of the risks, a rescue team must be present on the riverbank.

By this measure, the Apurimac goes off the scale. The Andes are young mountains, full of sharp planes and edges, with walls like sheets of broken glass. Unlike the Colorado, with its big volume and large waves, the Apurimac hurls itself from the peaks down a steep, rocky descent. Running north by northeast toward Colombia, it drops five times faster than the Colorado does through the Grand Canyon, carving its own, far deeper gorge. The Apurimac promised a non-stop adrenaline high.

We pushed the boat into the river. The crowd on the shore was grim and cheerless—we were paddling to our deaths against the locals' advice. The current took the boat and pulled it toward the distant ocean. We were off.

CNIB 17th Annual Car Raffle

1080 Portage Avenue, Winnipeg, MB R3G 3M3

Grand Prize: Win your choice:

- $20,000 Cash
- 2009 Pontiac G5 2dr Coupe (value $24,800)
- 2009 Pontiac Vibe 4dr Wgn (value $25,855)
- 2009 GMC Canyon Ext Cab (value $28,560)

2nd Prize $1,000

3rd Prize $500

TICKETS 4/$5.00

Grand Prize Draw – Saturday, Sept. 12, 2009 – 9:30 pm

Conducted @ *Assiniboia Downs* 3975 Portage Avenue, Winnipeg, MB

Draws will be held in order of 3rd to 1st prize. All draws open to all ticket holders.

See Reverse for Early Bird Draw

170,000 Tickets Printed   MGCC 1439 RF

No. 124551

McNAUGHT
PONTIAC • BUICK • CADILLAC • GMC

cnib
vision health. vision hope.

CNIB is a nationwide, community-based, registered charity, committed to research, public education and the vision health of all Canadians. CNIB provides the services and support necessary for people to enjoy a good quality of life while living with vision loss.

Early Bird Draws will be held on:

May 14, 2009   June 11, 2009   July 16, 2009   August 13, 2009

All Early Bird Draws will take place at 4:00 p.m. at CNIB,
1080 Portage Avenue, Winnipeg, MB R3G 3M3

vision health. vision hope.

The following lists of prizes are available for **each** early bird:

1 – **Cash Prize of $200.00**
1 – **Cash Prize of $150.00**
1 – **Cash Prize of $100.00**
1 – **Cash Prize of $50.00**

CNIB 17ᵗʰ Annual Car Raffle

1080 Portage Avenue, Winnipeg, MB   R3G 3M3

Grand Prize: Win your choice:

• $20,000 Cash	**2nd Prize**
• 2009 Pontiac G5 2dr Coupe (value $24,800)	**$1,000**
• 2009 Pontiac Vibe 4dr Wgn (value $25,855)	**3rd Prize**
• 2009 GMC Canyon Ext Cab (value $28,560)	**$500**

Grand Prize Draw – Saturday, Sept. 12, 2009 – 9:30 pm

Conducted @ *Assiniboia Downs* 3975 Portage Avenue, Winnipeg, MB

Draws will be held in order of 3rd to 1st prize. All draws open to all ticket holders.

See Reverse for Early Bird Draw

170,000 Tickets Printed   MGCC 1439 RF

TICKETS 4/$5.00

No. 124552

McNAUGHT
PONTIAC • BUICK • CADILLAC • GMC

cnib
vision health. vision hope.

CNIB is a nationwide, community-based, registered charity, committed to research, public education and the vision health of all Canadians. CNIB provides the services and support necessary for people to enjoy a good quality of life while living with vision loss.

Early Bird Draws will be held on:

May 14, 2009   June 11, 2009   July 16, 2009   August 13, 2009

All Early Bird Draws will take place at 4:00 p.m. at CNIB,
1080 Portage Avenue, Winnipeg, MB R3G 3M3

vision health. vision hope.

The following lists of prizes are available for **each** early bird:

1 – **Cash Prize of $200.00**
1 – **Cash Prize of $150.00**
1 – **Cash Prize of $100.00**
1 – **Cash Prize of $50.00**

CNIB 17th Annual Car Raffle

1080 Portage Avenue, Winnipeg, MB R3G 3M3

Grand Prize: Win your choice:

- $20,000 Cash
- 2009 Pontiac G5 2dr Coupe (value $24,800)
- 2009 Pontiac Vibe 4dr Wgn (value $25,855)
- 2009 GMC Canyon Ext Cab (value $28,560)

2nd Prize
$1,000
3rd Prize
$500

Grand Prize Draw – Saturday, Sept. 12, 2009 – 9:30 pm

Conducted @ *ASSINIBOIA DOWNS* 3975 Portage Avenue, Winnipeg, MB

Draws will be held in order of 3rd to 1st prize. All draws open to all ticket holders.

See Reverse for Early Bird Draw

170,000 Tickets Printed   MGCC 1439 RF

No. 124553

TICKETS 4/$5.00

cnib
vision health. vision hope.

CNIB is a nationwide, community-based, registered charity, committed to research, public education and the vision health of all Canadians. CNIB provides the services and support necessary for people to enjoy a good quality of life while living with vision loss.

Early Bird Draws will be held on:

May 14, 2009   June 11, 2009   July 16, 2009   August 13, 2009

All Early Bird Draws will take place at 4:00 p.m. at CNIB,
1080 Portage Avenue, Winnipeg, MB R3G 3M3

vision health. vision hope.

The following lists of prizes are available for **each** early bird:

1 – **Cash Prize of $200.00**
1 – **Cash Prize of $150.00**
1 – **Cash Prize of $100.00**
1 – **Cash Prize of $50.00**

CNIB 17th Annual Car Raffle

1080 Portage Avenue, Winnipeg, MB R3G 3M3

Grand Prize: Win your choice:

- $20,000 Cash
- 2009 Pontiac G5 2dr Coupe (value $24,800)
- 2009 Pontiac Vibe 4dr Wgn (value $25,855)
- 2009 GMC Canyon Ext Cab (value $28,560)

2nd Prize $1,000

3rd Prize $500

Grand Prize Draw – Saturday, Sept. 12, 2009 – 9:30 pm

Conducted @ *Assiniboia Downs* 3975 Portage Avenue, Winnipeg, MB

Draws will be held in order of 3rd to 1st prize. All draws open to all ticket holders.

See Reverse for Early Bird Draw

170,000 Tickets Printed   MGCC 1439 RF

TICKETS 4/$5.00

No. 124554

cnib
vision health. vision hope.

CNIB is a nationwide, community-based, registered charity, committed to research, public education and the vision health of all Canadians. CNIB provides the services and support necessary for people to enjoy a good quality of life while living with vision loss.

Early Bird Draws will be held on:

May 14, 2009   June 11, 2009   July 16, 2009   August 13, 2009

All Early Bird Draws will take place at 4:00 p.m. at CNIB,
1080 Portage Avenue, Winnipeg, MB R3G 3M3

The following lists of prizes are available for **each** early bird:

cnib
vision health. vision hope.

1 – **Cash Prize of $200.00**
1 – **Cash Prize of $150.00**
1 – **Cash Prize of $100.00**
1 – **Cash Prize of $50.00**

"Who-o-o-o-o-o-o-pie!" I cried.

"Whoop-whoop!" echoed Ben and Scott.

Ecstatic to be on the water, we paddled vigorously. Scott and Ben were up front; I was in the back, guiding. We splashed through a set of small standing waves and into the main current, which flowed flat and steady. I looked at all our gear lashed in the middle, amazed at how little effort it took to transport it all. It jostled in place.

Loaded with food and equipment, the raft weighed about 590 pounds. Hiking, the most we ever carried totalled 200 pounds or so. A trek made the muscles ache, and you didn't get anywhere while resting. Now, even when we stopped paddling, we clipped along faster than we ever had backpacking. I loved it.

About thirty children ran along a trail parallel to the river. Their parents had predicted we would die and they wanted to watch. They stopped at every set of small rapids, screaming and yelling as we rode through the choppy water and over the small falls.

"¡Mas! ¡Mas!" the children cried eagerly, laughing with delight.

The rapids were going to have to get much bigger before we were in any true danger. We were having a ball. This was about as dangerous as taking a stroll on the beach, though we didn't know exactly where the big rapids started. Our topographical maps were not of sufficient scale to show elevation drops with any precision. We had also discovered that we were missing one, which meant a portion of the river was a complete mystery.

The canyon walls closed in and soon there was room only for the river, muddy with silt, sloshing along the bottom of the sandstone gorge. We were once more in a world of brown, save far overhead, where a slash of cloud or azure blue domed above the canyon lip.

We stopped paddling and let the river work. I pulled out a bottle of water. Holding it in the air, I toasted the beginning of our rafting journey. "If we can't raft properly now, in two months we sure will be able to," I said.

"Either that or we'll be rafting the great whitewater in the sky," Ben replied with a chuckle. "Mind you, with the water we're going through now, my confidence is growing in leaps and bounds."

The river was tame here. It dropped over small cataracts or down small chutes, but nothing more than speed bumps. The canyon walls stretched up on both sides for thousands of feet. We were being washed along at the very bottom of a great crack in the earth. The current varied. There were times when the water became deep and very slow moving, as the river-banks broadened. The sun baked down then, basting us in sweat underneath our protective whitewater gear. At other times the river grew shallow as its banks became more constricted, and picking up speed it shot us along at a good pace. In these moments the sunlight rarely reached the river.

Occasionally, we banged into a submerged boulder or were bucked by a wave. Once the river bounced down abrupt, step-like drops in elevation. But the raft handled these jolts, thumps, and plummets with aplomb. My stomach fell into my boots a couple of times, but it wasn't much more than the Wild Mouse Ride in Disneyland.

We went for three or four hours, each taking a turn guiding. In the easy water, it was a good opportunity for us to work on our paddling skills and commands. We had to develop good control over the boat and discipline for the big stuff. Since any stretch of whitewater is a minefield of potentially killer rocks, whoever is steering has complete control. He issues commands to the paddlers in the front while using his own paddle to pry the boat in this direction or that.

Running rapids is like playing a video game: you make split-second decisions constantly. The boat frequently grounded in shallow water. Occasionally, it dropped through rocky chutes so narrow that the raft wedged between the canyon walls. But we were always able to free it.

Our worst fear was running into a boulder sieve—a section where huge rocks had fallen, ostensibly blocking the river's course. The river roars around them, washing away the scree that accompanied the slide, leaving the large rocks forming a tea-strainer barrier. Instead, without warning, the Apurimac widened, offering a large sandy beach and a gardenlike setting irrigated by a tiny tributary cascading down the canyon wall.

Scott angled the boat for the shore: "Forward paddle."

We called it a day, pulling the boat high up on the sand and securing it to a tree in case the water rose during the night.

Camping in the raft was a far more comfortable experience than hiking. While backpacking, we had carried the barest of essentials. Now we had an additional tent, a 20-quart container of water, a tarpaulin, and extra cookware. We would take turns sleeping alone, in the "masturbation tent" as Scott dubbed it.

We pitched the tents and started a cooking fire. We carried a small butane stove, but we wanted to save it for emergencies. It was extremely inefficient and required a full canister of gas to cook a meal. Each canister cost roughly $5 in Cuzco, so we bought only eight hours' worth of gas—enough, we figured, for days when it rained or when we couldn't find combustibles. Most of the driftwood, a type of cane that grew along the riverbank, was tinder dry. The brown leaves ignited better than newspaper.

The sun had disappeared behind the canyon walls and small trout-sized fish were jumping. Scott appeared with a fishing rod. "I'm going to catch us a big fish, mate," he said, affixing a piece of dried meat to his hook and casting out into the river.

I looked around: Ben cooking rice; Scott fishing. How long would it last? It was one of those *Twilight Zone* moments. I could feel it. It was as if the tranquillity was begging for something more ominous to happen. Call it a premonition, call it intuition, call it anxiety.

The Apurimac is one of the toughest rivers in the world. Its history is punctuated by death. It drops from 17,700 feet to 4,900 feet in only 37 miles. There had to be a wicked waterfall or a series of stepped cataracts to do that.

In 1953 a French couple put their kayaks into the Apurimac, hoping to make it to the jungle below. The woman drowned in the savage currents. In 1976 a German expedition gave up after the leader perished in a boulder sieve. In 1986 a team of kayakers ended their voyage down the Amazon when one of their number smashed his leg and was nearly killed. And in 1997 a six-man Swiss team tried to descend in a whitewater raft. Like so many others, their expedition ended in tragedy when two members drowned in a killer hole—one of the most dangerous features of a cascading current.

As I watched Scott serenely casting after the jumping fish, I pondered the figures. Out of six attempts to journey down the Amazon to this day, only two had been successful. All the others ended in death, disfigurement, and tragedy. We were being teased. The more pastoral and bucolic it seemed, the more I knew we were being invited to relax and underestimate the challenge before us.

Ben called us to dinner, dispelling my gloom.

Day 25: October 7, 1999

The sun was a long way from clearing the canyon walls when we left the next morning. The water was calm for a few hours, and then we hit some Class III rapids. They were exhilarating and relatively safe, but they got us wet. The boat behaved like a spirited filly, bucking and prancing.

These rapids were followed by another slightly rougher set. Then another. Each set we passed through got progressively more difficult and we began fearing the worst. The only solution was to stop, disembark, and scout ahead. We scrambled over the massive boulders that littered the canyon floor to get a view of the river's course.

We stood looking at the way the water moved, discussing the safest route to follow. Three sets of eyes and judgment were better than one. We plotted our course, trying to avoid the lethal by taking the simplest and easiest route. The river was probably at its lowest point—this being the very end of the driest season. In the constricted canyon, we had to execute turns and maneuvers quickly to avoid disaster.

The river fell down a narrow chute about 6 feet wide. The force of the water thundering through this barrel was indeed the voice of a god. It was impossible to follow it, as boulders blocked our view of the current. Even if the speed and violence of the current didn't toss us overboard, the bottom of the chute was a jagged bed of granite waiting to impale and shred the raft.

"We're going to have to portage," Scott said.

I nodded. We headed back to the raft and began the heavy work of unloading the gear and transporting it below the cascading current. It took us about an hour and it was less difficult than I had imagined. Unfortunately, Ben scraped his foot— nothing serious, but a distraction and an inconvenience.

Scott and I scouted ahead while Ben tended his foot. We hadn't gone far when we came upon another series of big, loud rapids. They were Class IV-plus. We thought they were runable and plotted a route that would take us through the worst of the whitewater. The scariest part was near the bottom, where the river threw itself over a 6-foot rift in the bedrock. If we went over the falls too far to the right, we would be dashed on a car-sized rock. The left side was clear.

"How is it?" Ben asked when we returned to the raft.

"Piece of piss, mate," I said.

We climbed in and pushed off the sloping granite wall. I would steer, Scott would be front-right, and Ben front-left. We paddled forward, sliding out of the eddy and back into the current. Ben and Scott tensed paddles at the ready as the boat picked up speed. We could see the spray and the leading edge of the turmoil. The sound of the rushing, falling water filled our ears.

I could see a whirlpool ahead so large that the turbulence of its lip would flip the boat. It might not suck the raft under, but, if we were tossed into its grasp, it would be a watery grave for us.

"Back-paddle!" I yelled.

We had to skirt the edge of the black, turbulent mouth.

Scott and Ben back-paddled desperately, and the boat slid away from immediate danger.

"Stop!" I said.

They pulled their paddles from the water and the current picked us up again, hurling us toward the falls. The raft dropped down a tongue of green water, with two swirling holes on either side—almost horizontal whirlpools churning beside the central current.

"Hard forward!"

A cluster of boulders choked the river 20 yards ahead. Only one passage was wide enough for the raft. But I miscalculated the angle, and we were pushed toward the sieve of boulders.

"Come on, guys! Give it all you've got!" I screamed frantically.

Scott and Ben dug hard into the rampaging water. I could see their biceps flex and bulge, the sweat splashing from their faces with the river spray.

"Come on, PADDLE!" I encouraged, the rocks looming.

The current slammed the back end of the raft into the first boulder. The force of the impact spun us toward the middle of the river—Hallelujah!—the direction in which we wanted to go. The current grabbed us, pushing us sideways into the widest channel flowing through the massive mound of boulders.

"Yeeeeehah!" Ben and Scott yelled as we rocketed out the other side, rushing headlong toward a waterfall—the final obstacle in this series of rapids.

We had to cut across the current again, to avoid being swept over the falls and onto the giant boulder that lay at the bottom on the right-hand side. I wedged my feet, leaned out over the water, and dug into the churning fury with the steering paddle. I pulled on it with all my weight and the boat pivoted, the paddle acting as the fulcrum.

"Hard forward!" I shouted.

Ben began to paddle vigorously, but Scott froze, his paddle suspended over the water.

"Come on, you fucker!" I yelled. "Paddle, paddle, paddle!"

Scott didn't move. We weren't going to make it across if he didn't dig in.

"Fucking paddle!" I screamed again, hoping he just wasn't hearing me over the pandemonium of the rapids. "Paddle!"

It was too late. With Ben paddling on one side, the raft turned broadside to the current. We went over the falls at about a 30-degree angle. The bow dropped first.

"F-U-U-U-U-C-K-K-K-K!"

As Ben and Scott vanished from my sight, the stern of the raft erupted under me, launching me skyward like a catapult. I flew over the falls and landed on the rocks below. I screamed in pain. Thank God I was wearing a helmet.

I gasped, trying to breathe, but I realized I was being pulled back into the river. I was lying atop my paddle, which was tethered to the raft—now upside down and careering downriver.

I clutched the paddle to my breast. The raft pulled me through the turbulence that swirled and growled around me. Spluttering, coughing, bleeding, battered, and bruised, I bobbed along behind the overturned boat. It came to rest in an eddy as the water began a more measured flow.

I could see Ben and Scott in the current, too—we all appeared to be alive. Ben climbed onto the overturned raft, uncoiled a line wrapped around his waist, clipped it onto the side of the boat with a carabiner, and leaned back. He used his weight to pull the burdened boat slowly upright, just as you would to right a small sailing dinghy.

"Why the fuck didn't you paddle!" I yelled at Scott as we sat dripping in the raft. "You almost killed us there!"

"I thought the rock was on the other side of the waterfall," he said.

"Don't you remember when we looked at it? You said, 'Holy shit, we'd better get across to the left side of the river quick or we're buggered.'" I was shaking.

"It's weird," he said. "In all the chaos, I must have reversed things in my mind. I was sure the rock was on the left. When you said forward, I just couldn't. I thought you were aiming us straight above it."

"Guys," Ben interjected, "I thought you said this was an easy run. Fuck! I think if I'd seen that one, I would have portaged."

"We would have made it through like clockwork if everyone had paddled," I maintained, glowering at Scott.

He looked away.

We climbed back into the raft—the gear remained stowed as if nothing had happened, the water rippling off the secured sacks. We pushed back into the current and continued in sullen silence.

The rest of the day was uneventful and we decided to make camp about 3 P.M. There were three more hours of sunlight, but we were exhausted. We were burned out from anxiety, concentration, and extreme physical effort. We needed time to recuperate. We needed time ashore.

That's one of the ineffable things about river travel. You may always be close to one shore or the other, but nothing provides the security of terra firma. The river is forever changing, flowing, moving, and mutating. A lethal threat could lie around the next bend no matter how pleasant the ride at the moment. Being on land is different. It's solid, safe, immutable, and always ready to welcome and provide.

The canyon was very narrow and there was no real shore. We picked a spot to camp on a tiny patch of sand between the massive boulders that choked the canyon. There was not enough room to pitch both tents. We would sleep together.

It seemed much later in the day than it actually was because so little sunlight penetrated to the canyon floor. It felt as though we were deep in the bowels of the earth at the bottom of a hole, not at ground level with cliffs and mountains rising up on both sides.

It was my turn to cook. I made mashed potatoes and sardines (which tasted like cat food, but the locals referred to it as "tuna") as millions of sandflies ate us alive. The bug repellant worked for about twenty minutes, until the sweat washed it away and the bugs came back.

Ben and I had bug hats with mosquito netting around the edge that could be pulled down over our faces and ears, an elastic providing a seal around the neck. The hats, which we bought in Canada, were hot, stuffy, looked goofy, and severely restricted our vision. But wearing one was much better than the alternative. Scott suffered without, his hands in constant motion shooing sandflies. He tried standing in the smoke from the fire, but that didn't work. Only darkness dispelled them.

Night was exquisite. I sat with a cup of Nescafé, my back against the rock, savouring the moment. No bugs, no blistering heat, no vicious whitewater, and no growling stomach. The air was clean and clear. A ragged strip of black velvet sky hung like a ribbon overhead, rimmed by the lip of the canyon. Shooting stars, looking like red and yellow scratches, appeared. I could even see the faint beating pulse of satellites crawling across the face of the heavens. Cellphones, television, faxes, computers—they seemed alien here, yet there they were, the 500-channel universe itself winking down on us.

Right now, though, life for us was not much different from

the way it has been for individuals in any age. It was a raft, the river, and us. It's a feeling as old as civilization, from the ancient Egyptians to Alexander the Great, to the Polynesian navigators who conquered the Pacific, to Sir Francis Chichester to us.

Scott laughed.

"What's tickling your feet?" I asked.

"Right now, in England, it's 6 A.M., probably rainy and cold," he said. "My mates will be getting up about now to go to work. Pretty soon they will be in the tube, pushing, shoving, and rushing to make it into the office."

He stared dreamily into the sky, too. "I wonder if we'll be able to see the Southern Cross after we leave this canyon and the cliffs don't block out so much."

"Probably," said Ben.

We were pals again and fell into our silent reveries. Periodically, over the white noise of the river, we could hear the crashing sound of slides and rocks tumbling into the canyon. It was a funny feeling knowing we could be crushed in our sleep.

Day 26: October 8, 1999

After a breakfast of oatmeal, we pushed off into the river full of optimism and joy over the great weather. There was a tremor of anxiety, since we were now on the section of river for which we had no map. We had no idea what to expect for the next several miles. The adjacent maps, depicting the river above and below, indicated that an elevation drop of hundreds of feet occurred in this stretch. That meant serious rapids or one hell of a waterfall.

It was often necessary to stop and scout the rapids. Each time, we planned and executed our descents with precision. We dropped through runs of powerful, exhilarating water, and we did it as if we were born to it. We traveled cautiously, taking everything that came with a minimum of fuss. It was wild and woolly occasionally, as the river washed through the rocky mountain country, but nothing to really scare us.

After about three hours of such calisthenics, we came out of a chute and were propelled into what appeared to be a relatively calm stretch of water, the river meandering and mellow. Water dripped everywhere from the last set of thrashing rapids. I began to think about lunch.

"Women!" Scott shouted.

"Where, where?" Ben said.

We turned.

"On the right shore."

I strained my eyes and, sure enough, there were two young women in swimsuits lounging with what looked like a picnic basket. They began to giggle and wave, beckoning us over. Scott, guiding at the time, turned the boat shoreward.

The young women came down and helped us beach the boat. The slimmer of the pair held a half-gallon plastic bottle of orange soda.

"¿Gaseosa?"

"There must be a god!" Scott said, reaching for the bottle.

The other woman held the picnic basket and a Canon autofocus camera.

"You know, maybe we're not in Peru anymore, never mind in the middle of a remote mountain canyon in the Andes," I said. "Perhaps we've been transported to somewhere on the Mississippi."

"Where are you from?" asked the one with the camera.

"Canada, Australia, and England," I said.

They nodded. "I bet it's pretty cold in Canada right now," said the slimmer teen.

"What? You know where Canada is?" I said incredulously. Until now, most Peruvians we had met knew nothing about Canada.

"We studied it in school," she said. "And Australia. There are lots of kangaroos there."

"Where are you girls from?" Ben asked.

"Cuzco," the one with the camera replied, stepping back to snap a picture. "We came out to visit Francisca's uncle."

"I'm Francisca," said the other. "My uncle lives in the village just downstream."

"There's a village?" Scott looked pleased.

"Sure. It won't take you much longer than ten minutes to get there. It has a road and everything. You will see people."

"How about a store?" I asked.

"Yes."

"Can you buy Sublimes?" asked Ben.

"Probably," Francisca replied.

We grinned. The small squares of chocolate and nuts were already a measure of civilization to us. If a town had Sublimes, it had everything we needed. Sublimes were comfort food.

"Would you take us for a ride in the boat?" she asked fetchingly.

"Sure," Scott said, "hop aboard."

They clambered in, leaving their picnic basket and camera on shore. We pushed out into the wide flat-water with the pair of them giggling like the schoolgirls they were. We got about 50 feet from shore when they said they must go and dove over the side.

Sure enough, about ten minutes after the girls left us, we saw other people on the shore—first a fisherman, then a gaggle of teens swimming, and hives of *campesinos* tending small plots. We rounded a corner and were greeted by a wooden-trestle bridge spanning the river. A fistful of dilapidated mud buildings leaned against each end.

We secured the raft below the bridge and began the steep climb to the bridge road. At the top, we found ourselves at the back of someone's house. We scrambled over a mud wall and walked through a pen of scrawny chickens, ducks, and pigs. We could hear a dog barking, but we couldn't see it. The door to the building was open and we could see a few wooden shelves holding bags of food.

"Hola?" I called.

A short native woman, her coal-black hair in a bun, appeared through a side door.

"Do you sell hot food here?" Scott asked.

"Not yet, later. Where did you come from?"

"From upriver," answered Ben. "Do you sell Sublimes?"

"No."

"Hmmmh, is there a store on the other side of the bridge?" I asked.

"Yes, they may sell hot food now."

"Gracias," we chimed and turned from the door.

We walked across the bridge, peering down at the red raft 80 yards below. It looked tiny and insignificant beside a brown-textured swath of the river.

A small store with three wooden tables out front greeted us on the other side. Local workers, disgorged by a large Mercedes transport truck, occupied two of the tables.

We sat down and ordered three "menus"—as the daily special was called—from a girl who emerged from the kitchen. A small chicken wandered underfoot, looking for stray scraps. Scott went inside and came back smiling. He held up six Sublimes.

"Enjoy them—apparently there's nothing downstream for a long way."

Lunch was chunks of chicken mixed with beans on top of rice. Very tasty.

Sated, we climbed back down the steep banks. Soon, the bridge and houses disappeared behind us. The canyon walls closed in again, steeper than ever, and the sound of rapids filled our ears.

Our progress grew much slower as scouting, analyzing, and finding a path through the cataracts absorbed more and more time. No matter how long it required to map out a safe route, however, it never took more than a stomach-churning four or five minutes to run any one section. Staying in the raft was the biggest challenge. It bucked and dived, twisted and turned, bolted this way and that. It plummeted down into a hole and bounced out stern-first, barnstorming downriver at breakneck speed. We glued foot restraints onto the floor to help us remain inside. Sometimes, when the raft lurched sideways, our upper bodies would be thrown over into the river, held to the raft only by the foothold.

After battling the river most of the afternoon, we confronted a set of Class V rapids situated just above a sandy beach, where we decided we would camp. The whitewater didn't look challenging until the current picked up serious speed in a narrow chute. Suddenly, we shot out of the chute and slammed into an overhanging ledge.

The impact threw Scott across the raft and into Ben. Like characters from the World Wrestling Federation, the two of them plunged overboard and into the frothing torrent—Ben clinging desperately to his tethered paddle, Scott clinging to Ben. The raft spun back toward the large hole we had just skirted.

I grabbed Ben and pulled him into the raft. Scott let go of Ben and clambered in too, grabbing his paddle. They began paddling vigorously to slow the tractor-beam of swirling water. We were so close to the waterfall that waves were swamping the raft. For a moment it seemed that the cascade behind us, or the currents it was creating, would pull the raft under.

Ben and Scott dug in with their paddles while I leaned heavily on the steering paddle, and we broke the river's grip. We were free, gliding downriver toward a tranquil back eddy and a stretch of sandy shore that would be home for the night.

We unloaded the gear and overturned the raft to examine the damage inflicted by the river during the day's beating. A wooden or fiberglass boat would have been destroyed in the pounding it had taken, yet the outer skin was barely scarred.

Although it was a slim possibility, we were concerned about the raft disintegrating at the wrong moment. We carried a kind of flat-tire repair kit containing spare fabric, contact adhesive,

AMAZON EXTREME

a curved, thick sewing-needle, twine, and a special tape for making temporary emergency patches. But that would help only with a repairable puncture wound. These rocks and this water could julienne the raft beyond repair. That was a real fear.

We also carried a small spare foot pump in case the larger piston hand pump broke. In the hottest part of the day, we expelled air from the raft to relieve pressure as the trapped air expanded with the heat. The cool night caused the air to contract, and every morning we pumped up the soft floppy boat. A flaccid boat and no pump could be equally disastrous.

There were long stretches of the Apurimac canyon that were impassable on either side by foot. The cliffs were impossible to scale without mountaineering equipment. We carried rock-climbing-grade rope, harnesses, and cams in case we had to scale such walls, but it was rudimentary gear. If the raft died in an area like that, we would be in the House of Pain. We'd have to try and bodysurf our way out, and that would likely be fatal.

Day 27: October 9, 1999

The next morning the ride was smooth and monotonous.

"Two cats are having a race across the Apurimac River," Scott said just before lunchtime. "One is English. His name is One-Two-Three. The other is French and her name is Un-Deux-Trois. Which cat makes it across first?"

"I think I hear some rapids coming," Ben said.

"The English cat did," I replied. "Un-Deux-Trois quatre cinq."

Scott scowled, miffed that I'd ruined his punchline. He wrinkled his brow. "These ones do sound rumbly," he said.

We strained to see what lay ahead. About 300 yards away a thin line of mist sat across the river obscuring our view. Ben, in the back of the boat, stood to increase his vantage angle.

"Do you see anything, mate?" Scott asked.

"Nothing."

The roar was getting louder. It sounded like a waterfall. Clouds of mist and spray billowed ahead.

"Let's stop before we get too close," Scott said.

We were all standing now. Ben steered the boat toward an eddy, and we secured the raft.

We picked our way toward the sound of thunder, Ben bounding to the lead like a gazelle. He stopped and turned face, aghast.

The river fell about 50 feet down two main waterfalls of about 10 feet, separated horizontally by about 300 feet of steep-dropping rapids. The top waterfall was larger, but not by much. Taken together, they were horrendous. The cascading water and massive hydraulic forces formed holes and whirlpools that made Cerberus, the monstrous three-headed canine guardian of Hades, seem tame. We could not hear each other over the roar.

Back at the raft we talked it over. It was doable, we decided. We would have to hit the waterfalls square and fast to break through the recirculating water, holes, and whirlpools at the bottom. That last hole, at the bottom of the second falls, was the biggest I had ever seen. If the raft hit it, the boat would most likely flip and we would drown. We had to stay far to the left if we hoped to skirt it.

"It's up to you, Ben," I said. "You'll be guiding."

"I don't know," Scott worried. "It's pretty god-damned big."

"It's huge," Ben said quietly. "Let's do it."

Before pushing off, we went through the drill one last time. We would start out on the far right of the river, drop over the larger waterfall, and paddle like hell across the current to the far left side before the raft plummeted over the second falls. We would then cut sharply right to avoid a huge boulder, and left again past the last killer hole. Nothing to it.

"Are you guys set?" Ben shouted.

Scott and I turned back and nodded. We grinned at each other like idiots.

Ben (left), Scott, and I at "la Punta Bonita," near Camaná, after dipping our boots in the Pacific to mark the start of our journey.

Camping in the Majes Valley. The vertical stick near the fire marks where the camp stove was buried.

On the second day into our desert crossing, Scott and I puzzle over our dated and possibly inaccurate maps.

Scott and I taking a few minutes of shelter from the relentless sun.

Scott and I trudging on. What appears to be the summit of the ridge at the top of the picture is merely a shoulder. At this stage all water is gone.

The oasis—the thrilling splash of green we'd feared didn't exist.

Rehydrating at the oasis, with the Southern Cross glittering in the sky above us.

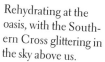

Curious children in Huambo, one of a series of villages along the rim of the Colca Canyon.

Taking a break with Willie, the farmer who rented us donkeys, on the ascent to the continental divide. The jagged peak in the background is Mt. Quehuishua, the source of the Amazon.

I celebrate with Scott on the summit of Mt. Quehuishua.

Scott surveying the continental divide from the summit of Mt. Quehuishua.

A view of the glacier from where the Amazon starts.

Commencing on the upper Apurimac, where the river wasn't much more than a large stream. After our ordeal in the desert, it was a relief to let the river carry our gear.

Scott and I portaging the raft—heavy work, but the only way to avoid a jagged bed of granite that could tear the raft to shreds.

Scott's view of me (left) and Ben (right) as we head into rapids two days above the Military Bridge.

After passing through a Class V abyss, we take a break to get our bearings and calm our shattered nerves.

Constable Ricardo serving breakfast at the Cunyac police station. He and his officers didn't think we'd make it down the Acobamba Abyss, but didn't want us to die hungry.

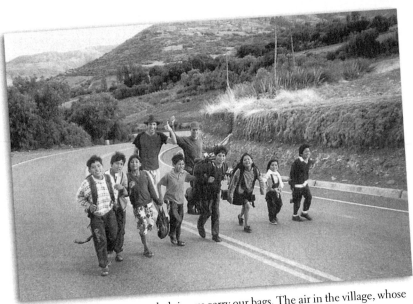

The children of Carhuasanta helping us carry our bags. The air in the village, whose economy depended on aniseed, smelled tantalizingly of licorice.

The yields of a tomato harvest on our portage around the Acobamba Abyss. The friendly farmers offered us as many juicy tomatoes as we could eat.

Ben taking a nap on the portage route while local girls giggle in the background.

Villagers pouring Ben a cup of pisco in Cachora, near the end of our journey.

A view of the river running between two mountains, from far above. This photo was taken during our descent to the river after the 38–mile portage.

I'm lining the raft while Ben remains in the boat to navigate with the paddle. Our progress over this section of the river, where we were working without maps, was extremely slow.

Ben and I scout the river from atop the never-ending jumble of boulders, two days away from the Pampas River.

Scott guiding the raft through Class IV+ rapids, a couple of days after flipping and losing much of our gear.

Our "cruise ship": The raft is converted for flat-water by using balsa logs, bamboo, and vines.

I try out the new rig while Scott luxuriates in a book. The bamboo extensions to our paddles made for effortless rowing.

One of the numerous army bases stationed in the jungle to combat the Sendero Luminoso.

Ben asleep at the helm. The magazine was a rare and welcome treat, purchased in Pucallpa.

A wary group of Indians in the "Red Zone," where sightings of nervous people armed to the teeth were common.

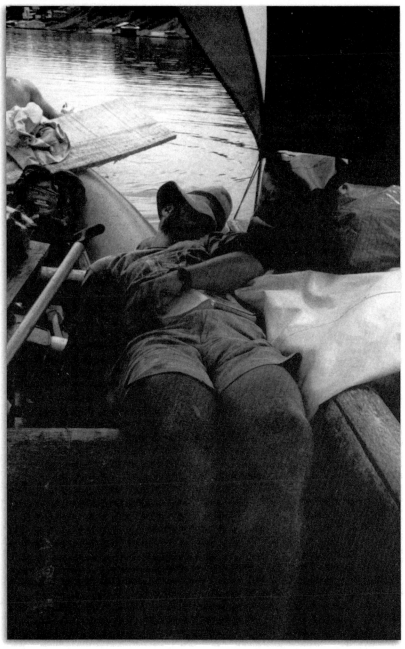

I strike the most comfortable sleeping position our raft offered. For over two months, we slept at night with our bodies draped over the balsa logs.

As my raftmates keep the boat moving, I cook a tasty breakfast of manioc-flour pancakes.

Learning Portuguese with the help of some local tutors near a beach at Santarem, "the Caribbean of the Amazon."

Rowing through the delta, which boasts the lushest jungle to be seen on the river.

Scott looking contemplative against a backdrop of roiling sky. Storms became a regular occurrence as we got closer to the Atlantic, making rowing—and living— extremely uncomfortable.

My stomach was in a knot. I cleared my mind. I looked ahead at the river and thought of nothing else. I smothered the cold shudder of fear. How do other people manage their fear? I wondered. I concentrated hard on being ready, staring at each bump, curl, and fluke in the surging current. I tried to slow the passage of time, to make it trancelike, dreamlike. To visualize everything first and make it happen.

"Easy back, fellows!" Ben was hollering. "And stop!"

The boat was just far out enough that it cleared the boulders and eddies of the right shore, but advanced no farther into the channel. It was crucial that we drop over the first falls as close to the right-hand bank as possible. About 20 yards from the brink, Ben lined up the bow. We hoped to propel ourselves over the falls with such speed and force that we would rocket through the clutching down-currents and undertows that swirled below.

"Ha-a-a-a-rd forward!" Ben yelled, and we charged the clouds of spray. "Come on, ha-a-a-rd, ha-a-a-rd, ha-rd!"

I leaned over the water and dug with all my strength. The thunderous noise of the river pulsed in my ears. I was afire with adrenaline. I pulled again and again on the aluminum paddle until the river vanished beneath me. I was left pulling mist as the bow plunged beneath me at a 45-degree angle, the raft diving into the froth below.

We landed in a roiling white hell. Icy water swirled around me as the bow sank below.

"Haaaaaaard FORWARD!" Ben hollered as the frigid fingers of the torrent raked my chest. "FORWARD!"

The boat seemed frozen amid the turmoil, even though our paddles pummelled the water. Ben was screaming at the top of his lungs: "FORWARD!"

It was little wonder. The waterfall we had just come over was inches from his back, threatening to pound the stern under. If the currents managed to push us even half a foot backward, we were doomed.

"Forwa-a-a-a-rd!" Ben was shouting while he paddled with all his might.

My arms were weakening. I glanced back. Were we advancing? We were. The raft shot forward as Ben angled the stern to get across to the other side of the river.

"BACK-PADDLE!" he commanded.

I dug the paddle into the loam-like water and turned my body slightly so that the shaft rested on my hip. Using my hip as a fulcrum, I pulled firmly on the handle with my left hand and the boat slid across the river, skating backward between two churning holes. Ben straightened the raft to face the next cascade.

"HA-A-RD FORWARD!"

We charged toward the second lip. I was confident this time because we had already survived the bigger drop. I was ready when we went flying over the brink. The nose of the raft collapsed, plunged into the foam, and sprang up clear a second later. This was how it's done, I thought.

The front end began to spin and I turned to see what Ben was doing. He was gone.

"Ben's overboard," I cried to Scott, just as I saw his head bob to the surface about 9 feet ahead of the raft—between it and the rocks. He was hanging on to his paddle, trying to grab a breath. He had a second to brace himself before the raft sandwiched him into the rocks. The back-end spun around and pulled us downstream backward, out of control. I lost sight of Ben going under.

Scott and I held on as the out-of-control raft gathered speed. The big hole, the one we had earlier stared at in awe, loomed immediately ahead. Scott and I began paddling like madmen, but, without someone on the stern to steer, the boat spun wildly. We hit the edge of the hole and the pull of its current stopped the spin. The raft seemed to hover on the edge as the slowly swirling black water drew it in and our paddling pulled it downstream. "PADDLE!" I yelled.

If we went into the hole stern first, we would surely flip and drown. Scott's paddle churned the water. The raft shuddered, poised on the cusp of the hole's slow steady boil. It was a brief tug-of-war, a seconds-long moment of equilibrium that ended when we exploded free and the raft shot downstream.

"Where is Ben?" Scott cried.

We looked upriver. Nothing.

A huge gasp made us turn. Ben was in front of the raft. I leaned forward and hauled him in, wet and limp. He was still gripping the paddle. He held on while the undertows and currents buffeted and clawed at him. He undid his wetsuit to reveal an ugly purpling bruise that stretched from his left hip to his knee—the product of the rock-slam.

"I was under the water at the last there," he said, "spinning and spinning around in a vortex. I was sure I was a goner, then I was yanked free again. Thank Christ I hung on to that paddle."

We pulled over and beached the raft. We sat eating lunch in silence. We were pretty battered and our confidence was shaken. Afterward, we portaged the next challenging whitewater and stopped for the day, rather than press our luck.

For me, it was the most depressing experience. We were not running the rapids; we were tentatively getting through them. We were bruised, and I didn't mind admitting I had been forced to think even more seriously about continuing. Did we really have the skills necessary to continue? I wondered. We had been lucky today, but when we did it over and over again, day after day, week after week, our luck was bound to run out. That was scary.

I tossed and turned all night, tormented by anxiety and fear. Big seething rapids threw me up and down, flinging me this way and that. I awoke drenched in sweat and gasping for breath, panicked about reaching the surface of a dream river in which I was drowning.

Shivering with fright, I promised myself that I would continue. To quit now was unthinkable. I pulled my sleeping bag around my shoulders and tried to relax.

Day 28: October 10, 1999

In the morning I tried to focus on the thought that the villagers in Pilpinto would never have thought we would make it so far. We had been on the river for five days now. Two smaller tributaries had added their volume to the Apurimac and, if there was rain higher up, the river turned the color of tobacco, making it almost impossible to read.

After our scare, we approached each set of rapids more cautiously. We used ropes to lower the boat down two stretches of impassable whitewater—a procedure easier than portaging, but not always possible.

We found the most perfect campsite we had encountered so far—a sandy beach fringed with trees. A small stream gurgled nearby. While exploring, I found pale-yellow-green melons growing near the stream. The flesh was white and similar in texture to watermelon, with seeds throughout. I sliced a piece. It was watery, with a faint, slightly sweet taste.

"Not bad." I passed it to Ben.

He nodded.

Enthusiastic, I headed back through the scrub to see what else could be found. I discovered some cacti, the flat-bladed variety that locals had earlier told us was edible. Some were blossoming with tiny saffron flowers. I cut off an ear and peeled back the outer skin. The exposed flesh was very slimy and sticky, but I stuck it in my mouth. It was fibrous, similar to asparagus—it would be better with cooking.

We sautéed the cacti and melon and added the stir-fry to our pasta.

Day 29: October 11, 1999

The morning continued calm and we drifted peacefully for the first few hours. We bumped through some Class III whitewater, then it was calm again. On the quiet water, we averaged about 5 miles an hour.

We passed under a decrepit suspension bridge at mid-morning. Some of the planking had rotted. There were sections missing and the occasional plank hanging as if by one arm. A trail clung to the steep canyon sides.

"This couldn't be the Military Bridge, could it?" Ben asked.

"No," I replied, "the Military Bridge has a road crossing it. At least I think it does."

In our minds the Military Bridge was a milestone—it would signal the second leg of our whitewater journey. I stared at the structure, wondering. Maybe? Naw.

Half an hour later another bridge appeared. This one was much more substantial, a trestle-style structure large enough to support a vehicle. A Toyota truck, with about thirty people standing in the bed, crossed the bridge.

"I think this is it, boys," said Scott. "We've made it to the Military Bridge, our first step in conquering this mighty river."

We drifted under the structure as another vehicle rumbled overhead. Ben guided the raft to shore.

"I wonder if there are any villages near here?" he said. "You'd think they would have something here servicing the vehicles passing through."

We could see nothing except the bridge and the dusty road.

"I wonder if this really is the Military Bridge?" I asked. "We were expecting this part of the run to take ten days, and it's been only six."

I looked around for clues. There was nothing. "Let's go for a walk and see if we can find someone to tell us. Perhaps we'll be able to find somewhere we can buy some food, too."

"Who's going to stay with the boat?" Scott asked.

"Let's draw straws," said Ben.

He stepped onto the shore and proceeded to pick three pieces of brown grass. "OK. Shortest straw stays with the boat."

Scott lost and sat down dejectedly; Ben and I sauntered off. "Bring back lots of Sublimes for me," Scott shouted. "And if you find hot food, don't forget to bring some back in a doggy bag."

We clambered up the rocks to the bridge just as a big rusty bus, with four whitewater rafts strapped onto the roof, coughed to a stop. Gringos poured out of the bus, stretching, talking, and taking pictures. Fit-looking Peruvian guides sprinted about unloading gear and pumping up the rafts. One of them spotted our raft. He said something to his friends and they paused to look at our boat.

"I guess we'll be having company for the next few days," said Ben. "This also means we won't be getting killed. They wouldn't be doing this section commercially if it was a killer."

The guides greeted us. "Hello, my friends," said one, a lean, fortyish man who shook our hands warmly. "My name is Benjamin." He owned the company and spoke almost perfect English—a boon, given our rudimentary Spanish. "Where have you guys come from and where are you going?"

"We started in Pilpinto and we'll be finishing at the Atlantic Ocean," I replied. "Is this the Military Bridge?"

Benjamin nodded. "I've kayaked a section below Pilpinto," Benjamin said admiringly. "It's pretty big there."

It felt strange to be talking to someone who knew the world of whitewater rafting and kayaking. Most people we met had not seen a raft before. Benjamin knew every explorer who had tried to conquer the Apurimac. He had met Mike Horn—the legendary South African who had made it solo two years previously.

Benjamin told us that the companies rafting this section of the Apurimac were pushing the envelope of commercial safety. There were many Class V sections and, in the two years that the companies had operated here, many had died. "But never with my company," he insisted. "I have the best guides and we take every safety precaution possible."

Benjamin told us there was a house about 3 miles down the road where we could get a hot meal. With that, he left to round up his Israeli clients. The world is indeed a village—from the kibbutz to the Andes, from Poughkeepsie to Everest. It didn't matter where you went these days, you could run into anyone from anywhere—and, in most cases, they would be better equipped than the most famous explorers of yore.

"This evening we will be setting up camp just a few miles downriver," Benjamin said. "Come and join us for dinner. We will talk more about the river."

Ben and I strolled down the dirt road and had a good hot meal. But there were no take-out containers, so all we could do was to buy a cold Coke for Scott and return to the raft. He wasn't amused.

"Mates, I've been sitting here on my ass for two hours and all you bring me is a bottle of warm Coke."

"They didn't sell anything else," Ben lied.

"What did you guys get?" Scott asked, not believing a word of it.

"Just a Coke," I lied, too. We couldn't carry the rice back in our hands, so why torture him?

On the opposite side of the river we could see the rafts with "Instinct" emblazoned on their sides, packed and ready to go. Benjamin followed in his kayak. He waved as he passed, and I pushed our raft out to follow them.

It was much easier following Benjamin's tour. The veteran guides knew the rapids well. They knew the dangers and what route to take. We were able to follow their course blindly, without having to scout for ourselves.

At 5 o'clock the Instinct crew beached their boats just above a set of Class VI rapids. In the morning the boats would be portaged. The group of twenty-six young Israelis busied themselves pitching tents provided by the company. We camped between them and the rapids.

I could see why the company had chosen this spot. There was a flat grassy area for the tents, and the view was spectacular. The surging whitewater below the camp had sculpted the side of the cliff into stunning swirls and ripples, making the granite itself appear to flow. There was also an abundance of cane for firewood.

Roberto, the youngest of the guides, came to fetch us when dinner was ready. We followed him to the cooking pit. The Israelis were spread out, sitting on logs. The guides sat by themselves, near the fire. The three guides who controlled the passenger boats spoke fluent English. The long-haired, well-muscled guide who navigated the gear boat spoke only Spanish. His skills were phenomenal. He handled the over-burdened boat without difficulty, moving her through the rough whitewater with ease.

Benjamin smiled: "I can imagine the kind of food you've been eating for the last while. Help yourselves to whatever you want."

I loaded my plate with pork steaks, applesauce, potato salad, and bean salad. There was cream of asparagus soup to go along with it. It was our best meal in weeks—and totally unexpected.

As we ate dinner, the guides told us what lay ahead. For the next couple of days, up until the Cunyac Bridge, there was nothing too dangerous. After the bridge, though, the famed and feared Acobamba Abyss began. Roberto had gone through the abyss many years earlier on an expedition with some friends. They barely made it out with their lives—and, he said, the water was much lower than it was now.

"The water is too high now," he added somberly. "It is coming up each day. If you try going through the abyss, you will surely die. For much of it there is no shore to step off on—just sheer cliffs coming down both sides. There aren't even eddies. You are flushed on and on, down waterfalls and endless rapids."

Day 30: October 12, 1999

It was a delight following the Instinct boats, but not without its moments—the worst when we got trapped in a hole. The current spun the raft sideways and threatened to push us back under the cascade.

"High side!" Scott screamed.

I jumped across the boat onto the high side. The idea was to keep all the human weight on one side to try to counteract the flipping force of the water. Tons of water pushed down on the opposite side of the boat, forcing it down. It reared up to almost 90 degrees, but our weight won and it dropped.

We were still trapped in the middle of the hole, the currents moving up and down beneath us like jackhammers. The boat was in the middle of the river, bucking and rearing, slowly spinning, but making no forward progress. Every so often the current spinning the raft pushed it under the cascading water and we would be forced to counteract the pounding to keep the boat from flipping.

As we rushed from side to side, I slipped and fell overboard into the hole. Unfortunately, my ankle was wrapped in the paddle tether. The current sucked me down, but the rope held me with the raft. I tried to reach up to untangle the line from my ankle. I couldn't—the current was too strong. I felt my strength fading. I concentrated on holding my breath, waiting for my lifejacket to pull me to the surface. It felt strange, in such a dynamic river, for everything to be so static. I seemed to be suspended somewhere beneath the raft at the end of a paddle rope. My lungs were bursting. I could see nothing.

Hold on, I thought. Hold on. Then I was jerked free. I came to the surface gasping for breath. Scott and Ben hauled me back into the boat.

The long-haired guide in the gear boat behind saw us caught in the hole. He angled his raft into the hole and slammed into us, springing us from the grip of the currents.

Out of the hole, the raft surged downriver, pulling us free of the river's death grip. I coughed and grinned.

We celebrated my rebirth with a dinner of steak and potatoes, with soup and salad. Fabulous! How many times can you say it's great to be alive!

We stayed with the Instinct tour as long as we could. They continued to look after us, providing delicious food and offering advice on some of the runs. Benjamin dropped through the most dangerous whitewater in his kayak, and the rafts followed. If they flipped, he pulled the foundering bodies to shore or back to the raft.

Some of the rapids were too big to take the clients through safely. Instead, the Israelis would walk to the bottom while the fearless guides braved the cataracts—often being flipped or bucked into the river.

We felt proud descending these sections of the river without being tossed. And we were proud to have made it to the Cunyac Bridge—the first section of whitewater was over. But we were now extremely worried about the next stage. To be warned by a land-bound farmer of the danger was one thing; to hear from an experienced guide that it was certain death was another.

Day 31: October 13, 1999

The metal structure spanning the river looked brand new, thanks to a fresh coat of bright-orange paint. Two trucks passed overhead; another coming the other way waited its turn. Just upstream lay a second wooden structure falling to pieces—a decaying mess of boards and spars. Children scampered over the wooden skeleton with fishing lines and bait. It was an image from countless childhoods immortalized by Mark Twain through the adventures of Tom Sawyer and Huckleberry Finn.

The metal bridge allowed the main highway between

Cuzco and Abancay to vault the Apurimac canyon. We tied up below the bridge with the Instinct rafts and climbed the steep bank into Cunyac, a small village with two parallel lines of mud houses flanking the road. Each house offered a display of crackers, soda, bubble gum, and other snacks and products for sale.

We bought six quart bottles of beer to share with our friends before they departed. We stood, laughter echoing off the canyon walls, sipping the beer as the rafts were loaded onto the waiting truck. We shook hands and they climbed into the vehicles.

Benjamin leaned out the window and gave his parting words of wisdom: "Remember, don't try to beat the river. Try to think with it—be its friend." And they were gone.

We returned to the river, paddled our boat a few hundred yards downstream, and pulled it onto a small gravel beach. A steep but passable trail led back up to the village. We had rice, flour, and a few condiments, but we needed more substantial food now that the Instinct larder was no longer available.

One house in the village had a table and two chairs in front. Scott and Ben grabbed the chairs and I sat on a milk crate. A middle-aged woman immediately appeared through a dark opening and came to our table brandishing a dishrag. She bent and dipped the cloth into the street-side gutter that gurgled with water from the hillside above.

"Do you have any hot food?" I asked.

"*Sí.*"

She disappeared.

Farther up the street, a girl of about eighteen carried a sickly-looking child. As she walked toward us, her sombre expression changed to a look of urgency. She ran toward the gutter and held the child above it. A stream of diarrhea washed toward us.

"Excellent, the drinking supply and the sewer in one," Ben said, grimacing. "I think I'm losing my appetite here."

The gray-haired woman reappeared holding a tray of what

looked like six deep-fried baseballs. The dark-golden globes glistened with oil. Scott poked his fork into one and oil oozed onto the tray. Lifting an eyebrow quizzically, Scott tried it: "Not bad. Deep fried mashed potatoes."

We dug in. In the middle was a hard-boiled egg, a kind of Peruvian version of a Scotch egg. After polishing off two each, we ordered another three. A tall, lean man in his mid-thirties came and joined us.

"My name is Ricardo."

He ordered a quart of beer and a cup. When it came, he poured a glass, downed the beer, and passed the bottle and cup to Ben.

In the course of our conversation we learned that he was a local policeman. There were four manning the bridge checkpoint. They examined every vehicle traveling between the Peruvian administrative districts of Cuzco and Abancay. The security was a holdover from the days when the Sendero Luminoso, or Shining Path, which advocated a Maoist transformation of society, commanded these highlands.

As he quaffed beer after beer—"I'm on a little celebration," he said—Ricardo regaled us with hair-raising stories of the savagery of the foe he and his colleagues faced.

Peru won independence from Spain in 1824, but for most of the last century the country has been in a state of political turmoil. From 1980 (when they hung dead dogs from Lima lampposts to draw attention to China's treatment of the Gang of Four) until the present, the most serious threat in Peru has been the sanguinary Sendero Luminoso.

Former professor Abimael Guzmán Reynoso of the National University of San Cristobal in Ayacucho was the movement's well-bred, well-heeled philosopher leader. The Shining Path was one of the most feared underground revolutionary groups in the world. Like his hero Mao, Reynoso believed in a scorched-earth policy. His troops inspired legends worthy of Mistuh Kurtz—small piles of hands or feet, entire villages slaughtered, groups of journalists waving white flags hacked to death with machetes, army patrols bushwhacked. Human rights agencies and United Nations observers estimate that brutality and "disappearances" in Peru during the mid-1980s were comparable to the number who vanished in Chile during the 1970s reign of terror.

As the beer flowed, Ricardo regaled us with unsettling stories of what lurked in the surrounding darkness. Just as this area was the birthplace of the Inca rebellion under the yoke of Spanish rule, so the *altiplano* and the *selva*, the heavily forested western flank of the country, had proved a fertile recruiting ground for every revolutionary movement since. It also provided an isolated and remote sanctuary.

The tipsy constable was initially struck dumb when we explained what we were doing. He clasped our shoulders. "Come and stay in the police station tonight," he said. "There are plenty of beds there—it'll be a welcome break from your tents."

We declined. If we slept in the police station, it would be an invitation for someone to steal our equipment. We promised to come for breakfast.

"You know about the Swiss team that had two members die near here?" he asked.

We did.

"Others, too," he added.

We nodded.

"Many."

He looked out into the darkness toward the bridge and the river. His walnut-colored eyes misted after a moment and he turned maudlin. "You must be careful," he said, his voice choked with beery emotion. "Be very careful."

We reassured him and left him to his revels.

Day 32: October 14, 1999

The police station was a small adobe building painted powder blue. It was only slightly larger than its neighbors. A faded gray sign, "Policía," hung on the mud wall.

We arrived in the early morning sunshine. The sparkle off the canyon walls and the river invited optimism. A policeman scampered over the top of a large lorry that had been stopped for inspection. Inside the main door, two officers sat behind a large desk. One stroked a mangy chick nestled in his lap.

"Good morning," said the man with the chick, rising and offering a hand. "My name is José. And"—he gestured to the shorter man beside him—"this is also José."

"Good morning," I said, bursting to say Hose A and Hose B. If only it had been a fire station!

"Ricardo will be here in twenty minutes," the officer added. "He is picking some fruit for breakfast." He grinned and handed the chick to his partner. "Let me give you the tour."

He stepped around the desk and led us into an adjoining dining room dominated by a large wooden table and eight chairs. One door led to a dormitory in which I could see racks of bunk beds. Another led to the back of the building, where José proudly displayed the lone cell. "We don't use it very often—we just assess big fines," he said with a wink.

We returned to the dining room and were greeted by Ricardo. He had a bag full of papayas, bananas, and oranges, which he cut into a fruit salad. On the stove simmered rice and fresh catfish plucked from the river.

"I thought all the officials in Peru were supposed to be dinks," Ben said in English so the police didn't understand. "These guys couldn't be nicer."

We had a superb breakfast, but the police officers remained skeptical that we would survive the Acobamba Abyss.

"Good luck, amigos," they said, robustly shaking our hands. "If you need help with anything, you know where to find us."

As we headed downriver toward the abyss, we were unsure what to do. Our first look at the approach to the gorge made up our minds.

The river was about 150 feet wide as it approached the canyon. Then, showing its reluctance to enter an opening perhaps a quarter its width, the river began to buck and turn, twist and thrash. We could see bobsled-run chutes and blind stops. Waves and troughs, some as high as 10 feet standing mid-current, loomed like giant green walls. The river squeezed itself into the canyon, beyond which lay we knew not what ugly geography. It was terrifying. The dark canyon walls, devoid of life, rose vertically above the wild river—boulders, slabs of prehistoric granite, disintegrating shale. It was hard to believe that anyone would voluntarily commit himself to such a maelstrom.

Portaging the abyss was our only option. Benjamin was right—the water had risen too high. It was coming up daily. The tributaries swelling the Apurimac also carried silt from rain upcountry that turned the river the color of dark stout. To run the abyss would be suicide. We pulled the raft off the water at the nearby hot springs and began our portage.

From what people had told us, we expected the hot springs to be a funky stopover at a relatively run-down attraction maintained by a native family. We were shocked to find a North American–style commercialized spa with a parking lot full of late-model cars. There were so many people that we worried about someone stealing our equipment. Resting on the beach, the raft attracted a crowd and became an easy target.

Scott came up with an ingenious idea. Using ropes secured to trees along the riverbank, we strung the raft out in the current. We could watch it bob mid-river from the hot pools. We paid our two soles and soaked our aching muscles in the tepid mineral waters that seeped off the slope above the four pools.

Afterward, we set up our own small fire to cook up a meal

of chili. Nearby, in the parking lot, a group of teachers with their pupils on a school field trip built a huge fire. They cooked a gargantuan pot of potatoes and roasted a pig leg on a spit over coals. We chatted with one of the teachers, Marie, who told us the daily meal supplied by the school was the only food many of the children saw. The teachers earned $60 a month. School trips did not happen often, and if they did it was possible only because of the generosity of local businesses.

Ben, Scott, and I discussed logistics after dinner. The portage was about 40 miles—some was road, the rest trails over precipitous terrain. We would ascend 4,000 feet above the river to the canyon rim. We decided the most important consideration was that we complete this section of the trip on foot, to maintain the integrity of our mission—to cross the continent under our own power. But the 600 pounds of gear and provisions were too much for us to carry, so we would need a vehicle and beasts of burden. We would find those ahead at Abancay.

Day 33: October 15, 1999

The teachers offered us a lift in their flatbed truck. The students were already crowded on the back, hanging on to a wooden rail that ran the length of the vehicle. We found room to stash our gear—or, rather, everyone agreed to sit or stand on our collapsed raft and bags. We jumped aboard.

The truck spluttered to life and lurched up the steep, narrow road. The wooden rail, I soon learned, wasn't secured properly. Every so often a pothole or a rut jerked the pole from its socket, sending us flying.

Close to the river there was very little agriculture. The slopes were too steep. Our overloaded truck navigated hundreds of switchbacks before the incline became less severe and the terraced farms appeared. The clusters of homes we passed through didn't seem as poor as those farther west in the Andes.

Most were recently painted and roofed with corrugated steel, not fashioned from thatch.

The children were dropped off one by one as the truck came to the area closest to their rural homes. Their gray uniforms were dirty and tattered. One boy jumped from the truck and almost immediately began weeding the family corn plot. The ride ended about 6 miles from Abancay, near the village of Cachora, where a trail led back down to the river. The truck took a turn there and left us with our gear to catch a bus into town.

Abancay is the sleepy capital of this region, seldom visited by tourists. Throughout most of the 1980s and the 1990s, as Ricardo had told us, guerrillas and bandits plagued these rugged remote valleys. They drew their most ardent support from those born and bred here. At the height of the guerrilla conflict this area was off limits, closed to outsiders and under martial law. I knew it was also to this impenetrable landscape that the Incas retreated in the face of Spanish slaughter. Rebellion is in their blood; history in Peru is pervasive and unredeemed.

There are about 95,000 people in Abancay, but it has no air service. Most people who stop are looking for momentary respite from the long, tiring journey between Cuzco and Ayacucho. We were still almost 8,000 feet above sea level. We booked into an inexpensive *hostal*, planning to stay the night, store our gear while we walked the intervening section of river, and return the following morning to the hot springs. We overdosed on chocolate bars, hamburgers, fruit, and fresh orange juice.

Day 34: October 16, 1999

I awoke shaking. I felt as though I was about to explode and ran to the washroom. My condition soon worsened—a raging fever, headache, nausea, diarrhea—and my brain was screaming. I could barely move.

Needless to say, we changed our plans.

Ben took the five-hour bus ride to Cuzco to get a copy of a video recorded by the Instinct crew. Scott and I promised to make our way to the hot springs and to rendezvous with him by the next evening at the Military Bridge. As with so many plans, this one went out the window soon after Ben left. By 3:30 in the afternoon it was obvious I was going nowhere.

Days 35 and 36: October 17 and 18, 1999

For fifty-two hours I was racked on a bed, unable to eat. I was wasted, completely and utterly shattered. Any water I kept down came flushing out minutes later the color of Coca-Cola. I was too weak to make it to the washroom. Instead, I rolled over and evacuated and vomited in a bedside bucket. I consumed massive doses of Flagyl and prayed to make it through the day. The whole room stank of feces. My sheets were soiled from involuntary spasms of diarrhea. I had moments of lucidity and hours of writhing in sweaty febrile hallucination.

The fever burned itself out—or seemed to. I vaguely remembered Scott saying goodbye so someone would be at Cunyac to meet Ben. I staggered into the street to find breakfast. The only offering was Chinese food, which I managed to swallow and keep down. I returned to the *hostal*, packed, and caught the 3:30 bus to Cunyac and the Military Bridge. It was torture. With every bump and lurch, I felt sure I would mess myself. The bus was delayed more than two hours by major road construction. At one point I had to urinate in a bottle. My diarrhea, at least, did not return.

I arrived in Cunyac after dark and found Scott and Ben asleep in the tent on the riverbank. They had pitched camp on the same beach we had used a few days before, but now it was a much smaller sweep of gravel. Heavy rain had swollen the river, and the current had bitten off large chunks of the beach. The water lapped a couple of feet from the tent.

Ben had arrived just ahead of me. He, too, had been felled by sickness in Cuzco and had boarded the bus only today. Scott spent the night alone in the middle of the deluge. Thunder-like cracks split the night. "Boulders," he said, "falling into the canyon."

"Shit," I muttered.

These boulders worked loose from the cliff above. Rocks as big as apples regularly shook free, plummeting toward the river. Occasionally, chunks of gravel and sandy scree showered the tent. Every hour or so a much larger slide exploded somewhere.

With the river chomping at the beach, none of us slept soundly.

Day 37: October 19, 1999

In the village we learned that the policemen who had befriended us were gone—transferred—and that a new, more officious squad had taken their place. They demanded to see our passports and asked where we were going. When they satisfied themselves that we didn't pose a threat to internal security, they let us continue.

The road rose out of Cunyac, climbing toward the lip of the canyon. It was a difficult trek. I was weak from sickness and hadn't carried a pack for days. Ben was ill, too, and looked like death. Scott remained cheerfully unaffected.

We walked most of the day and covered about 15 miles along the upper canyon. It was not without small pleasures. Patches of blue wild potatoes and other wildflowers delighted the eye, and the wind blew a breath of aromatic eucalyptus.

A piquant licorice tinge to the air announced the village of Carhuasanta, whose local economy revolved around aniseed. About 3 miles from the village a group of children appeared offering to carry our backpacks. Scott and Ben declined, as their packs probably weighed more than the kids. I gave mine to a pint-sized boy who trotted beside me. His face lit up as he struggled with the heavy pack. My pack looked as though it had sprouted tiny feet and was running around. Scott and Ben relented.

"I'm only doing this because, otherwise, I'd keel over and die," growled Ben. "You, on the other hand, took the first opportunity you could to exploit these little kids. Maybe you should get a job managing for Nike."

"They do seem to be enjoying themselves," Scott said. "And they were begging to carry them. Man, my shoulders feel better."

We treated the kids to soda pops in a tiny store when we arrived in the tidy little town. They guzzled the fizzy orange *gaseosas*.

One of the boys tugged on the strap of my pack, offering to carry it farther. I waved him off.

Throughout the town, people sold aniseed processed in different ways—dried, fresh, in tea bags. We carried our packs to a small *hostal* and spent $2.50 each for the night. Ben and I remained fragile, and a night in bed would do us good.

Day 38: October 20, 1999

By morning, Ben was too sick to move. The rim of the Apurimac canyon was about 4 miles away. We were in a shallow valley that ran parallel to the river at a much higher altitude. Scott and I hiked to the rim for a look.

It turned out to be a fairly easy walk, mostly through terraces producing papayas, potatoes, onions, and tomatoes. As we got closer to the lip, the incline steepened and the terraces were replaced by scrub brush and tufts of *ichu* grass. Finally, the steep slope crested, giving way to a spectacular view on the other side.

A sheer, silver-gray cliff dove to the river almost a mile and a half below. The opposite wall of the canyon was so close we felt we could toss a stone across. I had read that the Grand

Canyon at its narrowest point is about 4 miles wide. Here the opposite rim of the canyon was about half a mile away. This gorge seemed more a huge bottomless crack in the planet than a canyon. The only sound was the wind brushing the crest of the cliff. The cascading, churning water of the Apurimac would be throwing up a deafening roar in the confined space of the canyon floor, but not a whisper reached us here.

Snow-capped cones, some as high as 21,000 feet, shouldered each other as they peered over us—sentinels that had witnessed cataclysmic changes in their day. As we drank in the vista, an enormous Andean condor silently appeared on a thermal current out of the canyon and whooshed past about 6 yards from us. It had a wingspan of close to 10 feet.

"Poor Ben," Scott said. "I wish I was a poet so I could describe what the Amazon looks like when you're seeing it framed by the wings of a condor."

Day 39: October 21, 1999

Ben was better the next morning. We rose and trudged off, reaching the village of Cachora—the end of the portage—late in the day. We would get a lift into Abancay the next day to retrieve our gear, return, and rent donkeys.

Days 40 and 41: October 22 and 23, 1999

In the morning we took the bus to Abancay, where we picked up our gear and purchased enough food for about three weeks. This was the most we could stuff into our bulging dry-bags. Our topographical maps indicated that there would be no villages, farms, or homes—just deep canyons and dangerous whitewater for the next fortnight at least. We had to hope we had enough food to see us through. Only when we got to the jungle far below would we be able to resupply.

A farmer named Juan agreed to pack all our gear on two horses and a mule for 60 soles, about $20 a day. He wanted

$40, since it was a two-day trip for him: one day descending into the canyon and one day climbing out.

The people of Cachora wanted little to do with us. They were only too familiar with extreme rafting and its adherents. Most recently they had comforted the terrified man who emerged from the canyon hysterically babbling about his two companions, swept away bloodied and drowned. Those we spoke with went to great lengths to try to dissuade us. They couldn't believe that there were other gringos willing to go down the same stretch of river. They stared at us pityingly—the way you would someone who just didn't get it.

The horses, Juan told us, were good-natured. They trotted over to my outstretched hand to have their noses rubbed. The ginger mule, his ears constantly back, was another story. He was an aggressive, bad-tempered animal whose rear hooves were to be avoided at all costs. The mule bared its teeth in a growl. Juan declared that the mule was twice as tough as the horses and able to carry a much bigger load over rougher ground. I smiled as the bitter animal was loaded with enough gear to sink a ship. I could swear its ebony eye followed me.

As we left the homes and fields of Cachora behind us, the trail traversed steep grassy slopes, high above the river, which gradually increased in pitch. The horses walked ahead, not needing encouragement, but the headstrong mule stopped every few feet until the slap of Juan's hand prodded it to move on again. Ben, Scott, and I carried our regular packs plus the gear the animals couldn't carry. The mule snarled whenever anyone got too close.

Alpine flowers, scattered about like so many Smarties, peeped up among the grass. Juan told us he hoped to become a guide if tourists began frequenting the highlands. "Do you think it is pretty enough to draw tourists?" he asked.

Of course it was, we assured him.

Juan nodded, just as the heavy raft tied on the mule's back slipped sideways. "Whoa," he shouted. "Caramba," he cursed. He pulled his T-shirt over his head and quickly tied it over the burro's eyes as a blindfold. "The beast would bite me if it could see me," he explained, as he jostled the load and tightened the straps. The mule stood at attention, trembling and shaking.

"How many animals do you have?" I asked, impressed with his husbandry.

"None," he said, slapping the ginger mule.

Puzzled, I bit: "What?"

"My neighbor's," Juan replied. "I rent."

"How much?"

"Sixty soles."

"That's what we paid you," Ben said with a laugh. "You're not making anything, Juan."

Juan smiled.

"I guess old Juan never made it into the business school of Cachora," I said in English.

After about 10 miles the alpine path was left clinging to the side of a sheer cliff. The descent to the canyon floor had begun. So steep was the incline, it felt as though I were walking on pointe.

Every so often the mule would kick out one of his hind legs, hoping someone was close behind.

"You know, that mule would taste very nice barbecued," Ben said, licking his lips.

Juan gave him a stern look—you would have thought he understood English. "The mule is a very noble animal," Juan said.

"Yes, it is—isn't it just," Scott said with mock sincerity.

As the slope became steeper, we got farther ahead of Juan, who spent more and more of his time whacking encouragement into the mule. We reached a tabletop plateau with a stream where a few wild grasses flourished. A small abandoned mud hut sat near the canyon wall and, nearby, a tree bore pale-green, slightly prickly fruit.

"Custard apples!" said Ben, who was familiar with tropical fruit. "They taste great, mates."

He grabbed a long stick and climbed the old, thick-limbed

tree. About 20 feet above the ground, he knocked the fruit down to Scott and me. Most were hard, but some were ripe.

"We can eat the soft ones now and bring the rest with us," Ben said from above. "They'll ripen in a few days."

I pulled back the thin green skin, revealing the pearl-colored pulp. I bit into the flesh—delicious. Sweet, creamy, juicy, but nothing like an apple or a custard.

"Why do you dumb Aussies call it a custard apple?" I asked Ben.

He paused, looked quizzical, and shrugged. Juan and the cantankerous mule arrived. The horses browsed at the bruised and rotten fruit scattered on the ground.

"We will be at the river in about another hour," Juan said. "We will be there just before dark."

An hour before, he had predicted we would be riverside within thirty minutes—*media hora*—half an hour, no more. He was sure. Positively. Fortunately, there were still two hours of daylight left.

The farther we descended, the drier the ground became, until the vegetation vanished and we were again in a scrubland of rock, debris, and cacti. An hour later, we were still descending the precipitous trail, but we could see a footbridge in the distance. The trail slithered down into the canyon, winding left and right, left and right. It was a long way to the river. And Juan was right about one thing—we did arrive just before dark.

After pitching our tent in a small clearing above the river, I strolled toward the footbridge and found a family from Cuzco camping there.

José and his eight-year-old daughter, Salina, were hiking in the district, rediscovering their heritage. This area, José told me, played a central role in Peruvian history—especially for its indigenous people. He explained that he was trying to give his daughter a connection to that past.

The military had only recently opened up the region, José

said. Things had been better since Guzmán, the leader of the Sendero Luminoso, had been captured in 1992 and sentenced to life imprisonment. Terrorism had significantly declined. José was also interested in the older revolutionaries.

Manco Inca, the last holdout to the Spanish, retreated in 1539 to these Andean badlands, the arcs of snow-capped peaks and near-bottomless canyons his panoply. José said there were Inca ruins everywhere. Where the Totorani joins the Apurimac, at Maucallacta, you could see crumbling stone towers. The lost city of Vilcabamba, he said, was in the Concevidayoc Valley, just to the east of us.

Hiram Bingham, the U.S. archaeologist who, in 1911, discovered the fabled ruins of Machu Picchu, walked past Vilcabamba's ruins several times. So did most others until the American Gene Savoy ventured into the region in 1964 and 1965 and mapped the hidden structures. They remain unexplored under the jungle canopy because of contemporary political turmoil and the country's poverty.

Three decades after Manco Inca's retreat, José continued, the Spanish dragged his son, Felipe Tupac Amaru, from these valleys, supposedly at the end of a golden chain. They marched him to Cuzco and, in 1572, beheaded him on the cobbled Plaza des Armas. His family dispersed. One of his daughters married a man from Surimana—the surly town we had been through a few weeks before—and settled there to try to forget about the coming of the white devils.

The family prospered and endorsed the Spanish colonial government, José said. But the indigenous people nursed great pride and wounds from the loss of their empire and the servile conditions imposed by the European and *mestizo* ruling class. So oppressive was the Spanish administration that José Gabriel Tupac Amaru II, the great-great-great-grandson of the last Inca, reluctantly became one of the New World's great revolutionary heroes.

Born about 1743, José Gabriel was well educated, wealthy,

and guilt-ridden. In 1780, declaring himself a loyal subject of the king of Spain, he revolted against the heinous colonial administration. He stirred native pride in Colombia, Ecuador, Peru, Bolivia, and Argentina. But he was captured in 1781 and, within two years, his nascent rebellion was crushed. The forces he unleashed, however, led Spain to replace the ruling colonial administration and to abandon the South American continent within two generations. In our own time, José said, militants opposed to the Peruvian central government invoked Tupac Amaru as their hero. It was throughout this area that you felt the strongest sense of indigenous pride and the greatest distrust of foreigners.

I was spellbound. José brought Peruvian history alive for me and gave me a deeper appreciation of the world I was traveling through. I wished I had taken more time in preparing for the trip to understand the history.

José was intrigued when I told him we were rafting the river. He didn't know it could be done—especially here. He had seen the water below the bridge in the daylight and said it looked like the lair of the devil: "*El diablo,*" he repeated.

Day 42: October 24, 1999

After the raft had been loaded, Juan, José, and Salina joined us on the riverside. This section of the Apurimac was one of the few areas where the canyon walls eased back enough to allow the trail to approach the river. That was why we chose it as the place to end our portage.

The Apurimac was swift here, having sluiced through the abyss. Just above the footbridge, it thrashed through a set of Class V rapids, composed itself for a few moments, and, about 100 yards downstream, erupted in a cacophony of whitewater that beckoned us. It was relatively calm in the eddy in which we were moored; the current fast and choppy, but flat, until the rapids. The raft, loaded with enough gear and food to last us for three weeks, tugged on its bowline.

The three Peruvians were talking animatedly among themselves when we came to say goodbye. They spoke rapidly to us in Spanish, but neither Scott nor I had a clue what they were saying or why they were gesticulating at the river. Ben put up his hands, saying: "Whoa. Slow down. No comprende so quickly." His tall body leaned against a pillarlike rock as he listened to them. Among the three of us, he spoke the best Spanish. He began to shake his head vigorously and wave his hands, saying over and over again "no, no, no." "Footbridge," he emphasized. "Footbridge."

Juan looked hangdog. He gestured at the far side. "The river is flat here," he said. "Surely you fellows are strong enough to get us across before the rapids start."

José nodded, and he pointed to Salina, who was pleading with her eyes, "Please."

I shifted uncomfortably, understanding now what was at issue. They were confident we could make it to the far shore before the troubled water began. But what if we didn't? They had no safety gear—no lifejackets, helmets, or cold-water clothing.

Salina looked to me like an eight-year-old putting on a brave face to please her dad. She was terrified just looking at the river. I could see that. She wanted to go across because her father said it would be fun. "We can do it, guys," Scott said, breaking the uncomfortable pause in the discussion. "I mean, how could we not? If we can't make it across this river in a hundred yards, there's something seriously wrong."

I was surprised. Scott had begun the expedition with great confidence, but, recently, the pounding on his body had undermined his swagger. His robust, stocky body had received many beatings and he had begun to take an "avoid it if you can" attitude. He had retreated within himself a lot over the last few days.

Ben seemed ambivalent.

It put me in an awkward spot. I thought Scott would be the one to keep us from trying anything too foolish. Now my own fear was on the line. I didn't like to admit it, but I too was terrified of the river. I still slept fitfully after the near-death experience of the last dunking, and I dreamt regularly of being pounded along the bottom and drowned.

The previous night, in the dark, I had admitted to myself that the Apurimac's savage indifference and interminable fury made my very soul weary. Every time the raft flipped, it thrashed you. I had been bruised everywhere. It was only luck that had kept me from dying in some savage vortex. I knew what it felt like to be held under until your lungs burned for oxygen, but the current wouldn't let you go. I knew how little confidence you felt after you'd promised anything and everything to whatever malevolent force was drowning you. I knew what this river could do. And I reviewed again what it had done in this very area.

In 1953 the Frenchman Michel Perrin and his Limeña girlfriend Teresa Gutierrez went into the river in kayaks at the Cunyac Bridge. Like us, they portaged the abyss and went in again near here. Gutierrez capsized within minutes and drowned. A well-financed German team attempted to run this stretch in 1976, but gave up when the leader drowned after putting his boat in the water.

I was scared of the Apurimac, and I didn't mind admitting it to myself. But I was prepared to stare down that fear and swallow the scalding bile that rose in my throat when I looked downstream at the waiting cauldron. Get back on the horse, I said. I just wasn't sure I wanted to do it with an eight-year-old kid.

I shifted from one foot to the other, mum.

Scott would be guiding, so ultimately it was his call, I figured. If he felt comfortable taking them across, why not? We would do it, I thought.

Ben, Scott, and I talked for a few minutes about the best strategy for reaching the other side and what measures to take if something happened. I followed Scott's blue-eyed gaze as he scanned the water for any hidden dangers. If he felt the risk was low, I thought, maybe . . . My own fear made me bite my tongue. No way was I going to put my foot down and nix the plan now. I wasn't brave enough to expose my own worries. Although not understanding a word of what we were saying, the three Peruvians smiled and nodded, pleased we were taking them across.

The river was the color of mud. A few hundred yards downstream it was a frothing, dirty-cream color where it smashed into a line of house-sized boulders and over a small falls.

We all got into the boat, and I shivered with a premonition of disaster. The mounds of food and gear weighed about 500 pounds. With five adults and a kid as well, the raft sat very low in the water. We were overloaded. The self-bailing floor was pushed down so far that river water sloshed around our feet. I didn't like it.

Salina sat atop the gear, and the Peruvian men sat one on each side of the tubes behind Ben and me.

"Forward paddle," Scott said, as José undid the mooring rope.

Ben and I dug in. The normally nimble boat was sluggish. Scott's voice increased a few decibels.

"Come on, guys. Ha-a-a-ard forward. Give it all you've got!"

The boat came into the main current at a 45-degree angle with the bow pointed upriver. Our paddles churned the water as the river picked up the boat and began to push it toward the waiting rapids.

"Harder! Harder!" Scott yelled.

I could hear the two Peruvians starting to talk behind us as we dug-dug-dug toward the far shore. The roar of the whitewater was getting louder. Scott angled the raft directly toward the opposite bank, but, by turning us broadside to the current, he gave us to the river. Our frenzied paddling was impotent against the force and increasing speed with which the Apurimac began to hurl us toward the whitewater.

We were only two-thirds of the way across when we hit the

top of the rapids. I could see the hole we had scouted—we were going to go into it sideways in slow motion.

José was pointing at his daughter and screaming: "¡No! ¡Nada!"

"We're going over, mates!" Scott yelled, as the bottom side of the raft crashed over the lip.

Everything went white and quiet. The screams disappeared. So did the world. I realized I was holding my breath and being sucked down by the swirling currents. My body was spinning and I had no idea which way was up. My only concern was that I wouldn't be hurled along the rock-covered bottom. The buoyancy of my lifejacket would, I hoped, pull me to the surface once the current released me.

I just had to hold my breath. Hold on. Hold on. I felt as if the river were squeezing me to death. Hold on. Hold on. I was bursting for air. Hold on. I couldn't tell which way was up. Where was the raft? Hold . . .

Suddenly, I burst into the air. I gasped. I sucked in air.

Under again. Up. Gasping. Trying to orient myself. Under again. Hold on. Up, gasping, under. Hold, up, under.

The hole spit me out and I was bobbing downstream, hurtling along in the current. I could see Scott—with one hand he was hanging on to a rope attached to the overturned raft and with his other he hugged the Peruvians bobbing nearby. Both were screaming: "Salina!"

I looked around frantically. Without a lifejacket, she hardly stood a chance. The river was tossing us merrily as it swept us along toward the next set of rapids.

I angled my swimming toward the raft. The current carried me past the other three and allowed me to grab a handhold. Salina. Where was she? My God, what if we'd killed her? I forgot about the river and began to feel panicky about finding the little girl.

There are prayers you say in childhood before bed and there are prayers that say themselves—prayers that rise unbidden, summoned from the very core of your being by the most extreme circumstances, the please-God-I-don't-want-to-die prayers. At that moment I begged whatever munificent power there was for a little girl I didn't know.

That's when I heard the whimpering. Salina! But where?

I pulled myself around to the other side of the raft and spotted the little brown hand clutching the perimeter line. She was still hanging on. She had held on to the raft as it went in one side of the hole and out the other. I grabbed her arm and tossed her quivering frame onto the overturned raft. I did a seal-roll up beside her and hugged her to me.

I clutched her to me as Scott and the others began to pull themselves toward the raft that continued to rock 'n' roll down the river. I felt sick. The Peruvian men were crying. I turned to get a look at what we were hurtling toward.

Ben's curly head appeared at the side of the raft and he pulled his lanky body up beside me. The other three continued bobbing on the outer rope, struggling to get to the raft.

I could see Scott trying to calm José and Juan, but it was no use. They came from a simple background and to be at the mercy of the river was terrifying. They could hear the coming rapids.

Out of control, the boat careered toward the whitewater. Massive limestone cliffs rose straight up on both sides and the roar deafened us. Salina clung to me in terror. The men still in the water were hanging on to the rope in prayer.

"Shall we try flipping the raft back upright?" Ben yelled.

"Good Christ, no," I said, shaking my head.

Salina was having trouble enough—if she fell in the water again, our chances of hanging on to her were non-existent. She was sure to drown.

"The next set is coming."

I could hear the roar increasing. I waved at Scott and he grabbed the two men, understanding immediately the danger. He looped the perimeter line around them and gripped it with both hands. Ben and I each held on to Salina with one hand and clung with the other to the lacing of the bottom of the self-bailing floor.

The raft was shaken like a leaf in a blower for the next minute. I let go of Salina. I couldn't see her in the froth of whitewater that flowed over us as the raft bucked and exploded beneath us. The floor became vertical on at least two occasions, threatening to flip backward, trapping us.

It was over as quickly as it erupted. We bobbed out of the whitewater and the raft spun slowly in an eddy until its nose snagged against some rocks. Ben and Salina lay beside me. Nobody said anything. I looked astern. Scott and the two men were still on the end of the rope, looking the worse for wear. We were about 20 feet from the shore.

Scott swam to shore with the line and pulled the boat in. José clasped Salina to him. He whimpered softly as she buried her face in his chest. She was screaming hysterically.

I lay thanking whatever forces there were in the universe that no one was seriously hurt.

It was our fault. We should never have let them talk us into taking them across the river. Up until that moment, each of us had placed only himself in danger. We knew the inherent peril, gauged our abilities, and threw the dice. It was a calculated risk. We were willing to take that risk to experience the journey of a lifetime.

Salina made no such informed choice. She put her trust in us. These were poor people living off subsistence farming. Adrenaline sports and extreme rafting were as foreign to them as English. They had trusted us. Our strange gear and foolhardy confidence led them to believe they would be safe in crossing the river. They were wrong.

Salina and her father sat sobbing for a long time. He held on to her even when they got up and began walking silently back upriver toward the footbridge. They were still on the same side.

Juan watched them go. He said nothing as he wrung out his

clothes. Finally he muttered, "You are crazy." He had been involved in a rescue operation for two members of the Swiss expedition who had drowned here. He finished wringing out his clothes, gave each of us a hug, and kissed us on the forehead. He considered us dead men.

We were too exhausted to do anything but sit for a long time.

I thought about other times in my life when I'd felt this way. It was a mixture of dread and jubilation, the residue of absolute terror, and the staggering ecstasy of simply being alive.

Coming back from New Zealand, I had been caught in a gale. It was blowing in excess of 66 knots. At its height, though, the storm raged over cyclone strength—consuming a 52-foot vessel with a father and two sons aboard just off Australia. I thought I was headed for the same fate sitting below deck, the hatches battened, trying to ride it out.

That's when the *Ondine* rolled over, flipped onto her side by a breaking wave. The mast was 20 degrees under the water, and tons of pressure were attempting to snap it off. The boat paused, suspended for perhaps fifteen seconds before it slowly started to right itself. One moment I was sitting on a settee eating a can of corn, and the next I was sliding down the wall onto the ceiling. As the *Ondine* resurfaced, I slid back down the wall and onto the couch, petrified.

The storm was unrelenting. I was thrown around and smashed about for days. I couldn't cook or sleep. And there was always the problem of water coming in. The bilge pump broke, and I had to bail the boat with a pot because the bucket had a hole in it. When I wanted to say time out, I couldn't. I had to keep going and keep fighting until it was over.

"My God," I thought, "once I get to land, I never want to do this again." But when it was over and I chugged into port, had a few beers, and told stories of the dangers I'd faced, my courage was restored. I had survived many storms like that, and I would survive this trial too.

We righted the raft. Our gear was normally stowed in four

115-quart dry-bags lashed securely to the floor of the boat with two cam straps. In a flip, everything usually stayed dry and attached to the raft. Not today. The extra provisions—the rice, dried beans, flour, pasta, and oatmeal—filled our dry-bags. We had been forced to leave some gear unprotected and secured only by straps: sneakers, sandals, foamies, cooking utensils, the tube of topographical maps, and the aluminum frame we used for carrying the raft. When we righted the raft, my heart sank. All that remained in the boat were the four secured dry-bags. Everything else had washed out. Losing the maps was bad. Worse was loosing every pot, pan, plate, cup, knife, fork, and spoon. Everything!

We were entering one of the most remote and dangerous regions of the world with a raft full of dehydrated staples and nothing to cook with. We could spend days hiking back to the village, or we could continue and jerry-rig a solution. We chose the latter. I think it was a combination of pride and stubbornness that made each of us continue. Or maybe we wanted to punish ourselves for what had happened.

I stood looking at the boat and tried to take stock. Nobody had been hurt. Scared, but not hurt. We had lost a lot of gear, but nothing that seemed indispensable. It wasn't as though we could get lost going down the river. If there was ever a time for character, this was it. It was all part of the challenge. Right?

The sun had risen high enough to warm the steep cliffs and chase the chill from our bones.

We scouted ahead before continuing. The river appeared to be an unbroken snarl of whitewater. We would tackle a set of rapids and enjoy a stretch of relative calm before the next explosion of whitewater combat. There would be no respite here. The narrowing of the canyon, the car-sized boulders, the cascades, the holes, the boils, the whirlpools—everything got more and more dangerous. Trying to control the raft in this turmoil was akin to riding a leaf in a gale.

We tried to stop and scout where possible, but often the river refused to allow it. We were lucky for most of the day and managed to get the raft pulled into an eddy. Then the river threw up a particularly frenzied set of whitewater and two massive holes. We saw that the entire river flowed through the second vortex and there would be no way to get around it. As the flow of the current emerged from the maelstrom, it curled back on itself, forming a standing wave that towered almost 9 feet high. The raft, hitting it like a brick wall, would be flipped back into the hole. We had no choice but to line the boat through.

The cam straps were cinched tight, and Scott and Ben walked downriver holding the line. The unmanned raft handled the river like a champ, bouncing merrily through the rapids and barreling through the first hole. The second hole, however, was its nemesis.

The raft skated across the roiling maw, but slammed into the standing wave and was flipped end-over-end back into the eye of the hole. Ben and Scott hauled on the rope as hard as they could, but the river drew the line tight, sending up a shower of water droplets from the tension. The raft windmilled, flipping over and over and over again as Ben and Scott struggled to hold onto the line.

I scrambled over the rocks as fast as I could to their aid. I slipped and scraped my shin on a sharp rock. I cursed, got up, and joined them pulling on the line. It refused to give an inch.

Pop! Like a sport-fish abandoning the fight, the rope suddenly slackened and the hole spat out the raft. We pulled it to shore, relieved to find the gear still attached.

For the rest of the day we continued to face a seemingly endless series of Class V rapids. We did well riding through without flipping. The success did a lot to mend our damaged pride and give us back a small piece of the confidence that had drained away earlier. The river gave us enough of a calm stretch to get out and scout one particularly bad stretch. For about 100 yards it roared through Class VI rapids, before jumping off a 9-foot drop. The raging current thundered over the lip slam-bang into an overhanging ledge and under the cliff-face. There was no way we could run it or line it. We would have to carry the raft and gear for about 1 mile along the right-hand bank.

Walking along the shore without any gear was a feat; negotiating the rocky canyon riverbank, loaded like a mule, was almost impossible. We were forced to scale enormous boulders, some almost 30 feet high, worn smooth by the river in flood. It could take twenty minutes just to move a few hundred yards.

We broke the portage into three parts. We began by each taking one of the 100-pound dry-bags. We emptied them at the far end of the portage and returned to the raft with the empty bags. For the second trip, we divided the 220-pound food bag equally into the three empty dry-bags and topped them up with the remaining gear—pumps, throw-bags, cameras, and so on. Lastly, we returned for the raft. This was the most difficult item to carry.

On this portage we were lucky. A large pool of water some 300 yards long lay about halfway along the route. We swam across this pool easily with the dry-bags on the first two trips. When we returned with the raft we paddled across, enjoying the mirrored calm of the giant puddle.

We pitched our tents in a small sandy area at the end of the portage and called it a day. The challenge now was to eat.

Ben lit a fire while I combed the shore for something with which to cook. I found an old rusty shovel blade wedged between some rocks. It took me about ten minutes to free it. Half the blade had rusted away completely, but what remained could be salvaged and used as a frying pan. I was amazed how much garbage lay trapped between the rocks—cracked plastic pop bottles, old plastic bags, rusty cans, and bits of Styrofoam speckled the ground. So much for the pristine wilderness.

I spotted a dark-green object protruding from a stretch of gravel. It was an old plastic gas can. The bottom half was shredded, but the top half, which included the filler hole, was still in good shape. It could be a pot. As children, we had put plastic bags of water into roaring fires and had been amazed that the bag didn't melt, even after the water began boiling, because the liquid always kept the plastic below its melting point. I wondered if the same principle would protect the gas can.

Walking back to our camp, I saw a tarantula—it was 10 inches across from foot tip to foot tip. These hairy creatures do not spin webs. They sit motionless, waiting for dinner to come within range, and—zap! I picked up a yard-sized length of cane and gently prodded the spider to see if it was alive. In a blink, the tarantula spun toward me and leapt at my hand. Fortunately, the stick was long enough that the spider's pounce fell short of my finger and it tumbled to the ground. It landed by my feet and scuttled away.

I continued back to camp and found Scott carving a wooden spoon with his Swiss Army knife. Ben sat in front of the fire contemplating a large tin of sardines and a package of rice.

"This is what I've decided," he said. "I'll dump the sardines out onto the rock here and cook the rice in the tin. It'll make only a couple of tablespoons each, but it'll be better than nothing. We can make rice all night until we're satisfied."

"What have you got?" Scott asked.

"A frying pan and maybe a pot. I'll have to cut it in half first and plug the filler hole."

He looked incredulous. "Don't you think it will melt?"

"Probably, but it's worth a try." I borrowed Ben's Leatherman and walked toward a clump of cane. I found a piece to plug the hole and cut the jug in half, discarding the perforated bottom. I now had a small bucket. Then I walked down to the river and filled it with water to see if the hole was properly plugged. It leaked slowly, but not badly. I returned to camp with the new cooking pot.

The first batch of rice was ready and Ben divided it onto

three flat rocks. He added two sardines, covered in tomato sauce.

"*Voilà*," he said. "Dinner is served."

Ben and I ate with our fingers; Scott used his new spoon.

Ben put another batch of rice over the fire. I licked my lips. "I'm going to try out the gas can to cook some of the beans," I announced.

I filled the makeshift pot halfway with water and dumped in two cups of dried navy beans. I arranged two flat rocks at the edge of the fire and set the gas can over the rocks. We watched nervously.

The plastic sides above the waterline curled from the heat and I began to think we should have tested it first without the beans. But the bottom remained solid. After about ten minutes, the water began to boil and soon the beans were bubbling away contentedly.

"Hurrah, lots of beans for dessert," said Ben.

Buoyed by the success of the beans, we decided to use the shovel blade, too, and make some Mexican food.

Scott made a salsa with the fresh tomatoes and onions we had brought in Cachora. We made a dough of flour, salt, and water, and cooked tortillas on the shovel blade.

We went to sleep sated, trying to put the morning's horror out of our minds.

Day 43: October 25, 1999

I slept fitfully, and something heavy and cold sat in the pit of my stomach. Fear. All night I was tormented by visions of huge, bucking rapids tossing the raft hither and yon, black yawning holes pulling me under, and the suffocating sensation of drowning. Throughout it all, I could hear a little girl's screams.

When I couldn't sleep, I felt my body tumbling, tumbling, tumbling. I closed my eyes and I saw the waves—high, ominous waves like clumps of black earth waiting to tumble over me and bury me alive. I could hear the rapids in the darkness. An endless nightmare of violent, suffocating tumbles through water and rock and darkness, the river howling and gushing around me.

No matter how bad the rivers were in Alberta, I always ran them with a sense of exhilaration. That excitement had long ago been dispelled by the Apurimac. In part, I enjoyed the adrenaline rush at home because I knew that, if anything happened, Foothills Hospital was only an hour or so away and the best medical care in the world was available. Here, there was no hope of expert medical care—heck, it would take days, weeks maybe, to go for help and lead back a rescue party if anyone was seriously injured.

The novelty of running rapids had long ago worn off. The pride with which I had started the journey had also thinned. I no longer felt as confident or as smart as I had at the beginning. The fun had gone and I merely hoped that I'd be around to enjoy dinner, no matter how unpalatable.

My physical health had deteriorated too. Racked by intestinal bugs and intermittent fevers, even my muscles had begun to degenerate from the unbalanced diet. When I tried some chin-ups on an overhanging branch a few days before, I could do only half the number I normally did.

We couldn't find firewood in the morning, so we tried to use the plastic pot on the butane stove. The focused heat took only moments to melt the bottom, however, releasing a wave of watery oats. I was dejected.

We sat and tried to swallow a cold breakfast—uncooked oats, sugar, and river water shaken vigorously in a jam jar. Hungry, tired, and feeling a long way from anywhere, we readied once again for the river.

The cliffs seemed to come even closer to the river's edge

and we encountered many stretches where there was no shore whatsoever. The river filled the canyon from one perpendicular cliff to the other. These were the most dangerous sections because it was impossible to scout ahead, or even to pull the raft over and take a break.

Traveling without maps, we figured we would be able to orient ourselves at the confluence of the Pampas River, a sizable tributary of the Apurimac. But we had no idea how much farther it would be before the rivers merged, so we continued our haphazard journey downriver.

As the riverbank reappeared, we went more cautiously—scouting rapids, lining the boat over the worst whitewater, and descending only when we felt it safe. Our progress was excruciatingly slow and it was difficult to imagine in the sunless canyon that, somewhere downriver, the water broadened out into a placid sea.

By evening, our growling stomachs begged for substantial food. Scott pulled out the plastic container he was using to protect his camera. He dumped a cup of rice into it, wrapped it in a T-shirt, and began pouring in steaming water heated over the fire in the sardine can. Once enough water was added, he covered the plastic container and waited. The lukewarm watery congee that emerged was crunchy and barely edible, even when topped with sardines and the last of the salsa.

After dinner we set to work to bake pan bread for lunch. I mixed a dough of flour, yeast, sugar, and salt. I kneaded the mixture for twenty minutes, let it proof, and formed it into small flat loaves. I cooked thirty-four flat breads on the shovel over the open fire. We ate three each, fresh off the fire, with butter and jam. The bread tasted scrumptious compared with the half-raw crap we'd been eating for the last two days. We stored the rest for lunch next day.

Our success with the bread inspired us to try oatcakes in the morning. With jam, they were even better than the cooked porridge. But as we headed out on the river, the ominous cloud of dread returned.

Again, the canyon walls closed in on us and it was impossible to stop the raft, get out, and scout approaching rapids. We heard them, sometimes we saw them, and other times we came around a large boulder or hairpin turn to find ourselves plummeting down into them. We hit a treacherous set of Class VI just that way before lunch.

The raft dropped over a small waterfall and slammed into a rock. The impact buckled the raft and flung Scott overboard as if from a slingshot. He hit a huge boulder and fell hard on his leg. He screamed and let go of his paddle, grasping at his wounded leg. As we spun out of control, the current washed him off the rock and downstream away from the raft. The raging torrent pushed him up against the left-hand bank and threatened to bash him senseless on the face of the cliff. Luckily, he grabbed the nub of a small ledge. As Ben and I hurtled past on the raft, we saw him clamber up onto the rock. I vainly extended my paddle out to him, but it was more of a wave. It took us nearly 200 yards to regain control of the raft and steer into an eddy.

Upriver on the opposite side, Scott was a tiny figure at the base of an intimidating cliff. He waved his arms and pointed to his leg. The ledge sloped toward the river. Behind Scott, a slick, perpendicular cliff rose hundreds of feet. The canyon wall was similarly sheer upriver and downriver of the ledge. There was no overland escape from his damp, slippery refuge.

We walked toward Scott, on the opposite side of the river from him. This shore was the usual mess of boulders; however, it was possible to traverse. Ben carried the rescue throw-bag, a 30-yard length of buoyant rope packed into a nylon bag. A loop on one end of the rope projected from the mouth of the bag. If you held the loop as you hurled the bag, the rope would rapidly uncoil behind it. With a strong throw, the bag sailed through the air to the end of the rope, which was attached inside the bag to a piece of Styrofoam to keep it afloat.

Scott looked helpless and vulnerable. The roar of the rapids made it impossible to hear anything. He pointed to his leg and gestured as if breaking a stick over his knee, to indicate it was broken.

"It can't be broken," Ben said. "He's standing on it."

"Maybe he's just trying to point out that it hurts really badly," I replied.

Scott was now pointing to us and swinging his right hand, imitating the motion of tossing the throw-bag. But it was clear the rope wouldn't be long enough. The river was too wide.

"It won't reach!" Ben shouted. He couldn't hear us.

We shook our heads, but Scott continued miming his throw-bag motions. Finally, to demonstrate, I walked down to the water's edge and threw the bag as hard as I could. It landed in the middle of the river, not even close to the opposite shore—a good 55 yards or more away.

"He's going to have to swim out of there," I said, reeling in the line. "There's not a hope in hell that we'll be able to rescue him."

Scott now pointed up at the cliff and placed his body in a spread-eagled climbing position at the base. He pointed to us.

We looked at each other, puzzled. Then we got it. He wanted us to ford the river, scale the canyon wall, and lower a rope to him. Sure, we had climbing gear, but our 55 yards of rope wouldn't be nearly enough to mount that kind of rescue operation. Scott couldn't see how far the cliff stretched above him. He was underneath the cliff. We would never reach the top, Ben and I agreed. We emphatically shook our heads.

I'm sure Scott felt that this was just a conspiracy against him. We appeared pretty apathetic about the whole situation as we sat on the rocks, watching him and doing nothing.

"He thinks we're fucking him over," I said to Ben.

"Yeah, nothing we can do about that."

Scott scowled at us. The noise of the Apurimac mocked us.

"It's like that scene in *Deliverance*," I said.

"Where Burt Reynolds breaks his leg?"

"Yeah."

"They made it. We'll make it. He's just got to suck it up and get back in the river."

"Yeah, easy for us to say," I nodded.

Scott looked truly miserable. There was nothing we could do for him. Nothing.

I rotated my arms as if swimming. It was his only escape. I pointed to the rescue line and gestured to the bottom of the rapids. We could fish him out of the river with the rope.

He looked panic-stricken and pointed to his injured leg.

We turned our backs on him and made our way to the small eddy at the base of the rapids. We sat on the rocks downriver, waiting for Scott to jump into the whitewater. He just sat on the wet slippery ledge.

"What's he doing?" Ben muttered. "Even if his leg is broken, he's got no other choice."

Ben was frustrated. "WE CAN'T RESCUE YOU!" he yelled. "We can't rescue you," he repeated slowly and concisely, as though the clarity of the statement could be transmitted to Scott via telepathy.

I sympathized with Scott; he faced a painful ordeal. After an hour, though, I grew impatient.

Scott sat on the ledge waiting for Godot or God himself to descend from the sky and carry him down the river. Every ten minutes or so, Ben or I would windmill our arms. He would shake his head and point to his leg.

"Perhaps if we start eating lunch he'll get hungry and swim down," I said.

Ben chuckled. Scott stood up.

"I think he's about to do it," Ben said. "Quick, get the video camera—this will make some great footage."

I handed Ben the camera. I thought it a touch mercenary and hard-hearted, but he was right. I picked up the throw-bag. It was like those wildings you read about where the participants carry digi-cams and latter get nabbed by the police with their crimes immortalized on homemade video. We were going to capture either a dramatic bit of river rescue work or Scott's death. Great footage.

Scott procrastinated for about another ten minutes, eying the river furtively, searching for the right spot to launch from, before jumping into the frothy whitewater.

Immediately he disappeared. We scrutinized the churning water, searching for his head. Nothing. Shit.

"There's an arm," Ben shouted.

"A leg. Another arm."

Bits of Scott's body appeared and disappeared as he tumbled down the rapids. His head appeared again and we saw him try to grab a breath. He seemed to be screaming in pain at the same time. Ouch. He went under again. The current pounded him the way Mike Tyson once pummelled his opponents.

Ben and I watched anxiously. I tensed, ready with the throw-bag. We had to get him before he was washed the next 55 yards downstream and into a waiting set of murderous rapids. Where was he?

He popped to the surface in front of me. I hurled the rescue bag. It fell short.

Scott, gasping for air, was able to swim to the shore. He pulled himself up onto a rock and lay there, mugged, shaken, his lower torso and legs floating gently in an eddy.

He was safe. I waved over at him and he managed to nod his head. We still couldn't hear each other over the river.

I climbed down to the water, retrieving the rope. Frothy scum lined the edge of the river. Amid the foam, I spotted a shoe—two shoes.

"Holy shit!" I exclaimed. "Check these out, Ben. Scott's Nikes. What are the chances of that!" He had lost them three days earlier in the catastrophic flip. "Of all the millions of nooks and crannies for them to get washed up on in the river, and we just happen across them."

Scott was too busy feeling sorry for himself and regaining his breath to see what I'd found. I tossed them into the raft, and Ben and I paddled across to Scott. He was not a happy camper.

"Thanks for the rescue, guys," he said sarcastically.

"There was nothing we could do," I replied, his shoes hidden at my feet.

"You didn't even try," he pouted. "And my leg is fucked—even more fucked now after the swim."

He gestured down at his knee, swollen the size of a softball and stained an ugly yellow and puce.

"What could we do?" Ben asked. "I don't know how we could have tried harder."

"What happened to your bootie?" I asked, nodding toward his bare foot and trying to change the subject.

This was the tensest moment we'd ever had as a trio.

"It got ripped off in the river," Scott grumbled. "I'll have to go barefoot now."

I held up the Nikes.

Incredulous, he broke into a grin. "Where'd you get those?"

"On the shore, mate," I said. "The Apurimac took one pair and she gave back another."

Ben laughed.

"Maybe the river likes me after all," Scott said.

"Nah, she's just teasing you," Ben quipped. "You're the one she's going to have for dinner."

Scott removed his remaining neoprene bootie and tucked it in a dry-bag. He slid on his running shoes, taking care to lace each one tightly. We ghosted back out into the current, drifted for a bit, and stopped the raft in an eddy above the next rapids.

We would have to portage. With Scott still feeling a bit shaky, we didn't feel it wise to continue. We decided discretion was the better part of valour. We would camp here.

Day 45: October 27, 1999

I had another bad night worrying about the rapids we would have to face, especially with Scott on one leg. From the first set on, though, the river was kind to us and spared us any nasty surprises.

We portaged and lined anything that looked remotely challenging, as we needed to rebuild our confidence. To be honest, mostly we portaged. Actual time spent riding the "waterslide" was minimal. As a result, our progress was extremely slow. We probably didn't advance more than two miles. The whitewater was difficult and impassable. The day was one of constant mental anguish. I was beginning to wonder if we should be here at all. People don't belong in the bowels of the earth.

We were making do with meagre rations of undercooked crunchy rice and beans. We ate it with grubby fingers and washed it down with silt-laden, polluted, unfiltered river water.

This trip was no longer an exciting challenge giving us a breathtaking ride. Rather, the river was grinding us down, like so many beach pebbles.

We came to an abyss of sheer walls. We only just managed to guide the boat into a cliff-side eddy that allowed us to climb onto a rock to get a look. There was no way to portage, and the water ahead looked ferocious.

"Shit, mates, that looks really bad!" said Scott.

He was standing on the wet, foam-streaked boulder, straining to see downriver. I climbed another rock, slightly higher, trying to get a better view. It was impossible to make much out. The river disappeared through a tiny crack ahead of us. Waterfalls, killer strainers, anything could be lurking just beyond our view, but we had no choice. The sheer cliffs rose over 3,000 feet over our heads. We were trapped. Retreating upriver was impossible, and climbing out was not an option.

"We've only got one choice," I said, a sickening knot growing in my stomach. "We're going to have to ride whatever this abyss ahead has to offer. It's either that or sit where we are until we starve to death."

Ben didn't say anything. In the dim light of the canyon his sunken gaunt face was etched with stress and worry. Scott looked worse. His eyes were moving quickly back and forth from the raft to the canyon walls, to the river, and back to the raft again. A problem-solver by nature, he was trying to find a solution, but was drawing a blank. There was no safe way out of there.

Whitewater is frightening partly because of the roaring it produces. The more powerful the water, the louder the roar. From childhood, we have all been conditioned to be afraid of this noise. Lions roar, monsters roar, ferocious dinosaurs are said to have roared too. And now the river roared at our folly. The thunder reverberated off the walls of the canyon. "OK, let's do it," I said quietly.

Between the boat and the narrow throat of the abyss we had some hefty whitewater to run. We would have to be careful. If we flipped before the abyss, we'd be washed through the unknown stretch out of control—bodies, boat, and paddles tumbling, falling, and flailing.

One good thing about being heavily burdened was that it made the raft more stable. The two heaviest bags were on the bottom, keeping the center of gravity low. People don't make good ballast. They get thrown around like rag dolls no matter how tightly they are braced against the thwarts or wedged into the foot cups. The extra weight also provided momentum that made it easier to break through walls of recirculating water, the boiling white froth that booby-traps the bottom of most rapids.

I was glad I was guiding the run—not because Scott and Ben weren't capable, but I just liked the feeling of controlling my own destiny in a situation where death lurked behind every miscalculation. I also thought Scott would be too timid and Ben too aggressive for my liking.

Scott and Ben took their places up forward. Ben almost always sat on the port side because the foot cup on the starboard side was farther forward to accommodate an air valve on the floor. Ben's long legs simply wouldn't fold up to fit into the right-hand position.

Scott twisted around and tightened the cam straps securing the gear by another few inches. As we were about to push off, we heard a rumbling above the sound of the river. I looked up and saw a car-sized boulder bouncing down the canyon walls. It detonated just upstream of us with the force of a small bomb.

"I hope that's not an omen," Ben said.

"Maybe the river was trying to get us there, and by the time she figures out she missed us we'll be through this shit ahead," Scott replied.

We paddled forward a few strokes and exited our eddy.

My guiding wasn't perfect, but we made it through without flipping. I straightened the boat out as the cliffs came together on both sides and we slipped into the mysterious abyss. Before us we could see the cause of the spray and mist that obscured our view from the rocks above. The water cascaded over a series of drops, each progressively larger than the previous one, a staircase to a whitewater hell.

We tumbled over the first drop, barely escaping the hole that yawned at the base. We should have hit the second one with more speed. I tried to increase the momentum, but the river had other ideas. Powerful boils and jets of upwelling currents wreaked havoc on my efforts to keep the raft under control. The ebullient boils played with our boat, spinning it, stopping it, pushing it this way and that. Paddling was useless. We dropped over the lip of the second waterfall in slow motion. I was lucky just to be able to keep the nose of the raft pointed downriver.

The slow speed of the raft helped us maintain stability until we found ourselves suddenly beyond the turbulence and moving downstream, picking up speed. The walls of the abyss rushed by as I tried to steer through another set of rapids, dodged a standing wave, bucked through a second set of rapids, and slid through yet another. The raft shot through the sluice box at about 8 knots—we were flying and I had scant moments to analyze the water pattern ahead or make a decision.

Ben and Scott screamed at the top of their lungs: "Hole on the port side at two o'clock . . . boils to starboard . . ." I couldn't hear what they were saying. Dread filled my ears with the pounding of my own heartbeat. It drowned out even Apu Rimac's frightening roar.

The canyon narrowed into a gateway not more than 30 yards wide. As the river hurled itself through the narrow gap, its velocity increased tremendously and the whipping current created two gargantuan holes whose churning waves collided mid-river, throwing up a rooster tail. Brown water sprayed into the sky as though forced from a giant fire hose. Never in all my experience had I seen such powerful, intimidating water.

I aimed to raft between the twin hillocks of boiling water, and we smashed head-on into the rooster tail. The force of the water pushed the nose of the raft up, up, up.

From my seat in the back, Ben and Scott rose straight up and were soon almost over my head, the raft practically vertical, pointed at the heavens like a rocket about to take off. It teetered for a second before twisting and turning over. Fortunately, we landed right-side up, but facing upstream.

Now it was the stern being punched upright by the rooster-tail wave. I was catapulted onto the pile of gear. I clung to the cam straps as the boat and my body were engulfed in muddy water. I didn't know if we were upside down or right-side up. The water cleared.

I sat up and found we were out of the narrow abyss and moving downriver. I got back into position and steered the raft to the first hint of shore. We sat breathing heavily.

We celebrated that night with a creamy pasta soup with sardines, sliced carrots, and onions. We also used the Nescafé jar to drink a communal coffee, passing it among ourselves like communion.

After hot drinks, we got the production line going to make bread. I created the dough, Ben did the flattening, and Scott cooked on the shovel blade. We made forty loaves—five each for lunch over two days and three to consume after production! Delicious!

Day 46: October 28, 1999

The next day was another long slog of portaging, lining, flipping, swimming, scouting, walking, slipping, cursing, and paddling. We called it quits at the brink of a series of cataracts. The necessary portage could wait until the morning.

We lit a big cooking fire and I pulled out bags of dehydrated food, eying them with disdain.

I heard a shout from Scott. He was standing by a waterfall. He pointed and I saw dozens of fish trying to climb the rapids. Most were unsuccessful, leaping high, landing amid the current, and getting washed back down. Some landed on the rocks, bounced once or twice, and fell into the pool below. One in every ten of the ruler-sized fish was successful in scaling the 6-foot falls.

Ben joined us, lugging a 60-pound stalk of green bananas balanced on his shoulder. "We're eating well tonight," he said. "I just found these growing next to that stream coming down to the river. It's Eden there. A little waterfall—perfect for a shower under the palms and—best of all—a banana tree."

He laid down the green fruit. "So how are we going to catch the tasty little bastards?"

I jogged back to the campsite to fetch the "bread bucket," a clear plastic container we had salvaged. I lay on the rock and held out the container as far as I could toward the waterfall.

Within a minute a fish jumped and I was able to maneuver the bucket to catch it.

"Good job, mate!" Ben shouted. "I'll bet he wasn't expecting that."

I tossed the fish onto the rock and Ben whacked it on the head with a stick.

"Fish number one," said Scott. "I'm going to get my mosquito netting. I'll be able to rig that into a fish net."

Within ten minutes I had four plump fish.

Scott had a better idea and attached some of our mosquito netting between two long pieces of cane. He held the makeshift net under the waterfall and the fish rained onto it. We had a dozen in no time.

We returned to the campsite and built an extra fire to accommodate the feast. My stomach growled ferociously.

Scott cooked the fish, sprinkling them with salt and roasting them one by one on the shovel blade.

Cooking the bananas involved a bit more work. We stuffed the green fruit, four bananas at a time, into the middle of a roaring fire. After about twenty minutes we pulled the fruit, blackened, from the flames. The skins split to expose the now soft vanilla flesh, which we scraped into the bread bucket and mashed. We repeated the process until we had roasted about twenty bananas. After we added butter, salt, pepper, and garlic powder, they tasted startlingly similar to mashed potatoes. For the first time in days my stomach felt satisfied. None of us could eat another bite, and we lazed around the crackling fire like beached belugas.

"True westerners we are," Ben said, "only content in the face of overindulgence."

Scott belched loudly. "Just give me roast bananas and trout every day for the rest of my life and I'll be happy. That's not a lot to ask, is it?"

Day 47: October 29, 1999

We reached the confluence of the Pachachaca River, a translucent green current that, after it joined the Apurimac, added greatly to its width and depth. The rapids grew in size with the river. They were truly big now, with wall-like standing waves. But our skills had been honed to the point that we were seldom flipped.

We were no longer afraid to admit our fear and to portage. When the water was catastrophic, we spent a full day transporting our gear just a few hundred yards.

The confluence of the Pampas River surprised us, not only because we had been traveling without a map. We had anticipated a much more violent meeting of two large waterways. Instead, they met and embraced like long-lost brothers.

The air was warm and the sun, truly visible for the first time in ages, hung over a gauzy horizon. The sky turned the color of pomegranate as we enjoyed our first spectacular sunset in weeks. Darkness came much later than we were used to. The worst of the Apurimac's whitewater was behind us.

It was like an anti-climactic end to a horror film—not with a bang but a whimper. The landscape broadened and we were in a warm tropical valley as luminous as the gorge had been dim. It was as if we had emerged from the Underworld and been given a second chance at life in the light.

PART 3 THE CLOUD FOREST

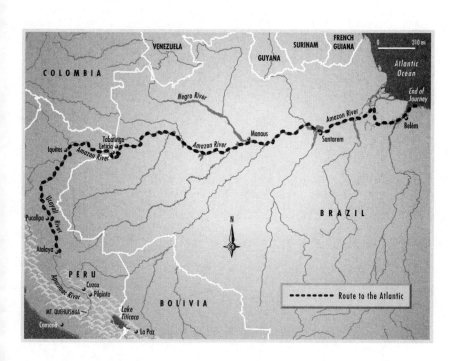

Day 49: October 31, 1999

We had difficulty believing we had made it. As we paddled along, the dense foliage along the banks and the expansive horizon were proof we were now in the "cloud forest." We still faced some rapids, but they would be nothing compared with what we had been through.

The three of us were quite beaten. In no way could it be said we had conquered the river. Benjamin was right: to even think such a thought was to court death. The river must be a friend.

We set up camp on the opposite side of the river from a small village of planked huts. A crowd gathered on the shore. Unable to contain their curiosity, about thirty boys and a handful of adults plunged into the river and swam the 60 or so yards across to us. They emerged dripping from the river, bidding us welcome.

They were completely puzzled when I told them we had traveled from the source of the river. To them, life beyond their own reach of the river remained largely incomprehensible.

"The river goes forever," said one small boy. "I once spent a full day following it upstream with my father, fishing. It keeps going and going."

"Well," I said, "we started a long way up."

He seemed pleased with this answer. I asked one of the men if it was possible to buy food.

"Sí," he replied.

This time I drew the short straw to stay with the gear. Scott and Ben paddled the raft across the river and I lay against a piece of driftwood, writing in my journal.

Sweat trickled down my chest and I sipped on a bottle of water drawn from a jungle spring that bubbled into the Apurimac. If you swallowed too much of the Apurimac during a dunking, you were guaranteed a dose of diarrhea. But there were innumerable small streams joining the river, and we figured they carried fewer parasites and intestinal bugs, so we filled our bottles from them. We drank this tea-colored water without adding bleach with no ill effects.

I didn't want to think of the viruses, parasites, and tropical diseases I might be contracting: malaria, hepatitis, yellow fever, tetanus, giardiasis, dysentery, cholera, typhoid, Chagas' disease, or trypanosomiasis (which is blamed for Darwin's lassitude on his return to England after *The Beagle* voyage), leishmaniasis (transmitted by sandflies), dengue fever, rabies . . .

I dozed in the sun until Scott and Ben returned, beaming.

"Mate, we've got a little surprise for you," Ben said. He pulled two Sublimes out from his pack. "But that's not all." His hand disappeared once again and he pulled out a big bottle of rum.

"What a way to celebrate our entry to the jungle!" I said, unscrewing the top and taking a big swig. "Wow! Here's to the god-damned Amazon jungle!"

The sky was a shimmering curtain of crimson, violet, and

gold. Howler monkeys and myriad unseen birds chattered in the dense vivid-green canopy, a chorus rising in volume as the roseate light dimmed. Darkness arrived suddenly, as though someone had thrown a switch, and the din increased.

"We invited the guy who sold us the food to come across for a drink," Scott said.

Sure enough, a few minutes later, a dark face appeared in the firelight.

"Hola," I said, offering my hand. "Me llamo Colin."

"Alfredo," the short lean man replied, shaking hands firmly.

He wore only a pair of faded Adidas shorts and carried a cane fishing-trap under his arm.

We chatted and drank until Alfredo spotted our tiny travel chess set.

"It's a game," Ben said slowly. "We play with it for fun."

Alfredo picked up the chess set and started to open it.

"Careful," Scott cautioned. "There are many pieces in there. We don't want to lose them."

Alfredo dumped the pieces into his cupped hand and stared at them for a second, before placing them on the tiny plastic board.

"What the hell!" I said. "He's setting them up correctly."

Alfredo turned to me: "You can start."

I won, but only after a long, closely fought game—and Alfredo had drunk more rum than I had. About 11 o'clock he disappeared into the darkness, telling us to join him for breakfast.

Day 50: November 1, 1999

We ate breakfast—a meal of chicken, salad, rice, and bananas—at Alfredo's hut before continuing on down the meandering river. The Apurimac was much broader now and its wild mountain streak had been replaced by a more sedate pace. What rapids we encountered, the raft rolled over as if slipping into an armchair.

Although the banks were a verdant jungle rather than an inscrutable rock-face, they remained as impenetrable—a veritable emerald wall. We were still 4,900 feet above sea level and the climatic conditions produced pea-soup fogs worthy of London. It was spooky traveling downriver through the soft-gray billowing banks of fog, punctuated by squeals and roars and other jungle noises. For the most part, we passed through rainforest disturbed only by an occasional farm—no more than a clapboard hut, a clutch of banana and papaya trees, a yard full of scrawny fowls, a fat pig, and children.

Paddling became monotonous and painful. Hour after hour after hour, the repeated motion was a killer. We began to discuss rowing instead of paddling. One person pulling on two sets of oars can provide almost as much power as three paddling. We decided that, at the first opportunity, we would rig the raft for rowing.

We still weren't sure where we were exactly, but more and more people appeared along the banks or out on the river fishing. Most used bamboo rafts rather than dugout canoes. These vessels were surprisingly maneuverable considering they were little more than a collection of logs.

We asked several different people how far it was to Luisiana, the village we knew we should be approaching. Like Juan with his *"media hora"* answer for everything, we came to realize that people on the river had their own sense of time and distance.

Shortly after lunch, we asked a man in a dugout canoe how far to Luisiana?

"In your boat, half an hour."

An hour later, about 2 P.M., we asked a man poling a raft: How far to Luisiana?

"You'll not get there till about 8 tonight."

At 3 o'clock we stopped at a small knot of huts and bought a box of crackers. We asked again how far it was to Luisiana.

"A mile and a half," the plump, gray-haired man said with certainty. "Not far."

A group of villagers who were looking at the raft agreed.

"Maybe two," they assured us. "It will take you about an hour."

An hour later, with no sign of the town, we asked some teenaged boys. "How far is it to Luisiana?"

"One hour," shouted one.

"Five minutes," cried the other.

At 5:30 we called it a day. Luisiana, wherever it was, would have to wait.

Day 51: November 2, 1999

We stumbled onto Louisiana moments after pushing off in the morning and, a short distance farther on, arrived in San Francisco, a decrepit government outpost of about 4,000 people with road access to Lima. The Ayacucho highway arrives here and jumps the river via a bridge, the first below Cunyac and the last across the river until the Atlantic. This is, in more ways than one, the end of the road.

San Francisco is the largest settlement on the Apurimac, a regional military headquarters supported by a civilian supply industry. It is a jungle cesspit of dank, mouldy buildings and a population equally ruined by rot. The streets are lined with poles carrying the offerings of a non-stop diesel power plant humming away on the edge of town. Small children played among the garbage, and vultures cavorted amid the detritus on the riverbank—the only indigenous creature to celebrate modernity's encroachment on the rainforest. To us, the squalor was irrelevant. Here we could replace our lost cooking utensils, pick up nails, twine, and rope to modify the raft, and maybe even enjoy a hot shower.

Most of the shopkeepers we spoke with were surprised we were going downriver. Didn't we know it was the last stronghold of the Shining Path? They insisted it was suicide to continue.

Later, we drank Coca-Cola and discussed their warnings.

"It's probably exaggeration," I said. "How many times did people warn us about *banditos* back in the mountains? We didn't encounter one thief."

"True," Ben said. "In places like this, one incident happens and gossip spreads like wildfire. Probably someone was killed by the rebels a few years ago and everyone has lived in terror since."

We nodded. We took solace at least in the local watercraft— long, skinny boats with extremely shallow draft. We figured if they handled the worst of the river, we would have no trouble in the raft.

We camped just downstream from the garbage that lined the bank. Hot showers didn't seem to exist outside Iquitos or Pucallpa. It was Scott's turn to do the cooking and he grinned foolishly doing rice and beans in separate pots. "Man, we're living in luxury now."

He handed me a brand-new tin plate and fork: "Now you get to eat like a civilized man again. Yesterday, when I saw you climbing up that tree to pick those oranges, I could have sworn you were turning back into a monkey. You were just swinging through those branches."

"He's too ugly for a monkey," Ben piped in. "Perhaps a sloth."

"What kind of appreciation is that for getting you guys oranges for dessert?"

"They were shitty oranges," retorted Ben. "Dry and full of seeds. I think what you were getting could more appropriately be called greens."

We had purchased a small shortwave radio and, occasionally, through the evangelical programming broadcast by jungle missionaries, we picked up the BBC. Ironically, one of the shows was a documentary on a new malaria-like disease transmitted by sandflies in the cloud forests of Peru.

What news to go to sleep to!

Day 53: November 4, 1999

The low jungle wall ran unbroken along the river and beyond to the low sloping hills in the distance. Far away we could see the neat squares of coca plantations, meadows, and orchards. The river was running at perhaps 4 knots. By noon the farms disappeared and the old-growth forest sat primeval and silent.

The Apurimac's youthful restlessness was gone. In some ways, Scott said, his innocence had fled along with it. He felt seasoned, perhaps even somewhat indestructible.

Without warning, a helicopter gunship appeared over the forest canopy, rising like an extra from *Apocalypse Now*. It hovered facing us, its missiles directed at the raft. For several seconds it hung scant feet above the treetops, then banked sharply and was gone.

Like the solemn warning of danger from the local towns-folk, we dismissed it. Even the odd shotgun slung over the shoulder of a fisherman failed to register alarm. It was all merely part of the terrorist legacy, wasn't it? Not quite. It soon dawned on us that this region of Peru is still a war zone.

We saw no one for hours until a lone fisherman appeared on shore. "Let's stop and see if we can find anything to make our rowing frame of," said Scott.

We pulled onto the muddy flat, 7 or 8 yards from the old man. He tied his line of braided bark to a tree and walked slowly up to us. "Where are you going?" he asked.

"Downriver."

He shook his head.

"It is not safe. Especially in a boat like this with no engine," he said, nudging our raft scornfully with his bare foot.

"We're looking for some bamboo," I said. "You don't know if there is any around here, do you?"

Again, he shook his head laconically. "Come with me."

We followed him as he nimbly disappeared into the jungle. For about ten minutes we trailed behind him as he strolled through the bush. Finally he reached a pile of logs. "This is better than bamboo," he said. "Balsa."

The 5-yard logs looked unwieldy. But the old man grabbed one with his right hand and flicked it toward me. I was momentarily startled—it weighed almost nothing. I threw the log at Scott, grinning. I remembered the airplanes I had flown as a child. This is what they were made of.

"They'll be great," said Scott.

We carried two logs gingerly back to the boat and the old man used his machete to halve them. The logs were cinched into place with cam straps run through the raft's D-rings. We secured loops of nylon strapping on each side to act as oar locks and created wing-like platforms for the gear, giving us more room inside the raft. We even found a thicket of bamboo mature enough to provide paddle-shafts. Using duct-tape and twine, we attached bamboo extensions onto the paddles to form two long oars. It took about four hours, but the raft looked great. Most important, though, it made life much easier.

Finished, Ben tried out the oars. After a moment or two he found his rhythm and pulled with easy full strokes. "All right! We're geniuses," he crowed.

Before continuing, we decided to add a table and an awning. Our boat now was nothing short of a cruise ship.

The old man waved as we left, smiling as if he were watching the funniest show on earth. We did look a bit odd: three white gringos riding through the heart of the Amazon on a fire-engine-red rubber raft draped in balsa, bamboo, and vines.

I took the first shift on the oars, and Ben and Scott relaxed on the side tubes.

"I think I can handle this," Ben said, opening his book. "I haven't been able to do any reading in a long time."

We watched the shore slip by. With effortless strokes on the oars, I was easily going as fast as the three of us had been laboring on the paddles. It felt much better on my body, too.

We each took a turn getting used to the long, unwieldy oars, then pulled over for the night.

Day 54: November 5, 1999

Our first day using our new rowing system yielded impressive results. We rowed three hours each in ninety-minute shifts, so our energy levels remained high at the oars. I think we made better speed, and it was much easier.

The two people not rowing could also make lunches, snacks, and perform other tasks, so we got more done. With the sheet of blue plastic hung on the bamboo frame, those not rowing had pleasant shade. The man doing the work, unfortunately, sat exposed to the sun, dripping and sliding in his own sweat.

As we drifted down the river, the jungle was like a moving Rorschach test. We were in the bosom of the *selva*, as the Peruvian Amazon was known. It was easy to let your mind drift with the raft, thinking about what had happened, thinking about life . . .

At the age of seventeen I met my father for the first time ever. He had finally contacted my mother, curiosity getting the better of him. He was in Canada for only a few days before flying to New Zealand. It was strange seeing him for real after having imagined him all those years.

As a child I had listened to my mother's stories about him and formed a character in my mind. That's all he was, a fictitious character no different from Noddy or Jupiter Jones. The only tangible evidence that he really existed was the faded, handsome man in a picture that stared from my mother's antique dressing table.

At a young age I got a job delivering the local paper, the *Victoria Times-Colonist*. Money was scarce in our family, and I needed some sort of income to enjoy the same luxuries other kids had—going to the movies and buying the occasional Coke. Most of the money I made I saved diligently.

Through elementary and junior high, while living in Port

Alberni, I had a buddy, Steve, who shared my way of thinking. We spent evenings and weekends climbing trees (he had some great trees in his backyard), flying planes, floating model boats down the creek, and fishing at the secret hole on the river. Years later I found out that the hundreds of "trout" we had caught were actually Coho smelt released from the hatchery.

Steve's father, a German immigrant with a big heart, would fix my bike and show me how to use power tools. I remember when the soapbox derby was coming up and all the other kids were working on their racers with their dads. At school I listened dejectedly as Steve told me the plans he and his father had for his racer. After school, when we went up to his place, his dad had two pieces of plywood laid out on the garage floor. They had identical floor patterns cut out on them.

"Why do you need two?" I asked.

Steve's dad patted me on the shoulder and said that Steve needed somebody to race against. "Otherwise he'll win too easily with our great design."

The reason for my father's seventeen-year disappearing act was more than an escape from responsibility, he maintained, and we got along quite well. In the years that followed, I got to know him and was amazed at how similar our thought patterns were. I could talk to him for hours, not because I felt it was my duty, but because I really enjoyed listening to his perspective on things.

After bailing from Canada in 1971, my father moved to New Zealand. There he met his second wife and had a third child. He found work as a skipper on an offshore dredger. He was a binge alcoholic, as so many sailors are. He said a currency-smuggling caper gave him the money to start a successful video store. Several years later he and his wife split up. At fifty-eight and retired, Colin left everything to her, feeling he needed no material goods.

A survivor of three heart attacks and a major aneurysm requiring surgery, Colin couldn't sit still. He had to keep moving. Perhaps he felt if he stayed in the same spot for too long he would rot. He spent part of the year in New Zealand, part in Australia, and the rest in Britain. He timed it so he would be in each country during the best season—never too hot and never too cold. He returned to the same haunts—rooming houses or inexpensive character hotels. He thrived in areas where there was maritime history, where he could watch ships from foreign lands dock, listen to the evocative blast of their horns, and share the camaraderie of sailors in port.

He lived frugally, surviving on his pension and a few investments. He drank rum or whisky heavily on Thursday, Friday, and Saturday. In a drunken haze, he revisited the past, recalled old sailing mates, invoked proud ships, and summoned up the temptations of foreign ports. He lived with these shades the way real parents collect memories of children's birthdays and Christmases past.

I spent time in both New Zealand and Australia during the years I sailed about the Pacific. I got to know him better and a kind of bond developed between us. I discussed plans with him and he immediately shared my enthusiasm. His input always made sense to me, his thoughts usually concerns I hadn't yet voiced. I don't think we were close, but we came to understand each other.

I remember the last time I saw him in London, in 1997. I accompanied him back to King's Cross, where he was staying in a seedy hotel before flying to Australia. He shook my hand and wished me luck. He died within the year, slipping out of my life as quietly as he had entered. He wanted more than anything for one of his three offspring to have kids—"to pass on the Angus genes."

It hasn't happened yet, and I'm not sure it will for me. I wonder if I'd feel differently had he been around for all those missing years. I don't think I harbor any resentment, but I should have hugged him when I said goodbye and he should have hugged me. We were two ships from the same line passing in the night.

The jungle remained unbroken, thick, and foreboding. The noise emanating from its dark-green recess was louder than ever—a kind of green noise indelibly alive, unlike the white noise of dead air. There were thousands of sounds blended together—caw-caws, cicadas, parrots, parakeets, monkeys, insects, hummingbirds, predators and prey—more life per square yard than anywhere else on the planet, all declaiming their inarticulate existence in one undifferentiated shriek. It came from all directions at once, everywhere and nowhere, out there and in here.

We found a muddy shoal suitable for camping and, soon after we lit a fire, several Indians appeared out of the jungle. They were a scruffy handful of armed, hard-eyed locals and they looked at us darkly. It's funny how much respect rifles command in the hands of men who have nothing to lose.

"Hola!" I said, waving.

"Hola," one grunted.

They hung back on the edge of the flickering firelight—the orange light dancing across their dark, middle-aged faces. They sat on their haunches, staring at us as we cooked.

"Where do you live?" Ben asked.

"In the jungle," a heavily muscled man replied in a raspy voice. "Our homes are hidden."

"Why the guns?" I asked.

"Protection," the same man replied.

"Protection from what? Sendero Luminoso?"

"Sí."

"Where do you get your guns from?" I asked. They seemed like extravagant purchases for people who eked out a living from the forest.

"The army gives us guns to protect ourselves."

"But the Sendero Luminoso aren't nearly as bad as they used to be?" Ben queried hopefully.

The apparent spokesman shook his head.

I dished out three plates of mashed potatoes. Usually we offered to share food, but there were too many of them and their intimidating presence kept me from suggesting they join us.

A short fellow with a simple-looking face spoke: "You going to eat all that?"

I nodded.

He stroked the wooden stock of his rifle. "Can we have some?"

I shoveled half the potatoes from each plate back into the pot and handed it to him. He wolfed a handful and passed the pot to the next man, who did the same. The potatoes vanished in seconds. They watched sullenly as we ate our share.

"I'm not even going to bring out our little tin of instant coffee," Ben said in English. "If we have to start giving all these guys coffee, it'll be finished tonight."

I nodded.

We talked quietly among ourselves while our taciturn guests remained in the fire's penumbra, camouflaged silhouettes against the jungle backdrop. Around 9 o'clock I headed for the tent. Ben got up too.

"Can we borrow your flashlight?" a voice from the shadows asked. "It's dark and it would help us find our way home."

"No," Ben said. "I want to read."

"Señor, it is dark, it will be hard for us to find the way."

For a big man, Ben didn't lose his temper often, but he would be pushed only so far. "If you can't find your fucking way home without a light," he said, his voice rising with every word, "why did you stay until it got dark?"

The jungle rang with his voice and, when it fell silent, the men were gone.

"Let's make sure we're out of here at first light," I said.

"Yeah," Scott added.

Day 55: November 6, 1999

I awoke about 6 A.M. and peeked out of the tent to see ten men sitting around the dead fire.

"Let's not be intimidated this time," Ben whispered.

We weren't.

We ate our oatcakes as the natives drooled. They didn't look as though they'd missed many meals lately. If they had been starving, I might have felt bad, but I was angry they were spoiling our breakfast.

Ben gave them a bag of candies to distract them. They gobbled them up with nary a *gracias*. We pushed into the river as fast as we could, without seeming to flee.

As we put more and more river behind us, the day became a delight: sunshine, the jungle slipping by, the river doing a perfect imitation of Old Man River. Scott and I played a tough, tactical chess battle. The three of us were engaged in a makeshift Amazon Chess Championship and were contesting it fiercely. I knew from the energy Ben and Scott put into the games that every win mattered. Just as I thought I had the better of Scott, I realized I was in time trouble. Ben was nearing the end of his rowing shift and I would replace him. If the game hadn't finished, the result wouldn't count in our ongoing tournament.

"Hey," Ben said softly, interrupting the game and sounding apprehensive. "Check these guys out."

I followed his line of sight. A movement on the shore caught my attention. The thatched hut was almost invisible. I would have missed it except for the half-dozen men who were standing beside it, animatedly pointing at us. They gestured for us to come ashore.

Ben quickened his stroke.

The men began to shout in Spanish. We couldn't hear exactly what they were saying, but we could guess. Two of them had guns.

"Keep going!" I shouted to Ben. "These guys mean business."

"For sure," Scott said, his voice quavering, "and pretend we don't understand anything they say."

Ben pulled harder on the oars, angling the boat downstream. I turned toward the men and yelled, "Hola," giving them my best "stupid" impression.

"Think we should wave?" Ben asked.

"Faster," croaked Scott. "Faster."

The men saw that we were pulling away and they grew more and more agitated. The shouting became more frantic. I heard a single dominant voice hollering "Stop! Stop!"

The two men sighted their rifles, aiming at us.

"Holy Shit! They're going to . . ."

Scott's voice was drowned out by the fusillade.

I saw the muzzles jump and heard the report. Terror like I'd never felt before ripped through my body. Death would surely follow soon. In one quick instinctive motion I slid over the far side of the boat, trying to make myself less of a target. My left hand and my left leg were draped over the inner tube while the other half of my body hung in the water.

Scott leaped into the middle of the boat and lay prostrate on the floor. Ben hauled on the oars like a madman. But the shifted weight of our bodies hampered him and the left oar hit me on the head with each stroke.

I heard a second volley. Ben kept rowing, I clutched the side of the boat, and Scott made like a pancake. It seemed interminable, but after five or ten minutes Ben said, "OK—we're around the bend." Scott and I pulled ourselves back into sitting positions.

"Fucking, fucking, fuck," Ben cursed, his knees keeping four-four time.

I felt like throwing up. My heart was going like a jackhammer and my legs were doing the pneumatic shudder as well. Whitewater seemed rational compared with this terror. "I wonder if they have a boat," I stuttered.

"I didn't see anything other than a half-submerged dugout canoe," Ben whispered.

The jungle screeched and howled, indifferent to our

predicament, perhaps rejoicing at the end of our hubris. We had blamed our anxiety on the sense of danger cultivated by the fear-mongers. Now it was real.

Our minds projected our paranoia onto nature itself. Our imaginations ran wild. Martin Sheen emerging from the water, his face painted in grotesque camouflage, eyes ablaze with murderous intent. Evil was everywhere and nowhere, guns drawn, ready to mow us down.

I traded places with Ben and started rowing, and rowing, and rowing. I wanted to put as much distance as possible between us and our attackers. We moved at an impressive speed, and the cardiovascular workout calmed my shakes. I settled down after a while, but I can't recall ever having been as scared, even in the desert. Then it wasn't fear, I knew that now—it was more self-awareness. I was going to die because of a mistake I had made. It was going to piss me off, but at least it was comprehensible. This wasn't.

"Do you think they were trying to kill us?" Scott murmured.

"It's hard to say," I replied. "You'd think they'd have been able to hit the raft."

"Maybe," Ben said.

"Those guns were lowered when they fired," I said. "They may have been aiming over our heads—but it didn't look like it."

"If they were trying to scare us, they certainly did a good job," said Ben. "I'm going to have nightmares about those two gunshots for the rest of my life. Did anyone shit themselves?"

We laughed.

For the next hour we continued in silence, watching apprehensively for any sign of pursuit coming from behind or along the bank. We tried to stay midstream so no one from the bank could surprise us.

A small cluster of shacks appeared on the right-hand side of the river, so I steered far to the left, just to be safe. I couldn't shake my fear. Small figures appeared on shore. I could hear more yelling, although they were too far away to understand what they were saying.

I kept rowing.

The crack of gunshots sounded once again. This time the reports came from farther away and behind me. I couldn't see who was doing the firing. I didn't care. I kept rowing.

"I HATE THIS!" I said, trying to get more and more speed out of the oars.

I looked over my shoulder and I could see more activity on shore. Shit. They were scrambling toward what looked like a pair of motorized launches.

"WHY CAN'T THEY LEAVE US ALONE?" I shouted.

Scott and Ben watched the activity as men poured out of the huts and into the boats. I pulled on the oars and, with the current's help, desperately tried to put more distance between us.

"Please, God, don't let those boats have engines," Scott said.

It took only a moment for the deafening roar to reach us, as the outboards leapt to life.

"No-o-o-o-o-o-o-o!" I screamed.

I could see the first boat with seven or eight armed men speeding toward us, a fantail in its wake. A yellow sun hung overhead in a picture-blue sky, the jungle shimmered a million shades of verdigris, and the river seemed a swath of molasses. This couldn't be happening. It was as if time slowed down. I pulled on the oars.

The first volley was a surprise. Unlike the earlier gunfire, it wasn't preceded by sharp explosions. Instead, all I heard was a splatter of firecrackers, like popcorn hitting hot oil. It took me a moment to realize why: they weren't using some old carbine; they had semi-automatics.

Another broadside salvo and that was it. I dove for the river, and Ben and Scott simultaneously hurled themselves over the side. We hung on to the raft, keeping it between us and the approaching speedboat.

The cannonade continued.

They must be firing over the boat since it hasn't exploded, I figured. But that's about as rational as I got. The three of us cringed behind the raft, petrified as the launch came around to our side.

We held our hands up as best we could as we treaded water. A half-dozen soldiers trained weapons on us. I could see now that they wore the insignia of the Peruvian armed force—the good guys, I hoped.

"Swim to shore," the officer-in-charge commanded.

The three of us began swimming for the encampment we had tried to avoid. The military latched on to the raft and towed it along behind.

Once we were ashore, the commander interrogated us. What were we doing on this bit of the river? He thought we were Sendero Luminoso. Indeed, our boat, covered with logs, cane, vines, and bright-blue plastic, did look like a suspicious vessel.

After we explained, he calmed down. They hadn't been shooting to kill us, he assured us.

"Are there more of your men farther upstream?" Ben asked.

The commander looked puzzled.

"We were shot at by some men farther upstream, about 6 miles up."

The officer shook his head. "They weren't our men. What did they look like?"

We were not close enough to get a good look.

The commander sucked in his cheeks and said: "Did the leader have a really skinny face?"

Again, we hadn't noticed.

"It would have been Sendero Luminoso," he said. "I'm wondering if it is the group we've been after for the last few months."

"No matter," he said, and with that his attitude completely changed. He was curious about our adventure and wanted to help out in any way he could. The incident on the river had just been a bit of excitement for him. Nothing to worry about at all.

"You can spend the night under the protection of my men," he told us warmly. "You don't want to camp out in this jungle alone."

Most of the soldiers didn't look any older than fifteen. They wore assorted clothing, and some sported colorful bandanas—an L.A. street gang. They looked more like bandits or mercenaries than bona fide military personnel. To think those kids had been firing semi-automatic weapons over our heads!

The raft was moored on a muddy bank, just below the barracks. All the buildings were constructed with cane and bamboo, roofed with a thatch of palm fronds. The windows were open spaces that allowed the warm tropical air to breeze through. Several corrals were filled with pigs and cows—food for the soldiers. Outside the perimeter fence we could see defensive bunkers to protect the outpost from a land-based assault.

An octagonal hut sat atop the highest piece of ground—its windows gazed over a 360-degree view of the jungle. From here we could see how our raft or any other boat stuck out, coming downriver. Inside the shack a pale man, who said he was in charge of the bivouac, interrogated us again. He asked us many questions: What were our nationalities? What were we doing on the river? Where were we going? His manner didn't relax and he didn't smile. I felt uncomfortable. If any of us spoke out of turn, he gave the offender an icy glare.

"You plan on continuing down the river," he said with an air of resignation. "This area is full of rebels. We have lost many good men. Do you think you can make it through the heart of their territory?"

I didn't know what to think. All I knew was that I didn't want to hear another gunshot for the rest of my life—and this man in front of me was saying the worst was yet to come.

"What do you think?" asked Ben. "We don't really know what to expect."

The officer shrugged: "You might make it or . . ." He ran his index finger across his throat.

Our conversation was finished. He stood up to leave and pointed to the parade ground outside. "You can pitch your tent there."

Day 56: November 7, 1999

We left the base an hour before sunrise. The soldiers warned us against traveling at night. It was the most dangerous time, they said, for the rebels were most active under cover of darkness.

We slept fitfully and were filled with dread as we pushed into the river. A garnet scar on the eastern horizon was the only herald of approaching dawn. We had hoped that the army might offer an escort, but it didn't—and we didn't ask.

Ben and Scott looked more tired and ragged than I'd ever seen them. They sat peering into the darkness in search of who knows what demons they thought were out there waiting. I probably looked no better, but rowing allowed me to vent a lot of my fear with physical exertion.

The oars had acquired a long braying squeak that accompanied each stroke. As color returned to the jungle, the hours passed and we creaked down the river. I couldn't relax. Each hour that passed without incident just seemed to build up the suspense. The light had banished the shadows from the river, but not my mind. I expected to meet someone with a gun around every bend.

At 2 o'clock we came across another military checkpoint. We had been told of this camp and they were expecting us, too, having talked to their comrades upriver by radio. We stopped for only a few minutes, long enough to exchange pleasantries with a handful of soldiers.

As we floated along, I continued to dwell on the most morbid thoughts. Before leaving Canada, I had read about several adventurers who had died exploring the flat-water of the Lower Amazon. In 1989 Indians attacked two Americans—one was killed and the other severely injured. Two years later another three travelers—two Frenchmen and a Peruvian—were murdered. In 1997 an apparently corrupt army officer robbed and executed a group of Japanese adventurers.

Coupled with what we had been through, those tales chilled me. I thought about my going-away party and the phone call I got from a Peruvian man. He had read an article about our proposed expedition and tracked me down. "Be careful," he warned. "I live in Canada now and I love Canada. Here you can walk anywhere and feel safe. Nobody here will take another's life for a pair of running shoes. But in Peru it is different." At the time I had laughed it off with a joke. Now I thought he was a prophet of doom.

The hours ticked by and nothing changed. The oars brayed, the vegetation stayed thick and lush, and nobody shot at us. The soldiers had said we would eventually reach a third military checkpoint, which marked the end of the most lawless territory. Until we reached the city of Atalaya, though, 250 miles away, there was still some danger.

We reached the third checkpoint at about 4 o'clock. The commander came down to greet us and ordered a squad of young recruits to guard our boat. The soldiers, mostly *mestizo*, were from scattered cities throughout Peru. Their faces and modern clothing were a stark contrast to the local Indians who sauntered and lounged near the barracks. They looked prehistoric—faces painted, torsos draped with bows and arrows, clothing made from hammered bark and assorted animal skins.

At the top of the hill the army had built a soccer pitch and the soldiers were staging a pickup game against the Indians. Both sides handled the ball impressively. We watched for a bit—the Indians scored a lovely goal. It gave us a moment's respite from our apprehension before we headed back to the boat.

Five minutes after setting off, I reached for my knife, which was normally jammed into one of the balsa logs. It was gone. Panicked, I checked for the digital video camera and found its dry-bag open. The padded bag was there, but the camera was gone.

"Did you put the video camera somewhere?" I asked Scott. He shook his head.

"It's been stolen. Ben, stop the raft!"

Ben propelled the boat toward the shore. We had to go back. I had that horrible gut feeling that I would never see the camera again. So much for the documentary we hoped to produce.

Ben and I walked back along the riverside to the barracks and found the commander at the viewpoint. "My video camera," I said, "my camera has been stolen. You said your men would guard our boat."

The commander looked at me sympathetically: What could he do?

"I don't know who stole the camera," I said. "It could have been the boys guarding the boat or perhaps they were slacking off and someone took advantage of the situation."

He called for the squad that had guarded the boat and quizzed them sharply in rapid Spanish. I understood little of what was said.

He turned to us: "My men disobeyed my orders and watched the football game. Probably someone from the village below stole your camera. I will see if we can find it. Wait here."

We waited for almost an hour. Finally a group of soldiers came up the hill and I could see they were carrying something. As they got closer, I saw it was my camera.

"We have found your camera," the commander said, handing over the Sony.

He didn't offer an explanation, and I didn't ask for one. I was just happy to have my baby back.

We returned to the raft and continued a short distance downriver before setting up camp. Our fear was palpable. We were terrified of what lurked in the jungle and fearful of what might be traveling on the river. We kept as low a profile as possible. We dragged the bright-red raft over the shore and hid it in a thicket of cane.

Our tents, too, were camouflaged in foliage. We finished our cooking before dusk, so the small fire was extinguished before its light betrayed our presence. We spoke in whispers—sound travels forever over water.

With no fire, swarms of insects—mosquitoes, cockroaches, blackflies, sandflies, moths, ants, spiders, bees, ticks, chiggers, wasps, a thousand species of bugs—made themselves known. They buzzed and hummed around our eyes and bit our feet. We were in bed by 7 o'clock, but it was not a restful night. The insects gnawed on us and we were haunted by the kind of inchoate fears that stalk the dreams of children.

Day 57: November 8, 1999

We were under way by first light. At 10 o'clock we spotted two men fishing from a 13-foot dugout canoe. They were unarmed and we decided to approach.

"Hola," I called.

They stared at us. One stopped bailing water with a half-gourd and looked at me. I saw not a glint of recognition in his eyes. They were both naked save for their tattered sports shorts.

"How far to Atalaya?" Ben inquired.

The man shook his head and continued bailing in short, quick strokes. The other man poled the canoe toward us. As it drew abreast, he flipped his paddle to the man who had been bailing and grabbed our bowline. They began to pull us slowly toward the muddy shore.

We looked at one another, puzzled. "Where are you taking us?" I asked.

Neither of the Indians replied.

There were three of us and only two of them in an unstable canoe. We could overpower them. Ben and Scott both shrugged. "Let's see what they're up to," Ben said.

A primitive village materialized along the shore. Men and women stopped carrying bananas, put down fishing rods, paused from thatching roofs, and gave us their attention.

The two Indians dragged us up beside a swath of dugout canoes tethered to cane poles driven into the mud. The village parking lot.

A crowd gathered, most armed with rifles, others carrying machetes along with bows and arrows.

"What do you want with us?" Ben asked.

"We are waiting for the chief," replied a machete-brandishing man with only one arm.

We sat quietly and two dozen natives watched us. Some wore long dark cloaks, or *cushmas*, made of cotton or perhaps kapok. It was difficult to tell what the lustrous but dingy-looking material was. A few wore only a pair of faded shorts. Most were barefoot and all shifted uneasily, fingering their weapons as they evaluated our boat and equipment.

After several minutes, the crowd parted and a short man bearing a huge gun appeared.

"Who are you?" he asked.

"Tourists," I replied. "We are attempting to voyage the full length of the river in our raft."

"Are you working with the Sendero Luminoso?" he asked.

"No," I said. "We are hoping to drift peacefully down the river."

"Everybody has guns though," Ben added, "guns, guns, guns, guns. Guns are no good."

The chief, who sported the same bowl-cut hairstyle as the others, stroked his firearm: "Guns protect us from the Sendero Luminoso."

He spoke to us as if he considered us retarded.

"Are you working for the American government?"

"No. We are here by ourselves exploring your beautiful country."

The chief paused. A murmur rolled through the crowd.

"Don't you have farms to look after and families to feed back where you come from?" he asked, flummoxed.

"No, we have no families."

The chief turned impatient. His interrogation was going nowhere.

"Are you sure you're not involved with the Sendero Luminoso?"

We shook our heads.

"We're going to have to search your bags," he said.

A man stepped forward and motioned with the muzzle of his rifle for us to step from the raft. We did.

Two men pulled our bags off the boat. One by one, each was emptied. The camera tripod puzzled them the most. The men talked among themselves. One held it up and aimed it as if it were a gun. Another motioned to the chief.

"Is that a weapon—a gun of some sort?" the chief asked.

I said no and mimed taking pictures.

"Why not hold the camera in your hands?" the chief asked.

I couldn't really explain it well enough to make him understand. The men moved on and rooted through the rest of our gear.

"Can I see your permit to be on the river?" the chief asked.

"We don't have a permit," I said. "We asked the army for permission and they said a permit is not needed."

"You need a permit," the chief replied.

"We don't have a permit," Ben said.

"I can't let you go on, then," said the chief.

"So what should we do?" I asked, trying to remain calm.

"We will keep your boat and gear and you can hike back to San Francisco for a permit."

"How can we hike back?" Ben exploded. "The jungle is impenetrable, there are no roads, no trails, and it is hundreds of miles!"

The chief shrugged. "Not my problem."

I restrained Ben.

"We don't need a permit, Chief," I said. "Every official we talked to told us that we would be fine without one. Why don't you let us go? It makes no difference to you."

Another man appeared at the back of the crowd and pushed his way forward. He was wearing long cotton pants, a buttoned shirt, and neatly combed hair. He was obviously *mestizo*. To our surprise, he spoke English.

"I am teacher," he said. "I live in Atalaya, but I work here as teacher. Where you from?"

"I come from South Africa," Scott replied, "and the other two are from Canada and Australia."

Obviously the teacher held a position of great respect. Everyone stood quietly as he spoke to us, including the chief.

"I study English for three years in school," the teacher explained. "And always I look for chance to speak with English people. I no often get chance." He grinned.

"The chief won't let us continue because we don't have a permit," I told him. "We don't need a permit and, even if we did, there isn't a hope in hell we could hike through the jungle back to San Francisco."

The teacher nodded: "You would probably not make it past the Sendero Luminoso. It is not good idea."

"Can you tell that to the chief?" Scott asked.

The teacher turned to the chief. After several minutes of conversation, he turned back to us.

"The chief wants to know if you have any ammunition or money you could give him for a gift?"

We had neither to spare. Our funds were almost completely gone until we reached Pucallpa, a city with a bank. As for ammunition, we never had any. I shook my head.

A long discussion ensued between the chief and the teacher.

"We've got some clothes we could give as gifts," I offered.

The chief shook his head. He wasn't interested in our mouldy clothes.

"The chief has allowed you to leave," the teacher said suddenly.

We thanked him for his help, threw our bags back onto the raft, and rowed off before any second thoughts formed. It had been a stressful two hours, and I wondered what the outcome would have been without the help of the teacher.

The hot humid weather created a haze that rested heavily on the rainforest and the river, welding water and sky. Scott was rowing now, his powerful strokes churning through the water. We had been told that Atalaya marked the end of the guerrilla stronghold and the end of guns. I wondered if that would really be the case. Guns were so prevalent in the jungle that it seemed unlikely they would vanish completely.

After our long ordeal with the village chief, we avoided people on the river and stayed away from the tiny settlements we saw in the occasional break in the jungle. Several times, men gathered on shore waving us to come in. We kept rowing.

Black clouds rolled in later in the afternoon, bringing a stinging cold rain and lightning. The temperature dropped and we were soon shivering and soaked. Scott and I huddled under the blue plastic tarpaulin to trap body heat. I curled up in a tight ball, letting the hours pass. About an hour before complete darkness, Ben beached the raft on a sandbar.

We set up the two tents and laid the tarp over them to create a small covered communal space. Then we cooked a dinner of Chinese noodles, tuna, and potatoes.

Day 58: November 9, 1999

The following morning I climbed out of the tent to find that we were surrounded by Indians bearing a small arsenal. They had been silently standing in the downpour for some time and were drenched. Their black hair hung down on their faces, giving them all the look of drowned rats.

"Hola," I said.

"Hola," came the reply from the nearest man.

After some talking, the men seemed to relax a bit. They were as nervous about us as we were about them. Unlike the Indians upstream, this group did not want to detain us. They wished us luck and disappeared into the torrential deluge.

The river had risen through the night and now was a swirling mahogany color studded with boils, whirlpools, and standing waves. It was nothing compared with what we had been through, but it was challenging with our cumbersome rowing rig. Having the heavy gear extended off each side on cane wings drastically shifted the raft's center of gravity, making it much more liable to tip. We had to execute maneuvers with greater care, but nothing untoward happened.

About 2 o'clock we passed the confluence of the Mantaro River. Like almost all the Apurimac's tributaries, the Mantaro joined from the west side. Where the Mantaro and the Apurimac merged, geographers had created a new river, the Ene.

We bade goodbye to the Apurimac, a river we had grown to know, and continued down the Ene. It flowed strong and fast, carrying us rapidly toward Atalaya. At one point the narrow rock walls compressed the Ene and increased her velocity to about 6 knots. She rolled and boiled and we saw a number of large whirlpools, but nothing threatened the raft.

Beyond the steep banks draped with rain forest, we could see rolling grasslands and distant highlands covered with a dark-green mat. We encountered almost no one on the river, and that night we camped once again on a remote sandbar.

Day 59: November 10, 1999

We awoke to bright sunshine, warmer temperatures, and a pristine jungle. It was not to last. The Mantaro River joined the Ene and formed the Tambo, a river the size of the Columbia in Washington State. We knew now that we were close to Atalaya. More and more people appeared on the river and they were no longer stern-faced. They waved with broad smiles as they sped past on motorized boats. Few of them brandished weapons. And then we saw the city itself.

Atalaya displayed a face of rickety shacks along the river, some on stilts hanging over the current. We pulled up to a small floating bar tethered to the shore. An assortment of jungle boats was tied up—dugout canoes, wooden *lanchas*, and speedboats. Atalaya is the last Peruvian port you can reach from the Atlantic by sailing up the Amazon River system. Motorized tugs and barges easily navigate the 3,700 miles. There are no rapids. It would all be smooth sailing from here—except for the weather and the human factor.

Days 60 to 64: November 11 to 15, 1999

We were unable to find any maps, but everyone we spoke with said the river was flat right through to the Atlantic. There were a few small villages and towns, they said, between Atalaya and Pucallpa, a city of about 200,000 people some 370 miles downriver. Still, we decided not to trust that they had services.

Weight wasn't really an issue for us without rapids to worry about. We bought potatoes, cabbages, carrots, beets, bananas, and oranges, spending our last $30 of ready cash stocking up on food. We also replaced the bamboo oar shafts, which continually splintered and snapped, with hardwood poles. Although heavier and not as pliable, the hardwood wasn't so susceptible to fatigue fractures. Our awning evolved and we jettisoned the bamboo frame. In its place we erected the two long poles from the dome tent and strung the fly over this framework. Voilà! A streamlined sunshade. The fly was quick and easy to remove if the wind picked up.

We slipped back onto the river, organized and well supplied. My hands were developing thick leathery calluses from rowing. I could row indefinitely, without feeling any pain. Even my body seemed to have adapted to the physical hardships. The aching joints and muscles were gone.

About 3 miles downstream from Atalaya, the Tambo joins the Urubamba to give birth to the Ucayali. The river from here was a true highway. Its banks resembled a quilt of small farms, villages, and logging operations. We spotted all kinds of shacks and huts nestled amid the second- and even third-growth forest. River traffic picked up: canoes, small motorboats, barges, aluminum flat-bottom skiffs, and supply boats. The normality dispelled the anxiety of the "Red Zone."

We were still thousands of miles from the ocean, but already there were signs of our journey's end. The first harbingers were the pink and gray dolphins. We heard them gulping down air before we saw our first one. They sporadically broke the surface, grabbed a quick breath, and dove back to the murky depths. They sounded like sixth-grade boys making fart jokes.

The gray dolphins were small and sleek, similar to the ocean dolphins I had seen when I was sailing the Pacific Ocean. The pinks were wrinkled, Beluga-like creatures. They were said to be blind—vision was useless in the turbid soup in which they lived. Like bats, the dolphins have developed a biological sonar system that scientists believe they use to navigate and locate food.

Most of the fish in the local markets were whiskered for similar reasons: river water at best is the color of charcoal. These freshwater dolphins are found, worldwide, in only one Chinese lake and four rivers: the Ganges, Plata, Orinoco, and Amazon. They are also reputed to have aphrodisiac properties. Local lore and legend holds that a dolphin eye dried and grated into a woman's food will drive her mad, and that a male dolphin is capable of Zeus-like shape-shifting that allows him to walk on land and seduce virgins.

On the first night out of Atalaya, we found a spot to camp in an extremely muddy but flat area. Ben prepared dinner while Scott and I tried to locate and fix a slow puncture in the raft. It was losing air, and every three to five hours we had to pump it up. Most likely the damage was caused by one of the thorns that seemed part of every indigenous plant's armor.

We deflated the raft as you would a bicycle tire, removed the inner tubes, and reinflated them, covered with soapy water. After an hour we gave up. We couldn't find the puncture. We reassembled the raft and inflated it. Until the leak was located, we resigned ourselves to periodically pumping up the boat.

We were eating a dinner of potatoes and yams covered in an onion and tomato sauce when a loud splashing caught our attention. Ben shone his headlight toward the river and two red coals glowed back. A caiman. Two more rubies glowed nearby just above the waterline.

We slept warily.

Hours slipped by quickly as the boat slowly but steadily continued down the river—oar stroke after oar stroke. The river meanders in infinite oxbows, forks, and loops as it wends its way through the jungle. We found ourselves lost in tree-choked mazes in which even the current seemed to disappear. Every fork presented a gamble. Without a map, we were at the mercy of the river gods.

With so much time on our hands we did too much thinking and psychoanalysis. Each moment of every day was no longer consumed with survival. It was just like the ages of man—with agriculture and spare time came philosophy and neurosis. For instance, I began to obsess that Scott's greatest downfall was his two-second attention span. He was forever adopting a new plan or goal he wanted to achieve. Some of them were great ideas, too, but the next day they were forgotten and he was on to something else. It drove me crazy.

We encountered some Danish men who were building a tall ship. They had spent five years laboring in the jungle heat and the ship was exquisitely beautiful. They had used only the finest of woods harvested from the rain forest and were about a month from launching the boat. The excitement of this nearly finished project was contagious. Scott told us that he, too, wanted to build a tall ship. Now, I'm the last person in the world to quash anyone's ambitions because I believe you can do anything you set your mind to. Scott could, by all means, build a tall ship. All it takes is drive, determination, and focus. But with Scott I knew the project would soon be forgotten. It was.

Ben suffered from exactly the opposite trait—he was too much of a realist. While in the whitewater stage of the journey, Scott and I spent hours planning for the flat-water. We drew countless diagrams and designs of ways we could make the raft more efficient and livable. I even pencilled in a plan for a bamboo-framed kayak with a polyurethane skin. Ben glanced at our sketch and rolled his eyes. Too far-fetched, he said. Yet, when the time came, he eagerly participated in the conversion and was more than happy to bask in the extra comfort the changes brought. He would never have thought to do it himself. I'm almost the exact opposite. If it's whacky, why not? That's my attitude. Ben's down-to-earth pragmatism sometimes got on my nerves.

I didn't bother to ask how I rankled Scott and Ben, but you can bet there were things I did over the time we spent together that bugged them. Even three saints going down the Amazon in a tiny raft would have trouble not rubbing each other the wrong way once in a while. The miracle was that we had no meaningful disagreements. Our friendship deepened through it all.

The monotony of the endless green wall of jungle, our growing bitchiness, and the worry about time spurred us into rowing around the clock. Our return flights from Rio de Janeiro were booked for six months from the date we arrived in South America. They could not be extended, and we couldn't afford to miss them. At our current speed, we would not make it in time.

To be honest, we were also worried about the wildlife. The caimans were nothing. Our chances of being bitten by a poisonous insect, spider, snake, or scorpion increased exponentially every time we bedded down ashore. And, yes, the Amazon is home to the most deadly vipers in the world—the bushmaster, or *shushupe*, and the fer-de-lance. But we were more freaked out by the bugs.

Never have I seen so many insects. Every evening hundreds of the tiny creatures scampered over our bodies. They came in all shapes, sizes, and colors. Some were spectacular in their iridescence, shimmering like luminous blue-black diadems in the emerald light. Others were garden-variety creepy-crawlies. Still, a 6-inch cockroach gets your attention faster than the domestic variety.

We were bitten frequently by ants. They swarmed across our feet and up our legs anytime we stood in one spot. Millions of winged insects were attracted to our fire. Inevitably they ended up in our food and our coffee. It got to the stage that we became so blasé about eating moths that we didn't remove their bodies from the porridge or the soup. Just more protein, we thought. We could have been in Thailand, where sweet-and-sour, candied, and savory insect dishes are loved!

By rowing through the night we figured we would save the two hours a day we spent setting up and striking camp. If we lived permanently on the raft, that wouldn't be necessary. But what clinched the decision to row around the clock was the mosquitoes. They were a voracious, airborne scourge. Every evening, as we came to shore, we heard the ominous hum of millions of the flying leeches rising from the fetid forest floor. Their roar filled our ears and they descended like a dark pall covering any exposed flesh. Nothing kept them at bay. Staying out on the river wasn't really a choice.

We decided to change shifts every hour from dusk until 9 o'clock, then do three-hour shifts through the night. We alternated each night so that no one was constantly stuck with the midnight-to-three shift. We each got six hours of sleep a night. Sleeping, though, took a bit of getting used to. There was no place to lie down on the boat. The side flotation chambers had two balsa-wood logs running across them. Using our lifejackets as pillows, we slept with one log under our necks and the other just below our hips. It was possible to get moderately comfortable.

We cut up the blue polyurethane tarpaulin to use as bedding. As well as holding in a bit of the heat during the surprisingly cool nights, it would shield us from the rain that fell several times a day. I knew there was a reason they called it the rain forest!

There was no point in using our sleeping bags. Everything in this humid, wet climate quickly became soaked, mildewed, and rotten. Our clothes putrefied. Washing them in the river only intensified the smell of decaying vegetation.

Fungus infections thrived and our feet were covered in red sores. Ben suffered the most. At one point he could no longer walk and the soles of his feet looked like Swiss cheese.

We figured we had enough gas to cook on the boat until we reached Pucallpa—if we were frugal.

As the first night approached, the light began to fade while I was on the oars. Scott was preparing dinner over the stove, which we had lashed to the table. Soon it was pitch black. As my eyes adjusted, I was barely able to distinguish the black-on-black outline of the riverbank.

Although we knew the river was flat, it was hard to suppress the irrational anxiety that a waterfall or killer whirlpool lurked in the inky darkness. We could also hear an occasional roar as the river cleared its throat—crunching through a semi-submerged logjam or biting off another bit of the bank. The current was often thick with clumps of weedy earth, uprooted trees, and detritus during the heavy rain. Although easy to avoid in the daylight, such hazards were potentially lethal in the dark.

The most frustrating part of night rowing was keeping the bow pointed downriver. The shadowy suggestion of shore wasn't enough on its own to indicate which way the current was moving—especially if the boat got turned around because we stopped for a moment to have a drink or piss, or maybe in the darkness we mistakenly steered in a circle. Once I spent hours rowing the wrong way before realizing my mistake.

Despite the discomfort, long hours, occasional wrong turns, and ever-present risk, we moved quickly downriver. We were also traveling almost insect free. The pain and sweat were worth it, if only for that.

Day 65: November 16, 1999

Five days after leaving Atalaya, the lights of Pucallpa came into view just before sunrise. Ben was rowing, Scott was asleep, and I lay watching the incandescent stars draw closer. Even though Pucallpa was at least 6 miles distant, the wind was scented with that lovely cologne Modernity—a mélange of diesel, kerosene, decay, and excrement.

The sense of smell is so evocative. I remembered how aware I became of my olfactory nerves while sailing, especially my arrival in Hiva Oa in French Polynesia, the first tropical island I hit after sailing across the Pacific from Mexico.

Out at sea, the ocean air is usually odorless, save for the smell of your ship. Although I could not yet see the island on the horizon, there was a magical moment when the air became redolent with the fragrance of bougainvillea, frangipani, and citrus mingled with the musky smell of a just-rained-in forest. It was Hiva Oa's natural perfume. By comparison, man's islands of civilization in the jungle fouled the air with the stench of money and the aroma of consumption on an industrial scale. What a difference from the scent of night-blooming jasmine that wafted occasionally over the river.

Pucallpa was an ugly smear on the lush green carpet of the Amazon forest. With a lumber mill and an oil refinery pumping twenty-four hours a day, tourism was not a big part of the economy. Pucallpa was a rugged port sitting at the end of a tenuous road that died there, worn out after coursing through the Andes and the Amazon jungle. We didn't plan on staying long.

"Pucallpa at last," Ben whispered. "Remember in Canada we used to say that at Pucallpa the cat would be in the bag? It's funny to see it become a reality." He was enraptured.

"Congrats, boy," I said, extending my hand. "Only 3,200 more miles to go."

Ben paused from paddling to shake my hand. Scott stirred. Rubbing his eyes, he grinned: "I smell Sublimes!"

Creamy yellow daylight spilled across the sky, and the city awoke squalid and bitter. Hundreds of slatternly huts leaned on stilts above the riverfront. Floating along the water's edge, an uneven line of clapboard, bamboo, and tin shacks squatted on large logs. The first people we saw emerge grimaced at the day and scooped buckets of water out of the river. Others came out to piss, defecate, or brush their teeth. The Amazon was truly the water of life.

Ben guided the raft toward a cluster of large commercial boats tethered to the shore. A crewman waved from the deck of a steel-hulled cargo ship bearing the name *Destroyer*. He pointed to the side of the barge-like vessel, indicating where we could tie up. We tethered the raft to the peeling oily side of the 98-foot ship. The air reeked of engine oil, rotting fish, and diesel.

On the rutted muddy streets, motorbikes buzzed every-where. For every car, there were twenty-five motorbikes. We flagged a three-wheeled taxi, the kind I always associate with India because of that great James Bond chase scene through the subcontinent's city streets. The driver took our patronage as a chance to display his own stunt driving skills, weaving through early morning rush hour as if on a slalom course.

The dirt roads turned to asphalt near the city center, which was a hive of activity. It was alive with people, market stalls, dirty stores, street salesmen, and, amid it all, the occasional modern office building.

Unhappy with the butane stove disaster, we bought a kerosene stove for 28 soles—less than $10. Pumped to full pres-sure, it roared like a rocket ship, capable of cooking anything in minutes. Kerosene was cheap and available. A 10-quart can cost $4—enough for a month, said the vendor. (By compari-son, a $4 butane canister usually lasted the three of us only one meal.) With a good stove, we could stay on the river for as long as we wanted.

That evening we joined the six-member crew of the *De-stroyer* for drinks. The boat was one of the many trading ships that plied the Amazon system. After the first bottle of rum, the cook, Frederiko, stood, cleared his throat, and sang sweet Pe-ruvian folk songs. It was a moving performance and a touching gesture. The flickering hurricane lantern and the rum cast a glow on the dark faces beaded with sweat from the humidity and heat. They fairly glowed with the warmth generated by un-expected conviviality.

Everyone was happy and I felt an unspoken companionship with the sailors. It was at moments like these that I understood why my father lived his life never far from docks and sailors. It was an almost spiritual moment. Shared time, shared experi-ence. Men taking common delight in the simple satisfaction of each other's company. A story told, a joke appreciated, a song offered. In a life devoid of the sacred, it was a moment of transcendence. It might also have been the rum.

I awoke on the steel deck of the *Destroyer,* lying just above the raft. Even without padding or bedding, the hard metal was a luxury compared with the discomfort that came from the contortions demanded by the raft.

We planned on going non-stop until we reached Iquitos, about 550 miles away. To get the maximum benefit of the current, we traveled down the middle of the river, which was now roughly 3 miles across.

One disadvantage of our nocturnal voyaging was that we felt isolated from the land we were traveling through. The shores seemed little more than a hazy smudge separating water and sky along the horizon. We learned nothing about the people or the geography we passed, and I realized too late how much richer the trip could have been with better preparation. It was a kind of grown-up thought that I hadn't really expected: the idea of doing something like this with more focus and more attention to detail, not just the best fun to be had on a summer vacation.

We had tried to pitch the trip to a couple of potential sponsors, without much luck. Perhaps now that we had surprised the naysayers, beaten the odds, and neared the finish, people would be less skeptical.

We tried to talk with every fisherman we encountered. If we could make ourselves understood, we would invite these men aboard and offer them one of the treats we had learned to concoct on the stove. With our plentiful fuel we produced pancakes, scones, caramel sauce, pizza, rice pudding, crumpets, and banana jam.

Within minutes, a blue sunny afternoon was transformed into a tropical hell—sideways rain, gale-force winds, threatening black skies. The river whipped into a frenzy with immense waves that tossed the raft like a cork. It was impossible to make headway. By nightfall the thick rain-clouds obliterated the sky, extinguishing the moon and stars. We rowed in complete and utter darkness, save for the occasional flash of lightning that lit up the seascape. Peals of thunder deafened us, pounding down on the river. Sleep was impossible. I lay with plastic sheeting pulled tight about my shoulders, dreading the shift call and the hours ahead rowing in the chilly deluge.

It was perilous trying to keep the raft moving downriver during such nocturnal tempests. The clay banks towered above the water by about 26 feet. The ravenous current, already clotted with debris, regularly devoured large chunks of the sandy clay, along with the trees and vegetation above. Huge clumps of earth and jungle slammed into the river. To be underneath the collapse meant certain death.

A lightning flash illuminated the danger. I had steered too close to shore and frantically rowed away. Minutes later I heard the roar as tons of dirt and rubble exploded into the river.

After my shift—wet, cold, teeth chattering—I tried to get back to sleep. There was no point in donning dry clothes; they would soon be drenched. Rain gear didn't work—rather, it created an environment for bacteria to thrive in and an incubator for the sores and infection we had grown accustomed to sporting.

Yet, despite the discomforts of the Amazonian storms, I would rather endure them than face the "Red Zone" again.

I swam in the murky waters on a daily basis—always during the storms, since the boat usually went too fast to keep up with during the calm. I enjoyed exercising the different muscles swimming forced me to use. Ben and Scott preferred to shower, using a cooking pot to scoop river water over themselves.

Scott tried his luck at fishing with some line and hooks we

had purchased in Pucallpa. Using as bait a piece of a fish that had jumped into our boat to die, Scott trolled the line behind. Almost immediately the line jerked and, hand over hand, he pulled in a small fish that looked like a shark with whiskers. He threw it back and tried for something more edible. Again, he got the same ugly catfish. After hauling in four of these denizens of the murky Amazon, he gave up.

"There are thousands of species of fish in this river and I have to catch the same kind four times in a row," Scott grumbled. "This fish that jumped in the boat looks pretty tasty. Too bad it's going rotten."

He slapped the chess pieces onto the board. "Game?"

Day 75: November 26, 1999

At 10 P.M. we reached the largest confluence in Peru—the meeting of the Marañón and Ucayali rivers. This is officially the start of the Amazon River (although the locals call it the Solimões). Ben and Scott slept soundly. I let them sleep as the landmark slipped by.

As day broke, I could see the change in the river—it was twice as wide as it had been. Around 2 miles across, I'd guess. This truly is El Río Mar, the River Sea. You can barely see the other bank. We could have been on a large lake.

Padre, a 10-mile-long island that stretches in front of the city of Iquitos and divides the river, protects the harbor. We navigated our way easily into the dirty harbor and tethered the raft to an apparently abandoned barge.

We fell asleep.

Days 77 to 83: November 28 to December 4, 1999

We planned to spend a week in Iquitos, trade capital of the Peruvian jungle, and treat ourselves to a cheap hotel. A fading, gracious promenade runs for a mile along the river, which can rise as much as 30 feet during the rainy season.

Founded in the mid-1800s, Iquitos didn't grow until the rubber boom at the turn of the century. Then it exploded with new wealth, profligate spending, and extravagant taste. As everyone who has ever heard of Iquitos will tell you, a cast-iron building designed by Alexandre Gustave Eiffel was shipped over from Europe in pieces. The oil rush in the 1970s preceded the cocaine boom of the 1980s, and now smuggling (drugs, exotic animals, and precious stones) is just one flourishing sector of the local economy.

We didn't want to leave the boat at the mercy of thieves, so we disassembled the log frame, deflated the raft, and loaded it into a decrepit pickup that doubled as a taxi.

We found a hotel overlooking Belén, dubbed the Venice of the Amazon, the low-lying southeastern swath of the city. It's really a floating shantytown, a slum under water for much of the year. Its shacks teeter on stilts and its inhabitants move about in dugout canoes. There is no plumbing and, if the river is low, as it was, the foreshore is a stinking boardwalk of sewage and garbage ruled by vultures.

Belén possessed a certain charm. We spent several hours shopping in its cheap raucous markets, which offered everything from bags of staples to armadillo shells, piranha teeth, and *chuchuhuasi*—the rum-soaked bark used as a health tonic. We even found a bar where home-brewed hooch was poured into bottles from gasoline cans.

On the other side of Iquitos, we found that the twentieth century existed in full splendor—Internet cafés, fancy restaurants, and ATMs. We spent three days e-mailing to different companies in the vain hope of acquiring a sponsor. I thought at least that manufacturers of the raft would be keen. We didn't even get a don't-call-us-we'll-call-you response.

Up until then I had presumed that money would be available from somewhere if we made it to Iquitos. Our journey was garnering headlines in Canada. Why were companies not interested in supporting us? We had $800 left in the kitty and 5,000 miles to cover. The visas that Ben and I required to enter Brazil would cost $100. Bus tickets at the end of the river would cost $450. That left $250 for food. There would be no more Sublimes—just the basics.

Day 84: December 5, 1999

After a week in Iquitos we were dying to get on the river again. The city was full of temptations—treats we couldn't afford. We filled the boat with the most basic and cheapest of staples: rice, flour, and beans.

The rainy season was full upon us and the weather was abysmal. Storms and gales flayed us and the river simply grew and grew—expanding phenomenally as tributaries added volume and bulk to the River Sea: the Maniti, the Vainilla, the Orosa, the Moahuanyo, the Palameta, the Pichana, the Cochiquinas, the Sta. Rosa, the Mayoruna . . .

Day 87: December 8, 1999

Three days out of Iquitos a weathered fisherman offered us his dugout canoe for 20 soles. The prospect of having our own canoe was too much to resist and we handed over the money from the meagre kitty. The canoe would be invaluable for exploring the flooded jungle. We towed it behind, its streamlined shape adding little resistance.

It also made a perfect sea anchor. During storms, ocean-like swells and waves sometimes accompanied winds so strong that, even with our best efforts, we were forced upstream. The canoe was our saviour. By lashing ropes to both ends of the canoe and sinking it, it caught the current like a parachute and dragged us downstream.

Sinking the canoe became part of the readying-for-the-storm routine. We always heard the wind and rain two to three minutes before it arrived. It was unsettling. It started like a bass rift as the deluge moved through the jungle. When we heard it, we dropped the tent-fly awning, stowed the loose gear, and submerged the canoe. We huddled under the plastic and waited for the onslaught. The canoe kept the bow pointing into the wind and waves, providing a more comfortable ride. If the wind blew at an angle, pushing us into the shore, we could steer by adjusting the two ropes that tethered the canoe.

Day 88: December 9, 1999

Three days after leaving Iquitos we came to a large army post that stopped and inspected all marine traffic. We were still 37 miles from the Colombian border. It was here that a rogue military officer, who coveted the expensive equipment, had shot the team of Japanese adventurers dead. We were slightly apprehensive.

A squad of soldiers led by a teenaged boy greeted us. They examined our passports, asked a few rudimentary questions, and waved us on. Take care, they cautioned, there are many narco-terrorists along the Colombian border.

For the next 80 miles or so, the Amazon was the shared border separating Peru and Colombia. Cocaine and smuggling were putatively the only industries. Both sides accused the other of harboring criminals, thugs, thieves, smugglers, drug dealers, terrorists, and guerrillas. The soldiers said to stay away from the Colombian side or risk being shot. They also warned us not to travel at night.

We decided to heed their warning and found a sandy beach on the left-hand side of the river. Surprisingly, the bugs left us alone and we slept soundly.

The following morning a lone fisherman in a dugout canoe arrived. "What are you doing?" he asked.

"We wanted to wait out the night before passing through Colombia," Ben said. "We've heard Colombians can be pretty aggressive."

"You're in Colombia right now," the fisherman chuckled. "I'm Colombian." He lifted his paddle in the air as a mock gun: "Pow, pow, pow!"

Ha-ha-ha.

When he'd finished laughing at us, he exchanged pleasantries with us and wished us well. We paddled quickly across the river and spent the day within a few hundred yards of the Peruvian shore. We made sure that we camped on their side of the river.

Day 90: December 11, 1999

Tabatinga and Leticia are really just one big city with an international border running through the middle. Leticia is in Colombia, Tabatinga in Brazil. People in both towns spoke Spanish and Portuguese. Tabatinga was the wrong side of the tracks—Leticia the neighborhoods of fancy shops, executive homes, and five-star restaurants. In Tabatinga, people said Leticia was lit up with drug money. Leticians shrugged and claimed they worked harder.

From the water we had no idea where one city ended and the other began. In fact, we pulled up 20 yards on the Brazilian side, strolled into Tabatinga, spotted the Portuguese signs, and realized our mistake. Ben and I needed visas to be in Brazil. We walked over to Leticia, passing the border guard snoring in a chair.

Sexy-looking girls sped past on motorcycles and scooters. How long had we been on that raft? One after another they flew by, sometimes tossing us a smile or a wave. I felt like a sailor who had been at sea too long.

We located the Colombian Immigration Office. An armed guard barred the door. We held out our passports and he led us inside. From one of the rooms came a chorus of grunts and moans. The guard knocked on the door. "You may have to wait a few minutes," he told us.

A young man with curly black hair and a mustache came out, buttoning his fly. Sweat dripped down his face. "What do you want?"

"Entry permits to Colombia from Peru."

He whisked out the forms and tapped the desk impatiently as we filled them in. He scooped them up, stamped our passports, and returned to his love shack. It had taken less than three minutes to clear Colombian customs. We strode out cheerfully, having expected the process to take all day.

The Brazilian visas required passport photos and photocopied documents. The consulate was open for only a few hours a day. We spent four days in Tabatinga and Leticia dealing with Brazilian bureaucratic delays. The consulate took two days to process our visas and, after that, we had to go to the police station in Tabatinga for an entry permit.

Surprisingly, in spite of appearances, Leticia was a fair bit cheaper than Tabatinga, so we did most of our shopping there. Fresh produce was cheaper in Brazil, we heard, so we waited to buy it there.

Each of us took a turn guarding the boat while the others went to town. We pitched a tent beside the raft. At night, two of us slept in the tent while the other stayed on the boat. It was too risky to leave it unattended.

Day 94: December 15, 1999

After our first night on the river again, a speedboat roared toward us in the dim morning light. It was the Brazilian Federal Police. Once again, completely unaware, we had skipped a checkpoint. All boats entering Brazil from Colombia were required to stop. How were we to know? The federales tied a line to the raft and towed us back upriver. Scott hung on to the canoe, which shuddered precariously from the speed.

We reached a floating wharf and were shepherded to a middle-aged man behind a desk in the sunshine. I carried my video camera under my arm, worried about leaving it unattended in the raft.

Our Portuguese was worse than our Spanish, yet the man

didn't seem at all frustrated by our presence. Through hand gestures and fragments of broken Spanish, he asked why we were sneaking past the checkpoint.

"We didn't know it existed," I said.

Did we have drugs on board? Cocaine?

"No," I said, shaking my head vigorously.

He paid no attention to my answer and handed us each a form to fill in. "Then you can go," he said.

The three of us sat down, quickly answered the usual name, country-of-origin, purpose-of-visit questions, and were soon back on the raft chortling about the experience.

Days 96 to 100: December 17 to 21, 1999

The river forked and we took what appeared to be the less-traveled branch. The jungle was pristine: towering palms, huge hardwoods, liana vines, Spanish moss, and impenetrable underbrush. Macaws flitted among the trees. I must capture some of this on film, I thought, and reached for the camera.

Gone!

Damn it!

Where? Shit. Back with the federales.

"I left my camera back at the police dock!" I said.

Scott and Ben looked up. After trying so hard to guard it, I had lost it. We couldn't row back upstream—the current was too swift and it was too far, about 200 miles.

"I'm going to go back," I said dejectedly. "At the next town or village, I'll catch a ride back up the river in a cargo ship."

I had a horrible feeling in my gut. Scott and Ben shared my anguish—the loss of footage from here on would affect us all.

Amaturá is a small town that seemed wealthier than its Peruvian jungle counterparts. The buildings were more substantial, constructed from either bricks or milled lumber. Most of the streets were paved, and some of the homes had television.

A small black river flowed in front of the town and directly into the Amazon.

We waited for three days, feeling very sorry for ourselves, before the arrival of a cargo ship, one of many maintaining regular supply routes throughout the Amazon system. My fare was going to eat up a large part of our remaining money, and there was a good chance the camera was long gone. I left Scott and Ben and boarded the 80-foot riverboat heading upstream. This *lancha* went back and forth between Manaus and Tabatinga.

The river here was a true highway. The *lancha* brimmed with people, cows, pigs, piles of dried fish, and all sorts of goods. There were three decks, and hammocks were strung wherever space allowed. I thought they were part of the boat—similar to the seats on a bus. I walked from hammock to hammock asking if they were taken. People gave me strange looks.

"Sí, sí," they said.

I found a lone hammock and no one about. I climbed inside and fell asleep. An hour later I felt a tap on my back. A wizened, gray-haired man stared at me. "You're in my hammock," he said.

"Excuse."

I muttered apologies and he seemed to realize I had made an honest mistake. He explained that the individual passengers brought the hammocks aboard. I started climbing out of his, but he told me to stay put.

"I have another if I need it," he said, extending his hand. "I am Marcos."

The journey to the checkpoint took twenty-five hours, as the boat stopped at villages along the way to load and unload, take on passengers, and let passengers disembark. Breakfast, lunch, and dinner were served on the *lancha*. Three Brazilian children, who tried to teach me rudimentary Portuguese, announced the menu to me. For lunch we had fresh fish. The communal atmosphere of the boat raised my spirits.

"Tonight we are having chicken for dinner!" one of the boys said excitedly.

I looked toward the galley and noticed that the chickens I had seen earlier with strings tied to their legs had vanished.

I arrived at the police dock at 2 P.M. The captain presented his papers for inspection and the vessel was cleared after little more than a cursory glance. I waved goodbye to my new friends and turned to the policeman. Today it was a different fellow.

Slowly, with hand gestures and bits of Spanish and Portuguese, I explained my predicament. He looked puzzled, abruptly got up, and went to a small shed that stood at the far end of the dock. Two black bags sat on one of the shelves. The policeman pointed to them.

I shook my head.

He shrugged. I felt sick. It had cost me $20 to come up the river and it would cost another $20 to get back to Amaturá. It was money we couldn't afford. In all, this calamity had claimed the camera and a week.

I asked when the next ship went down the river.

I was in luck, he said, the next boat would be coming at about 3 A.M.

Owing to federal regulations, I wasn't allowed to step off the dock on my own. I sat waiting, hungry and thirsty, for my ride.

The rain started almost immediately, sending the policeman scurrying to the staff quarters. I sat alone, wet and cold in the pelting rain.

At about six in the evening, a motorized canoe came peck-pecking to the dock. An Indian man and his family huddled under pieces of blue plastic—the same kind we used. He got out onto the dock as the policeman reappeared.

After the Indian family left, the policeman took pity on me. There were ten officers stationed here, he said—perhaps one of the others had picked up my camera. He motioned me to follow him toward the staff dormitories.

He led me into the cinderblock building. The walls were painted a pale blue and there were five bunk beds. Through an open door, I could see a group of men on a sagging couch watching soccer on TV.

My host rooted through duffel bags littered around the room and invited me to do the same. Some of the men in the adjacent room glanced in when they heard us rummaging about, but no one said anything.

After opening three bags without success, I hit the jackpot. Bingo! My camera was still in the dry-bag, jammed into a pile of dirty underwear. I was elated.

The policeman smiled. He seemed completely nonplussed that the camera turned up in his colleague's bag.

At 3 o'clock in the morning, right on time, a huge overloaded *lancha* docked. It was coming from Colombia, and most of the passengers, I learned later, were headed for Manaus for the new millennium celebrations. Ten policemen spent two hours searching every bag, nook, hold, cranny, and corner of the boat. After they had checked everyone's passport, I was allowed to board.

Wet and dripping from the rain, I found a spot on the wooden deck and curled up happily into a ball around my camera.

The following day I arrived back in Amaturá. Ben and Scott, resigned to never seeing the camera again, couldn't believe their eyes: here I was, with a face-splitting grin, the video camera slung over my shoulder.

Some of the tension among us was gone. We knew each other as well as it is possible for one man to know another. Intimacy grows quickly on a tiny raft. Our relationships had evolved as the journey progressed. Ben and Scott hadn't even known each other before meeting in Canada two weeks before we left. A lot of people had told us that three was a bad number because two always ganged up against the third. Sometimes that happened with us, but the rivalry also passed. Still, when you're staring at the same people day after day after day, even angels would get on your nerves after a while.

Nearing the end of the journey, we felt a deep kinship with each other. Having been through so much and faced death so many times, we could communicate with each other knowing we had all experienced the same things. We often talked about how we would hate to do something like this solo—not because of the increased difficulty, risk, or loneliness, but because there would be no one else in the world you could talk to afterward who would really understand where you're coming from. You can tell people what the journey was about, write a book, show a million photos, and they will grasp the achievement. But unless they have been there and shared the experience—hung suspended in a vortex praying for another chance at life, heard the crack of the rifles, staggered hopelessly lost in a desert without water, survived the mind-numbing monotony of the silent primeval jungle for weeks on end—then and only then can you viscerally understand what went on. We shared something with each other and no one else, and that bonded us.

Days 101 to 111: December 22, 1999, to January 1, 2000

We left Amaturá on December 22, hoping to make Manaus for the millennium celebrations. With a population of 1.2 million people, this jungle metropolis was bound to throw a great party. We rowed extra hard to make our nine-day deadline.

We celebrated Christmas in mid-river, not stepping ashore even once. We produced a meal using the few luxury items— spaghetti bolognese, potato salad, and Pringles potato chips. We gave each other a banana as a present—the same gift I had received on my birthday.

On December 26 we were buffeted by wind, rain, and

waves so large that Scott was seasick and couldn't eat. We couldn't row much at all, so lay under the tarps as the current's pull on the submerged canoe dragged us down the river.

Running out of food and fuel, we reached Manaus at 2 P.M. on December 31, looking to party.

Manaus is not on the Amazon proper. It sits about 9 miles up the Rio Negro. We rowed about halfway, before accepting a tow from an oil-refinery boat.

A huge oil farm announced the arrival of the city. Manaus is a rubber product. With the discovery in the nineteenth century of latex and its uses, the Amazon's rubber trees drew tens of thousands of fortune hunters from Europe. At the height of the boom, 1910, Manaus was the third city in the western hemisphere to have electricity. The population of 90,000 spent $8 million a year on jewelery. Some extravagants are reputed to have shipped their laundry to London and their children to school in France.

The excess of those days remains visible in the architecture. A handful of Victorian buildings remain—the most famous the opulent, pink-and-white Manaus Opera House designed to lure the world's brightest stars. Even Enrico Caruso came. Built in 1896 with a golden dome and a Florentine façade of Italian stone, the now-restored building features plush over-stuffed chairs, velvet boxes, ornate balconies, florid murals, and gilded columns. It has also been described as "an over-sized Italian biscuit tin."

The Municipal Market, constructed mostly of glass and iron from a copycat design of Les Halles in Paris, is also intact, as is the imposing classical brick Customs House built by the British from materials imported from England. The stones live on, but the rubber boom has long since burst.

In 1912 rubber trees smuggled out of Brazil by an English botanist were planted in Indonesia. It was the beginning of the end. Companies harvesting wild rubber couldn't compete with those operating rubber plantations, and the engine of the city's thriving economy seized up.

In the 1960s, in an effort to get Manaus back on its feet again, the Brazilian government declared the city a duty-free port, which transformed it into a shopping mecca selling everything from automobiles to jewelery and electronics. Brazilians flock there to beat taxes and tariffs. With the expansion of oil and logging, Manaus again became a boomtown in the 1980s, when the population neared a million and inflation raged at 200 percent.

We tied our faded raft to a dock in front of the city, close to several flashy high-powered speedboats. The family that owned the dock lived in a floating home connected to the rest of the wharf. They agreed to watch the raft and look after our bags.

We changed into our cleanest clothes and headed into the city, ready to celebrate the new millennium. The town was completely dead. We strolled up and down, looking for any activity. We found a nightclub with four patrons—three of them tired-looking hookers deciding whether to call it a night. Midnight came and went, and there wasn't even a pause in the dance music to mark the new millennium.

"Welcome to the year 2000," I said, holding aloft my lone beer ration.

"Maybe we can find somewhere with a bit more happening for the next millennium," Ben said, raising his glass.

We walked over to the central park and each of us slept on a concrete bench. The next morning I awoke to a hustling, busy city. People streamed past, only occasionally tossing curious glances at us.

On a nearby newsstand, the front page of a newspaper bore a picture of people celebrating. Fireworks were exploding in the background. Perhaps it was New York. "It looks like they celebrated somewhere in the world," Scott said, picking up the paper to see where the fun was. "Guess what, guys?" he said. "That was here!"

We'd missed it. While we sat like sad sacks downtown with the winos and the down-and-outs, the rest of Manaus was celebrating at Ponta Negra, a big resort area just outside the city limits.

"You don't win every time," Scott said.

Days 112 to 120: January 2 to 10, 2000

We spent a few days in Manaus and I really worked on my Portuguese, flirting with the local girls. Then we left on the final leg of our journey to the Atlantic Ocean.

At the confluence with the Amazon, we marveled again at the natural phenomenon the locals called the "Meeting of the Waters." The Negro is the sixth-largest river in the world, with a discharge four times that of the Mississippi. It meets the Solimões (as the locals call the Amazon) with fury. Along the front line the water roils and churns, a seething mass of whirlpools, waves, and turbulence. Behind, the waters of both rivers constantly rush and push.

The clash of these two great waterways would be spectacular enough, but the wonder is heightened by a distinct difference in color—the Negro is the color of café Americano, the Amazon a latte. The individual rivers of the Amazon drainage system are categorized according to their color—a product of the land the rivers chew through. The specific chemical, mineral, and organic material washed away by erosion and borne by each waterway, the composition of each river's suspended silt, gives it a hue. There are "whitewater," "blackwater," and "clearwater" tributaries of the Amazon. The white are murky tan-colored rivers, such as the Apurimac, which rise in the Andes and plummet, carrying loose rock and inorganic material, from the mountains toward the sea. The black, such as the Río Negro, are loaded with more organic humus material, washed out of the sandy soil of the highlands in Colombia and Guyana. They are said to carry twice as much silt as the white rivers and are generally the color of dark tea. The clear, which are rarely pellucid, include the Xingu, Tapajós, and Tocantins, which rise in the Brazilian highlands—old, eroded hills with little left to wear away. Each provides a variation on the famous Meeting of the Waters near Manaus.

Here, the currents of the Negro and the mainstream of the Amazon wrestle violently with each other. These two great flows run side by side in a two-tone, black-and-tan tussle for almost 8 miles. By the time they blend, the Amazon is truly a moving sea. We could barely see from one side of the river to the other, and occasionally the far shore would disappear altogether. The banks of the river were now more manicured and spotted with activity. What tufts of rainforest remained looked under siege.

The dolphins, happily, were as frequent as ever and provided a reassuring optimistic presence, frolicking and playing around the boat.

With the constant rain and tropical heat, our clothes started to rot on our bodies. Washing did nothing to stop the festering pong, so we had started to boil our clothes every third day. This treatment killed the bacteria and eliminated the pungent smell.

Day 121: January 11, 2000

We were now in the midst of the rainy season and the deluge was continuous. Our broad-faced raft found it impossible to buck the headwind even with the submerged canoe acting as a drag. We made no headway through the wind and swell.

When not rowing, swimming, eating, or sleeping, I constantly studied my little Portuguese phrase book. I had made it my goal to memorize every word in the index, and all the phrases and verbs displayed in the rest of the book. I practiced my new vocabulary on any boat people we passed.

The river also gave us time simply to think about life. It was a lot like being at sea. We had undertaken this expedition to get away from it all, but that had proved impossible. We could not escape the ugly face of commercialism, and it was impossible to escape our own desires and appetites. I missed the choices available in Canada, North American popular music, and newspapers. There were too many other things I wanted to do. It felt bittersweet that this journey was coming to an end, just as it had felt to give up sailing around the world. I had lived the rafting lifestyle, totally enjoyed it, and now it was time to move on to something else. But to what?

Day 123: January 13, 2000

It took us two days to reach Santarem, dubbed the Caribbean of the Amazon, at the confluence of the Amazon and the Tapajós Rivers. The area got its nickname from the royal-blue water of the Tapajós and its long, sandy beaches.

We pulled the raft onto one of the popular recreational beaches, as reggae and traditional Brazilian music blasted from the open-air bars. Our arrival seemed to intrigue the people, and they were more than happy to buy us beers to hear our tales.

Santarem has its own microclimate, and the weather was hot and sunny. My Portuguese was improving, and I believed I was beginning to understand most of what people said, so long as they talked slowly and used simple words. I guess that's saying I now functioned at the intellectual level of a Brazilian moron.

It was a start.

Days 130 to 146: January 20 to February 5, 2000

Ben squinted hard against the sun. We were four days downriver from Santarem. The glare off the glossy tourist map hurt his eyes nearly as much as its emerging uselessness.

"That's an island," he repeated, gesturing with an impatient nod at the right-hand shore that extended far into the distance. "How can it be?" I scoffed. "This passage here can't be anything but that one there."

I tapped hard at a spot of blue print, then at the gap in the left-hand shore.

Ben flushed. "Come and check the bloody compass!" he growled.

His sunglasses had fallen overboard a few hours earlier and he was losing his temper. It didn't matter. We were lost again. There was a maze of channels and we had no idea where we were. The water itself seemed unsure how to reach the ocean. We had found the beginning of the sprawling Amazon delta, larger than most European nations.

How could we have believed a $5 tourist map would work? The geography was a web of canals, ditches, and natural levees—an estuarial floodplain, or *várzea*, ruled by tidal currents. The coast was still 250 miles distant, and once more we were befuddled, our overconfidence painfully exposed. Only the arrival of the incoming tide made it worse.

We were very aware of the lunar cycles while on the river. The difference between a full and a new moon was ying and yang. If the moon was a sliver and the sky clouded, we were blind. As the new moon waxed, we eagerly anticipated each increment of extra light. When the moon was full, the river and the jungle were awash in shimmering silver. One evening, as the sun hung ablaze on the western horizon, a dazzling white disc of a full moon sat opposite on the eastern rim. For a few minutes the two stared at each other until the sun slipped beneath the olive jungle, leaving the sky to the night ruler.

I expected a stretch of easy, tranquil navigation. Scott woke me for my graveyard shift with a nudge of his bare foot. "Mate, wake up."

I sat up. My neck and back were stiff and sore. Scott climbed into the warm spot I had just vacated. "It's bright as day with that full moon," he said, pulling the cover up.

The moon had turned the jungle into an eerie daguerreo-type—you could see every leaf in the forest wall clearly and every detail on the river's surface. My fingers slipped into the well-worn grooves of the oar shafts and my body took on the efficient rhythm it had developed from months of rowing. An hour passed quickly as my mind drifted in the surreal river-scape. But soon the light began to fade. A dark shadow stained the face of the moon and obscured a good half of the orb. I continued watching in bewilderment as the moon disappeared—eclipsed by the shadow of the earth. The surrounding stars glittered brightly, but the moon was gone. So much for a nice bright night!

For the most part, rowing against the incoming current was a waste of time. Any hope we had of making progress against it was futile. We had continually to revise our end date. But it was an incredible bayou, an environment like no other we had encountered. Stilted houses perched along the shore, colorful wooden boats plied the waterways, and there was a never-ending soundtrack of birdsongs.

We were a sight for the locals—mostly subsistence fishermen who were incredulous at the apparition of our raft and its crew. They stared dumbfounded, sometimes with mouths agape. Asking them directions, as with anyone in South America it seemed, was useless. No one would say, "I don't know." Instead, they would send us off in directions that would only further confuse us.

One day a leather-faced fisherman told Ben, "Do not go on the river at night."

Ben stared at the long, raised scar splitting the man's chest. "Why?" he asked, knowing he wouldn't like the answer.

"Peeraches com heeflez."

"Pirates with rifles?"

"Is a big problem here," the man said.

We had heard. To us, they became the equivalent of the Sendero Luminoso, ideology notwithstanding.

The delta rose and fell with the ebb and flow of each tide,

and we had to pull in every twelve hours to await the tide's return. Navigation through the thousands of channels, forks, and islands was extremely difficult. The current flowed everywhere and nowhere. The tourist map, adequate for the long straight stretches of the river behind, was useless. Opposing tides also hampered our daily progress.

But the jungle was the most impressive we had ever seen anywhere down the river. Monkeys sat in elegant, stately palms, jeering as we drifted slowly past. The silt supported a lush, fecund ecosystem. The absence of agriculture and settlement meant that the luxuriant habitat flourished unmolested. As the river flooded its banks with every high tide, the waters flowed through the rich jungle. The daily inundation made the land useless for crops or grazing without expensive diking and water-control measures.

Early one morning, while Ben was rowing, I awoke to the sound of a diesel engine drawing closer. Three fishermen dressed in nothing but Y-front underwear approached in a dilapidated wooden scow. They drew within 20 feet.

"Bom dia," Ben called out.

"Bom dia," the man steering the boat replied.

Their boat moved in a slow circle around the raft. The man at the wheel fondled his crotch as he stared at us. I crawled back under my plastic. Ten minutes later, clearly bored, the men chugged off.

Later in the day I noticed two men in a canoe following us. They seemed to be gaining, so I rowed more vigorously. After a few moments I glanced back to see that the men had quickened their pace. I bent my back to the oars. The men stepped up their pace. I didn't like it.

The raft was too unwieldy. The men drew alongside about an hour after I had first spotted them.

"Bom dia," they said. "You passed our homes."

They seemed very friendly, but we were still too expectant of trouble to lower our guard.

"We thought you might like some coconuts."

They handed us a dozen ripe coconuts and disappeared as quickly as they had come.

We began to see regular hovels on stilts and, when we stopped, we were invariably greeted with warm hospitality. Although poor by Western standards, these people lived on a varied diet of freshwater shrimp, manioc flour, coconuts, and delicacies such as saie, a delicious palm berry, harvested from the jungle.

We stayed with one family for a full day while we weathered a large storm. They warned us against traveling at night.

"Peeraches com heeflez."

We had heard it all before. With the end so tantalizingly close, there was no point pushing our luck. Belém was only 60 miles away. Taking the advice of our hosts, we stopped in succeeding evenings at a hut and introduced ourselves to the owners. Tied up to such homes, we were relatively safe.

On our last day before reaching Belém we stayed at a church overlooking the river's edge. The whole community came over to visit us, bringing us fresh fruit and wishing us luck.

The city of Belém was filled with poor people. It was named after the biblical village of Bethlehem, and there was still no room at the inn. The first settlement dates from 1616, but any colonial legacy or historic atmosphere it once might have had has long since been obliterated by skyscraping tenements. More than 1.5 million people call it home.

The Atlantic Ocean was now only 50 miles away. We paddled past a swath of unkempt industrial waterfront and moored at the posh yacht club. It was free for international boats, so we thought we'd try our luck.

"What is the name of your yacht?" the fresh-faced coed in the office asked in English.

"*Los Labios*," Ben replied. We had christened the red rubber raft "Lips."

"And where have you sailed from?" she asked.

"Peru," I answered.

She gave us a form and pointed to a mooring buoy on a small map. We stayed free for three days, enjoying the luxury of the facilities: free showers, a swimming pool, and saunas. It was a fine way to end the trip.

Our tiny raft became an object of extreme interest moored among the luxury yachts. The first night we slept aboard our own boat. After that, a group of Spanish journalists with a chartered 50-foot sailboat invited us to stay with them on condition they could interview us to do a story on our journey. We happily obliged.

We readied our boat for the open ocean while we were in Belém. The final stages would be the roughest flat-water rafting we had done. We cut off the protruding wings with a borrowed handsaw and stored all the gear for the estimated four days in one dry-bag.

We placed it on the bottom of the boat to lower the center of gravity. We left the rest of our gear with the journalists. With the boat shipshape and tidy, we left Belém for the final stage of our voyage—the 30-mile crossing of Marajó Bay.

Surprisingly, the bay is filled with fresh water, so great is the volume draining out of the Amazon. The first night we tried to camp, still worried about pirates, but the landowner chased us off with a shotgun. We took our chances with the pirates.

Later that night, while I was rowing, I turned my head and heard the faint hum of an engine. I looked around and could see nothing at first. Then I realized that a wall of inky blackness was bearing down on us. I turned the boat toward shore and pulled on the oars, terrified. An unlit barge being pushed from behind by a tug slipped past the stern of the raft.

I yelled at the departing boat.

Ben and Scott woke up wondering what was going on.

"Go back to sleep," I said.

It would have mowed us under, and no one would even have known we had died.

The wind was calm and we awaited only the turn of the tide. A haze rested on the green bosom of the jungle and erased the horizon. Far off I could see a dark line of mournful, brooding clouds. The sea-reach of the Amazon stretched before me like an interminable waterway connecting every port on earth and every one of us. I thought of all the men and women who had passed this way down through time—the natives, explorers, adventurers, settlers, captains, admirals, interlopers.

Think of the first European sailors sitting here before an unknown continent, refusing to believe they were at the mouth of a river. Imagine them here, the sea the color of pewter, the sky the color of lead, and a primeval green mass steaming from horizon to horizon like a giant untamed beast—a jungle so dense it mocked their attempts to land and claimed any who ventured ashore. They grabbed what they could—robbery with violence, aggravated murder on a grand scale, as is proper with those who tackle a darkness. It was the same rapacious plunder Joseph Conrad decried on the Congo more than a century ago. It continues today.

The conquest of the earth, which mostly means taking it away from those who have a different complexion or slightly flatter noses than our own, is not a pretty thing when you examine it closely, Conrad warned. The days of drifting down the Amazon had forced me to consider it often. I thought of how, as a child, I had read all those stories about men captivated with the idea of filling in the blank spaces on earth. I had a passion for maps and regularly lost myself for hours in the glories of exploration. When I saw one particularly inviting place on the map, I put my finger on it and said, When I grow up I will go there.

But there are no more dark places. Even this immense snake of a river, its body curving far behind us into a vast country, its tail lost in the depths of the continent, is no longer obscure. No, not even this river valley, once a place of great mystery, can be said to be the ends of the earth—any more than London, Tokyo, or Mount Everest.

The tide began to ebb and the tranquil waterway, the River Sea, flowed somber under an overcast sky into an immense darkness.

Days 147 to 150: February 6 to 9, 2000

If you look at a map, the Amazon delta is a large triangle with Ponta Taipu at the bottom right-hand corner, where the coast swings southeast toward São Luis, Fortaleza, and Natal. Ponta Taipu was the end of our five-month journey. Twelve miles away there is a fishing town called Vigia, which we reached late in the evening. We decided to stay there for the night before heading out into the turbulent open waters of the bay. This was the last place where we would experience the beauty of Amazonian hospitality.

A group of fisherman approached us and gave us a couple of big fish for dinner. Rico, a plump, jovial man, offered to take us around the town. We felt safe leaving our boat and gear with his friends.

First, he took us to his house, showed us the shower, and supplied each of us with a clean set of clothes. I guess we must have appeared quite a mess to outsiders, wearing our ripped, stinking, faded clothes. After a dinner with his family, Rico took us on something of a pub crawl and treated us to beers. We stayed for two days when a heavy storm kept even the fishermen in port.

On February 8 we said goodbye to Rico and his family. I gave him my multi-tool as a gift. Ben gave the kids some Australian commemorative coins.

The Atlantic swells produced huge standing waves in the outgoing current that towered almost 10 feet in places. Our raft bobbed and pitched wildly, and Scott's complexion paled. He was soon seasick. The rain poured down until, finally, the hazy outline of Ponta Taipu appeared in the distance. It vanished in the rain and reappeared as the strength of the storm rose and fell. Although within about 30 miles of the equator, we shivered under our plastic sheeting.

We reached the point at the end of the day and decided to tie up to a fishing stake for the night, protected from the ocean swell by a mud bar. We would celebrate in the morning.

Camping ashore was impossible because it was a mess of mangroves. At high tide the waves would crash right through the stunted aquatic trees. Curled up and hungry, we lay under the plastic, sheltering from the cold rain and wind. By 10 o'clock the incoming tide had covered the mud bar that protected us and a swell rolled in. By midnight, full breakers assaulted the shallow water, crashing over and around us. The thick wooden stake bent precariously. I began to worry that the stake might let go and we would be washed into the mangroves. The waves crashed over the boat and drenched us completely, even through the plastic. I felt miserable, even a little sick. I slept badly, tossing and turning.

"MATES, WAKE UP!!" It was Scott.

I looked at my watch: 3 A.M. I dragged my body out of the plastic cocoon and looked around. There were lights everywhere. The incoming tide had pushed back the murky water of the Amazon and replaced it with the salty, star-sprinkled Atlantic. Glimmering phosphorescence shimmered in the breaking waves and sparkled over our boat.

"Wild!" Scott said.

"We've done it," I said. "That's the ocean!"

On February 9—150 days after we set off from "la Punta

Bonita"—our trip was ending on a magical note. It felt good, damn good.

"That glitter is the Atlantic Ocean!" I was ecstatic.

We dipped a cup in the murky brine and passed it around, its gritty taste catching in our throats. We had done it. This was it. Our grail. We tied victory flags to our paddles. We had made it to the ocean.

RELATED READING

Bernasconi, Maurizio, and Marco Tenucci. *Extreme Rafting: History, Techniques, Runs*. New York: Universe Publishing, 1998.

Fairfax, John. *Britannia: Rowing Alone Across the Atlantic*. New York: Simon & Schuster, 1971.

Graham, Robin Lee, with Derek L. T. Gill. *Dove*. Toronto: HarperCollins Canada, 1991.

Holman, Alan. *White River, Brown Water: A Record-Making Kayak Journey Down the Amazon*. Seattle: The Mountaineers, 1985.

Kane, Joe. *Running the Amazon*. New York: Alfred A. Knopf, 1989.

Kirkby, Bruce. *Sand Dance: By Camel Across Arabia's Great Southern Desert*. Toronto: McClelland & Stewart, 2000.

MacInnis, Jeff, with Wade Rowland. *Polar Passage: The Historic First Sail Through the Northwest Passage*. Toronto: Random House of Canada, 1989.

Odendaal, François. *Rafting the Amazon*. London: BBC Books, 1992.

Rachowiecki, Rob. *Lonely Planet Peru*, 4th ed. Victoria, Australia: Lonely Planet Publications, 2000.

Ross, Alec. *Coke Stop in Emo: The Adventures of a Long-Distance Paddle*. Toronto: Key Porter Books, 1996.

Starkell, Don. *Paddle to the Amazon: The Ultimate 12,000-Mile Canoe Adventure*. Toronto: McClelland & Stewart, 1994.

Ure, John. *Trespassers on the Amazon*. London: Constable and Co. Ltd., 1986.

AMAZON EXTREME

ACKNOWLEDGMENTS

People have often asked me: What is the best way to test yourself for an expedition? How do you know you've got what it takes? My answer is simple: if you can make it through the preparatory process, you can probably make it through the actual journey. In preparing for the Amazon, we spent many grueling months researching, learning new skills, working out logistics, dealing with bureaucracy, and stumbling through two new languages. Our finances were extremely limited, and our tight budget was a constant cause of worry. Throughout this process, many people helped to make the journey easier by offering assistance in various ways.

My mother, Valerie Spentzos, has probably had the hardest job of all: stressing and worrying throughout my years of travel. Despite her anxiety, she has always been supportive and has learned to accept my wanderlust.

This book wouldn't have been possible without the help of Ian Mulgrew. I would like to thank him for his patience, his excellent literary input, and the beers. It was truly a rewarding experience.

Others who helped along the way (or took me out to dinner so I'd include them in the acknowledgments) are George Spentzos, Jane Spentzos, Patricia Spentzos, Betti Angus, Dave Edlin, Mr. Sorenson (my cool fifth-grade teacher), Steve Besler, Dan Audet (my goofy sailing buddy), Michael Flynn, Janos Virag, Leah Bailly (my pain-in-the-ass roommate who brought me cups of tea while I wrote this book), Angela Legault (my evil landlady), Almarida Reynecke, Dena Cator, and my father, Colin Angus.

I would also like to thank some companies that are helping to make our next expedition down the Yenisey River a reality. Riot Kayaks, the premier Canadian kayak manufacturers, will be supplying us with top-of-the-line boats that will get us through the gnarliest of water. Aire rafts, Iridium Satellite telephones, and the *Globe and Mail* will also be assisting in our expedition.